The Teachers of
Spiritual Wisdom

The Teachers of Spiritual Wisdom

Gaining Perspective on Life's Perplexing Questions

DUNCAN S. FERGUSON
with JAMAL RAHMAN
and MARY PETRINA BOYD

WIPF & STOCK · Eugene, Oregon

THE TEACHERS OF SPIRITUAL WISDOM
Gaining Perspective on Life's Perplexing Questions

Wipf & Stock
An Imprint of Wipf and Stock Publishers
199 W. 8th Ave., Suite 3
Eugene, OR 97401

www.wipfandstock.com

PAPERBACK ISBN: 978-1-7252-9837-8
HARDCOVER ISBN: 978-1-7252-9838-5
EBOOK ISBN: 978-1-7252-9839-2

05/20/21

To the Teachers of Spiritual Wisdom

Two roads diverged in a yellow wood,
And sorry I could not travel both
And be one traveler, long I stood
And looked down one as far as I could
To where it bent in the undergrowth;
Then I took the other, as just as fair,
And having perhaps the better claim,
Because it was grassy and wanted wear,
Though as for the passing there
Had worn them really about the same,
And both that morning equally lay
In leaves no step had trodden black.
Oh, I kept the first for another day!
Yet knowing how way leads on to way,
I doubted if I should ever come back.
I shall be telling this with a sigh
Somewhere ages and ages hence:
Two roads diverged in a wood, and I—
I took the one less traveled by,
And that has made all the difference.[1]

1. Frost, *Collected Poems of Robert Frost*, 131.

Contents

Preface

THE THREE US, DUNCAN, Mary, and Jamal, have often thought back across the years of our lives and wondered just how we have arrived at our current place in life. And we have had wonderful moments of sharing the flow of our lives with family and friends. In this sharing, we have felt supported and encouraged, and these experiences have given us more clarity and understanding about our journey. We know that there have been many factors in shaping our lives including our historical and cultural heritage, our family situation and friendships, the years of education, the career paths we have taken, and our own internal voice, not always heard clearly and which we try to decipher daily. In talking together, we have reviewed the differences in our backgrounds and have found that each of these moments of honest sharing has expanded our self-understanding and, we believe, will make our entries more thoughtful and diverse.

There were several common themes in our sharing and one of them, which we had in common, seemed very important. It was the place of *wisdom* given to us by those who cared for us, by our reading and education, and by our common quest to live more honestly and compassionately. Wisdom has instructed us; it has been our great teacher. It has given each of us much needed insight and guidance, and our lives have been transformed as we have applied these insights to our way of being and our way of acting. The wisdom each of us has received across the years of our lives has come from different sources and reflects to some extent the roads we have taken and the choices we have made. Our hope is that in our sharing our honesty and diversity will enrich your life as it has ours.

We have prepared a volume containing some of the wisdom of the ages, and our goal is to let it speak to our readers in helpful and nurturing ways. Our design for the book is really quite simple: we have attempted to select ten of the most important questions of life, and then, after an initial reflection on the central question, we have expanded our response to the foundational question by asking nine related questions. We have then searched for statements of wisdom that speak to the questions. From these statements, we have provided brief answers to the foundational questions. Each of us has answered a third of the related sub-questions. We offer, then, one hundred entries, ten basic questions with each basic question having nine related sub-questions, anchored and informed by profound wisdom.[1]

We came to this task with our own religious beliefs and practices, and these will be reflected in our writing. Much of what we share will be spiritual in nature. We understand religion and spirituality as a way of engaging in depth of thought, feeling, and action, and as a way to encounter and relate to Transcendence. We seek a deeper level common to all those who seek union with the divine, a higher and more personal knowledge of Transcendence. It may be encountered in one form by external worship and be formulated in the creeds of a particular religious tradition. Often it will be encountered in apophatic ways, through prayer and meditation.[2] As we share from our spiritual heritage, we do so committed to respecting the views of each other and all who are sincere in their commitments to a spiritual way of life. Our approach will have aspects of our own heritage, yet will as far as possible be inclusive and non-sectarian, drawing upon the human family's great wisdom traditions. With humility before the most perplexing questions of our lives, we share some of what we have learned and hope it might provide insight and guidance for others.

As we quote the Bible, we will generally use the New Revised Standard Version. On occasion, we will alter the translation from the New Revised Standard Version when it uses the masculine gender for God. As we quote from other sacred books, such as the Qur'an, we will note the version if the translation differs substantially from the common English translations. We carefully footnote the source of the wisdom sayings.

---

1. There are many fine books that address the subject of wisdom. A recent one, excellent in many ways, is *The Cambridge Handbook of Wisdom*, edited by Robert J. Sternberg and Judith Gluck.

2. See, for example, the enduring classic describing mystical experience, *The Cloud of Unknowing and The Book of Privy Counseling*, edited by William Johnston.

Introduction

Our Earth Home

WE ARE KEENLY AWARE that we live in troubled times, regionally, nationally, and globally. Regardless of how we receive our information, often through different channels and points of view, the message from this information underlines the same issue: our problems are enormous, even overwhelming. We acknowledge that every age has had to address a range of challenging problems, and no doubt those in each of these different periods of time and place have thought that their situation was uniquely challenging. Human history has been filled with wars, the collapse of empires, the presence of extreme hunger and poverty, the suffering from disease and natural disaster,[1] the collapse of economies, the discrimination against those who are different, and the general quest for a measure of peace and meaning in life.

Our age has similar challenges as well, but another one has been added, *the threat to the welfare of our earth home*. We may be in the last few minutes of the survival of life on our planet if we place the history of the earth in the timeframe of twenty-four hours.[2] In fact, the symbolic Doomsday Clock of the *Bulletin of the Atomic Scientists* is set on two minutes before midnight when "the lights go out."

Not everyone can or needs to focus on this single greatest challenge of our generation; it is enough to get through the day or week with some sense of security and order. Yet the entire human family and all of nature's creatures and life forms do live with the reality that our earth home has

---

1. We write in the midst of the COVID-19 pandemic.

2. See the writing of Berry, *Great Work*, who maintains that saving mother earth is *the* great task of our generation. See as well the book by Swimme and Tucker, *Journey of the Universe*.

threatening problems that must be addressed. These problems and challenges have a way of spilling over into all of our lives and the setting we call home. As we become more sensitive to these problems, we begin to have anxiety about our future and long for some guidance and answers to the most perplexing questions of our lives. We do need wisdom to find our way and have a measure of security as we travel. We hope that our educational systems, our forms of government, our associations and organizations, such as a religious community, will help us address these problems and help us find our way.

We have studied the range of questions that encapsulate and articulate what it is that we face.[3] As mentioned, we have attempted to narrow these primary questions down to ten, with nine additional sub-questions for each. As we turn to these questions, we will try to point toward some answers, offering insight and perspective on these questions. We need wisdom!

Each of our answers to these queries will provide a quote from the great teachers of wisdom followed by a reflection and partial answer that we hope is wise and helpful. By wisdom, we mean a body of accumulated refection about the character and meaning of life.[4] Often, these expressions of wisdom will be rooted in universal common sense, although it may be expressed in the tone of the culture from which it comes. It is not so much pragmatism or a list of what to do next, but a deep truth that takes into account the complexity of life. Wisdom suggests an outlook and attitude that enable us to cope. It is a reflection on lived experience by the most perceptive and thoughtful people of the ages. Irish poet John O'Donohue writes that wisdom "is a deeper way of knowing. Wisdom is the art of living in rhythm with the soul, your life, and the divine. Wisdom is the way that you learn to decipher the unknown; and the unknown is our closest companion. So wisdom is the art of being courageous and generous with the unknown, of being able to decipher

---

3. There are many lists of these questions, one with as many as forty basic questions. We have learned from these lists and from our own questions and attempted to narrow them down to ten broad foundational questions with several sub-questions. It has not been an easy process, and we know that others might suggest different questions, ones perhaps more rooted in one's own culture, language, and life setting.

4. See Brueggemann, *Reverberations of Faith*, 232–35. The value of wisdom is given a high priority in several of the world's great religious and philosophical traditions, for example, the logos in Stoicism, the Tao in Taoism, and Dharma in Buddhism and Hinduism.

and recognize its treasures."[5] It will provide discernment and suggested patterns of thought, feelings, and behavior, with attention to probable outcomes. Joan Chittister offers the following observation about wisdom literature: "Wisdom literature endures precisely because it is not the history of a particular people, it is not the codification of the ethical mores of a single culture, it is not the teachings of science, it is not, in fact, devoted to the presentation of any particular body of knowledge. It deals with the spiritual, the ascetic, the Divine, and the nature of virtue. Its concerns life in the meaning of holiness and the fundamentals of happiness . . . It lifts the spiritual life from the legal to the mystical, from a study of the nature of religion to the depths of the personal spiritual life."[6]

It is important to note as we speak about wisdom that it has had a vital role in nearly every culture and historical period of time. We want to learn from these patterns of wisdom. Nearly always, in these historical cultures, wisdom has had a feminine face and has leaned toward right-brained descriptions, filled with intuition and mature emotion rather than exclusively left brained descriptions aimed at "how to" solutions.[7] In our time, we have been more inclined to find scientific and engineering solutions to our problems, and these are needed and helpful. We also need to understand the new research and knowledge that come from our study of the cosmos and our place in the cosmos. This larger frame of reference may be sending us other information that will expand our understanding of the place of wisdom in our lives. We need to hear from Sophia, the Greek goddess of wisdom, and her cousin, Athena. The Hebrew Bible points to *hokma*, a feminine noun meaning "wisdom" in Hebrew, as a central component of understanding creation and how to be her children rather than her master. The words for the divine presence in Arabic (*rahmah* and *hikmah*) are also feminine and imply that divine mercy and divine wisdom have feminine qualities. In summary, we might say the ultimate source of wisdom is the presence of Transcendent Love in our lives.

Because the wisdom selections we choose and the comments we make will reflect our own identity and values, we thought it might be wise to introduce ourselves and partially answer the first of the ten major questions, which is: "Who am I?" Often our focus will be more on a personal way of framing the questions as, for example, in question 1 (Who am I?)

5. O'Donohue, *Anam Cara*, 194.

6. Chittister, *Rule of St. Benedict: A Spirituality for the 21st Century*, xii.

7. See the description of wisdom in Matthew Fox's book, *Coming of the Cosmic Christ*, 21–22.

rather than on a more general way of phrasing the question, as for example, "What does it mean to be human?" We do so because we believe the reader should engage the questions in a personal way and find personal answers that are helpful and healing. Further, we often answer them in a personal way because we want the reader to have at least a preliminary understanding of who we are; our backgrounds and identities will be present in the selections we make and the paragraphs of interpretation we offer. Each of us will provide a response to the foundational questions, and then we will divide the nine sub-questions with each of us responding to three of them.

I (Duncan) will begin and then invite my gifted and trustworthy colleagues to follow with their brief self-introductions. My wife Dorothy and I have retired to the Pacific Northwest. My wife was a teacher and school counselor, and I spent my professional years as an academic and pastor. Our son, his wife, and their children live in Austin, and we make regular trips to Texas. Dorothy and I have deep roots in the Northwest, although my youth and teenage years were spent in California. I went to the University of Oregon for my undergraduate education, and following my seminary training, I did my doctoral studies at the University of Edinburgh and learned to love my Scottish heritage. I have served in congregations, four universities, and in the national offices of the Presbyterian Church (USA) with the responsibility of guiding and resourcing the PC (USA) in its mission in higher education.

My retirement years have given me the opportunity to continue my calling as teacher, pastor, and author. My career was filled with these endeavors. One aspect of my work that was especially informative and life changing was the opportunity to travel to many parts of the world. In these visits, my focus was on international education with a special concern for causes of social justice, peace, and interfaith understanding. I have continued in retirement in these causes, giving special attention to seeking a just peace in Israel and Palestine. More recently, I have turned my attention to our generation's most challenging problem, global warming/climate change. And, of course, I have given thought to COVID-19 as it has both threatened and changed the patterns of our lives.

I (Mary) am a native of Washington State, most at home where Douglas fir and salal flourish. My husband Steve and I are parents to two grown sons who live in the greater Puget Sound area. I met Steve as an undergraduate at the University of Puget Sound. Following graduation I went to the University of Hawaii and earned a Master of Library Science. I went to Wesley Theological Seminary in midlife and was drawn into the delight of biblical studies. This drew me to continue that work, earning a doctorate from Union Theological Seminary in Richmond, Virginia. The focus of that study was wisdom literature, focusing on Proverbs 31:10–31. Since 1994 I have worked at archaeological sites in Jordan.

I have served five United Methodist Churches, delighting in communities that sought to follow Jesus. I have recently retired and am listening carefully for God's next call for my life. We live on Whidbey Island where I am surrounded by incredible beauty. I love working with textiles: weaving, spinning, knitting, and quilting. Weekly visits from my year-old grandnephew bring much joy.

I (Jamal) am originally from Bangladesh and now settled and living in Seattle since the early 1990s. This city is adorned with breathtaking beauty, and I am grateful to call Seattle my home. Currently, I am co-founder and Imam of Interfaith Community Sanctuary and adjunct faculty member at Seattle University. Since 9/11, I have been working actively with a rabbi and a pastor on interfaith understanding. Affectionately known as the Interfaith Amigos, we travel the country sharing a message of inclusivity.

My parents and paternal grandfather, who was an Islamic scholar and healer, shaped my religious education. Because my father was a diplomat, we lived in a variety of countries in Europe, the Middle East, and Asia. My parents encouraged their children to attend worship services of the various religious traditions that were present where we were located. I am rooted in Islam, but from an early age I realized that interfaith relationships are not about the conversion of those from other traditions, but about completion, the shared goal of helping all people to become whole and a more mature human being.

During my formative years, my parents were posted to Saudi Arabia where I performed the Hajj pilgrimage and made frequent visits to Mecca and Medina. I was privileged to live in Iran and Turkey where Rumi is studied with great devotion. There, I was taught Qur'anic verses in tandem with treasured utterances of the thirteenth-century sage, Rumi, who it is said penetrated the inner secrets of the Qur'an. To this day, the words of Rumi resonate deeply inside of me and I quote him extensively in my talks and writings.

My parents were also posted to Burma (Myanmar) and India, and these experiences sparked in me a lifelong interest in Buddhism, Taoism, and Hinduism. Wisdom insights from these Eastern religious traditions have deepened my understanding of the Qur'an.

I received my BA from the University of Oregon and MA from the University of California at Berkeley. Subsequently, I chose to study Islamic spirituality with my parents who sent me to various teachers for personal and professional development.

At this time I am divorced, yet I have been blessed with an adorable daughter and angelic granddaughter. Since childhood I have had a loving relationship with my brother and sister. We have chosen to live in close physical proximity to one another in Seattle, and they share my commitment to the mission of the Interfaith Community Sanctuary. We are grateful to God for our Circle of Love comprised of family members and friends from our unique house of worship.

Foundational Question 1

Who Am I?

But now thus says the Lord,
the One who created you, O Jacob,
the One who formed you, O Israel:
Do not fear, for I have redeemed you;
I have called you by name, you are mine.

Isaiah 43:1

I AM A CHILD of God. This description is the core of my identity. I am connected to the transcendent Holy, whom I call God. She called me forth as part of this incredible creation called earth. The relationship is deep and God's faithfulness is sure.

Child of God suggests a familial relationship, and I am all too aware that this imagery is not helpful for those whose human families have lacked the ability to love fully and completely. I have stepped away from the image of God as Father. The image dominates much of traditional language in the church, and I find it troublesome. It would deny the feminine in the Divine. When God created humanity in the image of God, God created them male and female (Gen 1:27). Logically, God contains both the masculine and feminine. I find that the image of God the Mother is more helpful for my spiritual journey. However, all images of God are metaphors and no single metaphor fully expresses the completeness of the Divine.

I live secure in the love of God who is always faithful. I am loved as I am even when I fail God's dream for my life. That love sustains me, supporting me in times of difficulty, bringing comfort and giving me the courage to act. As a beloved child of God, I am part of the beloved community, that vast gathering of people around the world who work with love to bring forth *shalom*, God's deep peace, upon our planet.

I am but one of many of God's beloved children and am challenged to remember that when I meet another child whose opinions and ways of living are vastly different from my own. In fact, over the years, I have learned that the differences among the children of God is integral to God's plan, with each child having a role in the care of the earth and in expanding and deepening the love among God's children. We learn from those whose language, culture, and way of life may differ from our patterns of understanding and living. Do not fear, God tells me, so I dare to follow God's invitation and try to honor all of God's children in wise and caring ways. MB

FOUNDATIONAL QUESTION 1: WHO AM I?

You are a ruby in the midst of granite,
How long will you continue to deceive us?
We can see the look in your eyes;
Return to the root of your real self.[1]

RUMI

The Qur'an says that God molded the human from water and clay and then infused each of us with "something of His spirit." Beyond our ego-centered personality, deep inside of us, is a ruby-like divine spark.

The human mortal is a unique creation of God. We embody our personality, which, some tell us, is little more than a bundle of conditioned reactions to life's circumstances. But we also embody the divine essence. So sacred and precious is this inner essence that God in the Holy Book commanded the angels to bow to the human. With our unique inner essence we have the potential to rise higher than the angels, but because we also have free will, we can sink lower than savage beasts.

The Qur'an teaches that we humans are blessed with extraordinary honors and charged with awesome responsibilities. We are appointed as God's representatives on earth, and upon us is bestowed the Amanat or

---

1. Chittick, *Sufi Path of Love*, 339.

Divine trust. Allah trusts us to "enjoin the good and forbid the evil." In dealing with others we are told to be merciful and just, and in our relationship with the earth, the prophet Muhammad in a Hadith reminds us: "Protect and honor the earth, for the earth is like your mother."[2] Given all these high privileges and obligations, the human arrives on earth, says Rumi, "a little tipsy." We are bewildered and confused, but over time we realize that "this drunkenness must have started in some tavern." Slowly, it dawns on us that we are part of a mysterious cosmic design begging us to connect with the root of our real self and spread love and peace on earth in our own distinctive way.

If all this talk about our divine essence sounds abstract or exaggerated, consider the words of the 2020 presidential hopeful Marianne Williamson who said: "Our deepest fear is that we are powerful beyond measure. It is our light, not our darkness that most frightens us . . . You are a child of God. Your playing small does not serve the world."[3] JR

Sub-question 1a: Are we just a product of evolution with the exclusive goals of survival and reproduction, or do we have an additional and more substantial identity?

Self-centeredness bred into our bones by our evolution and experience on Earth has led us naturally to focus on local events and phenomena in the retelling of most origin stories. However, every advance in our knowledge of the cosmos has revealed that we live on a cosmic speck of dust, orbiting a mediocre star in the far suburbs of a common sort of galaxy, among a hundred billion galaxies in the universe. The news of our cosmic unimportance triggers impressive defense mechanisms in the human psyche.[4]

NEIL DEGRASSE TYSON AND DONALD GOLDSMITH

---

2. Fadiman and Frager, *Essential Sufism*, 90.

3. Williamson, *Return to Love*, 190.

4. Tyson and Goldsmith, *Origins*, 16. An earlier book by Timothy Ferris, *Whole Shebang*, is an excellent introduction to understanding the formation of universe (s), written for the educated layperson. So, too, is his book, *Coming of Age in the Milky Way*.

I think it is important in answering this question that we start with what is nearly universally accepted as the truth about human origins. We are part of cosmic evolution, and it does not advance the cause of religion or the status of human beings to hang on to older views of human origins that deny that humans are indeed part of the evolutionary process. *Homo sapiens* have many evolutionary ancestors, and the particular form of a human being is a part of the natural order, evolving over millions of years. It is likely that there were six human species inhabiting the earth one hundred thousand years ago.[5]

The evolution of the human species is a fascinating story and one for which we need the help of scientists and social scientists to understand. Our goals are modest, but important; we seek wisdom in placing the history of humankind in a framework based on the best scientific research, and then reflecting, with the aid of sacred books and wise teachers, on what it is that we have become.

It is true that survival and reproduction are integral to human life, and yet for most humans life has become more than just sustaining the species; what has been added says a great deal more about our identity as human beings. We have become a species that has the capacity to reflect on the meaning of life and to appreciate forms of goodness, truth, and beauty.[6] We do have a more substantial identity while remaining within the natural order. I find the works of Pierre Teilhard de Chardin, while being updated in current religious thought, especially helpful in the quest to integrate religious thought and scientific thought. He understands the place of God *within the natural order,* moving creation toward good ends.[7] He is careful to say that God is not the universe (pantheism) nor is God outside of creation, entering on occasion when necessary (traditional monotheism). God exists beyond the universe, yet is fully present in the natural order, a view that is often named panentheism. We need not choose between an exclusive scientific understanding of human origins and a religious or value-oriented perspective on the development of humankind. *It is possible and necessary to integrate them.* DF

5. See Harari, *Sapiens.*

6. See, for example, the writing of Delio, *Unbearable Wholeness of Being.*

7. Teilhard de Chardin, *Phenomenon of Man.*

Sub-question 1b. Are we fundamentally different from animals or is it simply that we have become more advanced in the evolutionary process?

Naturalism presents a hugely grandiose claim, and we have every right to be skeptical. When we look into the eyes of another person, it doesn't seem like what we're seeing is simply a collection of atoms, some sort immensely complicated chemical reaction. We often feel connected to the universe in some much more profound way that transcends the merely physical, whether it's a sense of awe when we contemplate the sea or sky, a trancelike reverie during meditation or prayer, or the feeling of love when we're close to someone we care about.[8]

SEAN CARROLL

Sean Carroll, a theoretical physicist at the California Institute of Technology, explores a range of questions in his thoughtful and profound discussion of "the big picture." Evolution, and particularly that part of evolution that traces the origin of humans, is certainly one of those big picture issues. It is interesting to note, as he shares in his excellent book, that Dr. Carroll was raised in the context of the Christian church. Gradually, over the years of his education in the sciences, he changed his beliefs and endorsed naturalism.[9] He maintains that one need not go back beyond what is and how it came into being; it is enough to find our place in the natural order. He does acknowledge that there are dimensions of human experience, consciousness among them, that are a bit hard to fit neatly into the worldview of naturalism and evolution.

I have great empathy for his journey, although I arrived at a different outlook, perhaps because my academic journey was in religious studies.[10]

8. Carroll, *Big Picture*, 13. His newer book, *Something Deeply Hidden: Quantum Words and the Emergence of Spacetime*, 2019, moves his observations to what is becoming a new worldview.

9. Naturalism is the view that the universe requires no supernatural cause and government, but is self-existent, self-explanatory, self-operating, and self-directed.

10. See the books by Richard Dawkins such as *The Greatest Show on Earth: The Evidence for Evolution*, *The God Delusion*, and *The Selfish Gene* for a more aggressive challenge to postulating the role of the divine in human origins and evolutionary development. Edward O. Wilson, a noted American scientist, agrees with both Sean

I am inclined to answer our question above with the affirmation of a scientific understanding of the universe, yet see it as the work of God. We are related to the animal world, have evolved in comparable ways, and have reached a point in our development that gives us a mind to understand, a conscience to determine right from wrong, a soul or consciousness that gives us self-awareness, and a will to choose the way of love and compassion. God has been in the process and given humankind a special role and responsibility to care for mother earth. DF

Sub-question 1c: In that we are similar in many ways with animals and share nature with them, should we treat them much as we should treat human beings? Do animals really suffer? Do we have the right to eliminate them?

To understand the human role in the functioning of the Earth we need to appreciate the spontaneities found in every form of existence in the natural world, spontaneities that we associate with the wild, that which is uncontrolled by human dominance. We misconceive our role if we consider that our historical mission is to "civilize" or to "domesticate" the planet, as though wildness is something destructive rather than the ultimate creative modality of any form of earthly being. We are not here to control. We are here to become integral with the larger Earth community.[11]

Thomas Berry

I can remember quite vividly my first reading of Albert Schweitzer's books about Jesus and the kingdom of God and learning more about the

---

Carroll and Richard Dawkins that naturalism and evolution provide our best explanations. Wilson's books are both profound and fair. See, for example, *On Human Nature, The Future of Life,* and *The Social Conquest of the Earth.* Michael Dowd, a thoughtful scholar and author, argues strongly for the integration of the scientific and informed religious perspectives in his book, *Thank God for Evolution: How the Marriage of Science and Religion Will Transform Your Life and Our World.*

11. Berry, *Great Work,* 48. Space does not allow a thorough review of the literature about climate change. One person who has influenced me is Wendell Berry who speaks profoundly about his love and care for the earth. See his work, *The Unsettling of American Culture and Agriculture,* now somewhat dated (1978), but it has a profound message about what was to occur in the next several decades.

first-century Jewish teacher, healer, and prophet. What Dr. Schweitzer said shook my somewhat innocent orthodoxy! I read more of his work and discovered what a grand human being he was, a musician, a scholar, and a dedicated medical missionary in Africa. I was moved by his commitment to the sacredness of life, valuing even the omnipresent African mosquitos. As I read more about his work, I discovered that he saw the earth, its systems, and its inhabitants as one sacred whole.

He wrote, "Late on the third day, at the very moment when, at sunset, we were making our way through a herd of hippopotamuses, there flashed upon my mind, unforeseen and unsought, the phrase, 'Reverence for Life'. The iron door had yielded: the path in the thicket had become visible."[12] I have often thought of his example and how his theological writing and personal reflections have led me through many thickets. I have not been able to be as consistent as he was in respecting all of life, but lessons from his life and writing stay central to my modestly informed conscience: that all of life is sacred, that we are part of an "elegant universe" that functions holistically, and that my careless intrusion may cause serious problems impacting other life in negative ways.[13] DF

Sub-question 1d. What qualities in human beings make them distinctive?

Apprehend God in all things, for God is in all things.
Every single creature is full of God and is a book about God.
Every creature is a word of God.
If I spent enough time with the tiniest creature—even a caterpillar—
I would never have to prepare a sermon.
So full of God is every creature.[14]

MEISTER ECKHART

12. Schweitzer, *Out of My Life and Thought*, in preliminary statements.

13. The Endangered Species Protection Act, passed by the Congress in 1973, has helped to preserve several species. This Act is currently being challenged. Brian Greene, a well-known physicist, has written a profound book entitled *The Elegant Universe*, and suggests that we need to appreciate the complexity and beauty of the universe and care for it in wise ways.

14. Roberts and Amidon, *Earth Prayers*, 251.

Humanity is deeply connected to all of creation, a creature among creatures, living off the bounty of the earth. We are part of the cosmic patterns that connect all that is. The rhythm of our lives plays in concert with the greater symphony of the cosmos. In Genesis we read that on the sixth day God commanded and the earth brought forth living creatures, all wild and domesticated animals on the face of the earth. Humanity is part of that day, creatures among creatures.

When humankind was created, they were assigned a task: "to have dominion over the fish of the sea, and over the birds of the air, and over the cattle, and over all the wild animals on the earth, and over every creeping thing that creeps upon the earth." After everything else is in place, God called forth humanity to take care of the rest.

Ellen Davies writes: "We have fallen short of God's intention that we should enact our resemblance to God through the exercise of benevolent dominion over creatures. Instead, through our greed, we have turned into a curse God's blessing of fruitfulness for the non-human creatures."[15] Our challenge is to reclaim our God-given role as caretakers.

One could argue, perhaps, that human beings have a superior self-awareness, the gift of speech, a more complex society, and a deeper spirituality. Yet we do not understand how other animals relate subjectively to the world or to the Divine. I would suggest that what distinguishes humans from other creatures is not exclusively our superior self-awareness, or intelligence, or ability, but primarily what makes humans unique is our responsibility to care for creation. MB

Sub-question 1e: Do you think we were created "in the image of God?" Is there a self-aware and subtle, even a divine image to our identity?

Let us create humankind in our own image, according to our own likeness; and let them have dominion over the fish of the sea, and over the birds of the air, and over the cattle, and over all the wild animals in of the earth, and over every creeping thing that creeps upon the earth. So God created human kind in the divine image, in the image of God were humans created; male and female, God created them.

Genesis 1:26–27

15. Davies, "Knowing Our Place on Earth," I-59.

Usually God forbids the making of images of the divine. The Ten Commandments forbid any images of God. "You shall not make yourself an idol, whether in the form of anything that is in heaven above or that is on the earth beneath, or that is on the water under the earth" (Exod 20:4). Through the prophet Ezekiel, God condemned those who, "From their beautiful ornament, in which they took pride, they made their abominable images, their detestable things" (Ezek 7:20). Things cannot fully reflect the image of God. Yet God creates divine images in living persons. Inanimate and manufactured things cannot reflect the image of God. Living persons can in some way do this.

God made humankind in God's image, in God's likeness. How can this be? The image goes beyond physical characteristics. God is spirit, and people cannot look like spirit whatever that might be. The image of God is metaphor for the way in which humans may embody the divine. Humanity is to reflect the characteristics of God: justice, righteousness, steadfast love, compassion, mercy, and forgiveness. These characteristics exist only in relationships between creatures. We live out the image of God as we treat others with respect, forgive one another, work for justice, and deal fairly with one another.

In Genesis 1, God is Creator. If we are to reflect the image of God, we are called to create. Our words do not have the power that God's do, but in many ways the words we use create our world. If we speak with kindness and gentleness, we work to create a world of peace. If we speak with anger, disdain, and condemnation, we separate ourselves from each other, creating a world of emotional devastation.

Every person is created in the image of God, according to God's likeness. It is easy to respond quickly, judging those who are different from me, distancing myself from others. Do I have the wisdom to look deeply into each person, even those who commit evil deeds, and see the image of God that is there?

God is utterly beyond our understanding, vaster than any metaphor, and deeper than we can imagine. And yet we each bear the image of the divine. Deep within each one is the holy gift and God's presence in our very being. MB

Sub-question 1f. If we have the divine image, what does that mean? How might it shape the values that guide our lives?

I was daily God's delight,
rejoicing before God always,
rejoicing in God's inhabited world
and delighting in the human race.

PROVERBS 8:30–31

Proverbs 8:22–31 contains another creation story where Woman Wisdom, *hokmah*, was the first creation. "The Lord created me at the beginning of God's work, the first of God's acts long ago" (Prov 8:22). She observed as God called forth the waters, shaped the mountains and the hills, formed the soil, and created the skies and ocean deeps. She watched as God brought forth order out of chaos.

Wisdom brought delight to God and found her delight in humanity. This is deeply moving language; Wisdom relates both to God and to humanity. The word, here translated as "rejoicing," can be translated as "playing." Delight, play, and joy are God's intention for creation. Wisdom models how humanity is to live. If Woman Wisdom is our model, we find delight in creation and joy in our relationship with God. We find ways to rejoice in one another and learn to play together, celebrating God's beautiful world. Joseph Campbell has underlined the point that God, the divine, has been understood as feminine in nearly all of the world's religions.[16]

We read this along with the Genesis creation story and we are reminded that humanity is called to care for the earth (Gen 1:26–27). Given the seriousness of global warming, this is a monumental task and we often feel overwhelmed. But God didn't give us this responsibility to care for the earth just when it was easy to do so. Our God-given call is more urgent now.

Wonder is the way we begin. We learn to look at the world, delighting in the beauty around us and grateful for the gift of life. Because it is so wondrously, delightfully precious, we work to preserve life, caring for all of God's creatures. For the sake of such beauty and because God has called us to care for the creation, I do what I can. I will not give up, for the image of God in me sees the world as precious and wonderful. Joy and responsibility weave together as we live in ways that reveal the image of God. MB

16. Campbell with Moyer, *Power of Myth*, chapter 4.

Sub-question 1g: How do we awaken and become aware of our divine identity?

"Know thyself and you shall know thy Sustainer."
"Die before you die."

THE PROPHET MUHAMMAD

Decades ago, one of my spiritual teachers said bluntly: "There is no short-cut to spiritual awakening. You simply have to do the "inner inconvenient work."" By this he meant that I have to do the work of transforming my ego and opening my heart. I have to come face to face with my own untamed ego and clenched heart. Daily, it is incumbent upon me to make continuous efforts to diminish my negative ego traits such as pride, envy, and greed and expand my divine qualities such as compassion, awareness, and patience. Little by little with self-mercy I have to strive to die to that which is false within me before I die a physical death. This lifetime work will bring me closer and closer to my inner divine spark, which is my Christ light, Allah's breath, and Buddha nature.

Alas, the inner work is difficult and needs continuous tending. We would rather studiously observe others and dispense to them admirable wisdom and practices. There is merit in this endeavor, but it is a poor substitute for the critical needs to focus on oneself. Lao Tzu said: "knowing others is intelligence; knowing yourself is true wisdom."[17]

To move closer to my true self, my teacher taught me a time-honored practice. Keep a small notebook with you at all times. Make a note of negative ego traits and divine qualities that arise in you during the course of your day. For example, if you felt a surge of jealousy, make a note of it. And, during the same day, if you were gracious with someone who was unreasonable, mark that down also. Every evening, review both categories with compassion for yourself. Express gratitude to Divinity for granting you awareness for those traits that need to be diminished and the qualities that need to be expanded. The light of merciful mindfulness will help you make choices to move closer to your higher self. JR

---

17. Tzu, *Tao Te Ching*, #33, with slightly different translation.

Sub-question 1h: Why is it that we are not aware of our divine identity?

As individuals responsible for the future of life on Earth, we hereby declare that we affirm the divine spark in the heart and mind of every human being and intend to live by its light in every sphere of its existence . . .

Fuji Declaration

The endorsers of the 2015 Fuji Declaration are an alliance of international change leaders, including Nobel laureates, heads of state, and scientists who, for years, have been studying the best ways to deal with the intractable global problems of social injustice and environmental degradation. The Declaration starts by emphasizing that we need to awaken to the divine spark that exists in every human being.

Why is it that we humans are unaware of our divine identity? Sufi teachers give three reasons. The first is illustrated in a classic story of the Mulla who travels to China for a financial transaction. The fictional thirteenth-century Mulla serves as a comic foil in Islamic spiritual literature to convey profound insights. When the bank officer asks the Mulla to prove his identity, he pulls out a pocket mirror and peers into it for long time. Finally, he declares, "Yep, that's me, alright. I certify it." This story testifies to our conditioned habit of defining others and ourselves by looking only at the surface external reality. We fail to perceive the inner reality, our divine identity. We judge others and ourselves on the basis of profession, bank account, and status in society. Outer attainments and affiliations matter, but are these more important than inner qualities such as our ability to love, capacity to be compassionate, and our willingness to forgive? The true worth of a human being is based not on the credentials we acquire but on what we become. About our bias regarding external credentials, a spiritual teacher asks, "When you hear a bird in song, do you feel the need to ask for its credentials?"

The second reason is that we received our divine identity as a free gift. We take our divine essence for granted and fail to acknowledge this most important and gracious gift. It is akin to the person who does not truly appreciate the full value of inherited wealth?

Third, a main purpose of our life journey is to discover and connect to our divine essence. This experience of discovery is life-giving. It enables us to see. Thus, Sufi sages are fond of saying that the mystery of our destiny is that we are foredoomed to forget so that we might remember, foredoomed to slumber so that we might awaken. And to awaken is to find our way. JR

Sub-question 1i: Are there ways that we might transform our ego and self-centeredness and increase our capacity to live a God-centered life?

God does not change humankind's condition unless they (humans) change their inner selves?

QUR'AN 13:11

The Qur'an teaches that we have three stages of the ego, and that we must move through these stages to help us change our inner selves to live a God-centered life. Essentially we are asked to transform the ego from a commanding master into a personal assistant. In the first stage we make a commitment to observe ourselves at all times. This switches on an internal light of compassionate self-witnessing. In the metaphor of the Hindu Upanishads, we are like two birds perched on the branch of a tree. One bird pecks away at the fruit, which could be sweet or bitter; this is often the unreflective story of our life. But we are also like the other bird that lovingly witnesses and guides our actions. The Qur'an asks us to be continuously vigilant because the untamed ego can incline us to wrongdoing. Through our abiding and merciful self-witnessing, we can diminish our ego's tendency to go astray.

In the second stage, we are encouraged to participate fully in the bazaar of life. Through our experiences, we expand our awareness and we realize that ours is a world of opposites. We have choices to make and we have a conscience to guide us. By resisting temptations of wrongdoing, we build our spiritual muscles. From our mistakes, we grow.

In the third stage, we make every effort to align elements of our personality with our higher self. It is a lifelong process. Rumi describes this lifelong process: "Marry your soul; that wedding is the way."[18] Mysteriously, as we apply ourselves sincerely to this inner work, Spirit helps us to mature and evolve into our fullness of our being. As we seek help from

---

18. Breton and Largent, *Love, Soul, and Freedom*, 190.

God, little by little, we mature and awaken to the Light. In the analogy of
the Sufis, God turns an ordinary stone marble into a ruby or a parched
section of ground turns green in a spring wind. JR

CHAPTER ONE: WHO AM I?

Resources and Practices

Further Reading

1. Thomas Berry, *The Great Work*

2. Denise Breton and Christopher Largent, *Love, Soul, and Freedom: Dancing with Rumi on the Mystic Path*

3. Joan Chittister, *Following the Path: The Search for a Life of Passion*

4. Ilio Delio, *The Unbearable Wholeness of Being: God, Evolution, and the Power of Love*

5. Kahlil Gibran, *The Prophet*

6. Maryam Mafi, translator, *Rumi: Day by Day*

7. Krista Tippett, *Becoming Wise: An Inquiry into the Mystery and Art of Living*

8. Edward O. Wilson, *The Meaning of Human Existence*

Suggested Practices

1. Set a quiet time each day for reflection, contemplation, meditation, and prayer. It need not be an extended period of time, although you need to be in a setting of quiet and comfort and be free from distractions. A few minutes per day, often as you start the day, can provide a positive spirit and good direction for the day.

2. Join a small group of other seekers dedicated to spiritual growth. The group may want to share answers to the foundational questions and the sub-questions in *The Teachers of Spiritual Wisdom*. We learn from others and need their support.

3. In time, the group may want to select another book or two, perhaps one with daily readings, that will provide you with wisdom and guidance in your spiritual journey.

4. Volunteer in a program offered by a religious group or social service agency that enables you to provide tangible assistance to those in need. ✴

5. Be conscious during each day of the need to be a person for others, a good listener, a friendly presence, and a joyful friend. Keep a journal recording your progress and the challenges you face.

✴ Talk w/ Meghan on Friday 9/17 to discuss ways to be of help.

Foundational Question 2
Why Am I Here?

In ordinary usage the word "meaning" implies intention, inten-tion implies design, and design implies a designer. Any entity, any process, or definition of any word itself is put into play as a result of an intended consequence in the mind of the designer. This is the heart of the philosophical worldview of organized religions, and in particular the creation stories . . . There is a second broader way the word "meaning" is used and a very different worldview implied. It is that the accidents of history, not the intentions of the designer are the source of meaning. There is no advance design, but instead overlap-ping networks of physical cause and effect. The unfolding of history is obedient only to the general laws of the Universe.[1]

Edward O. Wilson

DR. WILSON HAS A marvelous way of making complex issues clear and understandable. He argues persuasively that all we have as a clue to the meaning of universe and to those who inhabit it rests with the way the universe functions. There is no outside cause, no designer who created it and set it in motion. Science then gives us the best information about what we are dealing with as we attempt to find our way in world. Each event that we encounter is not placed there for healing, guidance, and direction in life by a gracious Creator, but by a random pattern of cause and effect. The worldview of science gives us the best information about how to understand the world we inhabit and how to find our way in

1. Wilson, *Meaning of Human Existence*, 12–13.

16

its complex and varied patterns. He does acknowledge that nature and sentient life have evolved in a remarkable way and now have built-in mechanisms, responses, feelings, and mind to adapt to the challenges of the natural order. The human brain, for example, evolved into an extraordinary resource to draw a map for guidance, but so has the spider's web enabled the spider to survive. "The human brain evolved under the same regimen as the spider's web."[2]

There is no God or transcendent principle that controls the flow of the natural order and human life. What is helpful to me is that his argument is so clear. If I endorse this scientific worldview, I know that when I look out the window, plan my day, wonder if I am on track and how to deal with anxiety and death, I look to the patterns inherent in the universe for clues to guide me. As I ponder my place and responsibilities, I know that I should devote myself to increasing human intelligence, finding patterns of social organization that lead to a measure of justice and peace, and at this moment in history, give myself to saving our earth home. Even a secular understanding of reality suggests a place for a *sense of vocation*. Dr. Wilson wrote: "We will find a way eventually to live with our inborn turmoil, and perhaps find pleasure in viewing it as the primary source of our creativity."[3]

This point of view does shape the contemporary worldview of many people, whether they are aware of it or not. In my outlook, I acknowledge the logic and persuasiveness of Dr. Wilson's view, but there seems to be so much left out, as for example the foundational ground of life itself, life's meaning, ethics, and the consciousness of human beings. This concern will be discussed as we move along in our search for wisdom. DF

FOUNDATIONAL QUESTION 2: WHY AM I HERE?

I was a secret Treasure and I longed to be known
And so I created you and the worlds, visible and invisible.[4]

THE PROPHET MUHAMMAD

2. Wilson, *Meaning of Human Existence*, 13.

3. Wilson, *Meaning of Human Existence*, 14.

4. Nurbaksh, *Traditions of the Prophet*, 13.

Sufis rhapsodize over this astonishing revelation that came to the Prophet Muhammad in a dream. Cosmically encoded within us is a deep and mysterious longing to know and connect with our Creator. Within every desire for anything in our lives is a yearning for our Beloved. The inexplicable unease we experience in our life even when our wants are fulfilled is expressed in the utterance of the beloved eighth-century female Islamic saint, Rabia: "There is a disease in my breast no doctor can cure; only union with the Friend can cure this."[5]

The Qur'an says that Allah is within and without. To connect with Allah inside of us, we have to do the essential inner work of evolving into the fullness of our being by removing the veils of our ego so that we move closer to our higher self. This work is critical. Sufi teachers explain the significance of this mission with a metaphor: A benevolent King sends you to a faraway country with a specific task. You go there and do many beautiful things, but not that one specific task. Upon your return, can you say that you have fulfilled your mission?

To bond with Divinity outside of us, we make a commitment to serve God's creation. We strive to be "a lamp, lifeboat, or ladder" to others. Our dedication to serve the common good makes our soul leap with joy! A twentieth-century Indian poet wrote: "I slept and dreamt that life was joy; I awoke and found that life was service; I served and lo, service was joy!"[6]

May the words of the Prophet Muhammad splash in your heart: "When you arrived here, everyone was laughing and smiling but you were weeping. Live such a life that when you depart, everyone is crying and weeping, but you are laughing and smiling." JR

FOUNDATIONAL QUESTION 2: WHY AM I HERE?

God has told you, O mortal, what is good:
and what does the Lord require of you
but to do justice, and love kindness,
and walk humbly with your God?

MICAH 6:8

---

5. Vaughn-Lee, *Traveling the Path of Love*, 48.

6. Quoted in the websites of Ram Dass and Deepak Chopra and on tagorefoundationinternational.com.

We are part of the earth's desire to sustain life. I stand in the chain of being with ancestors who have come before me and generations of descendants who will come after me. For me, meaning and purpose in life come from my relationships with family, others, and with God. I am all too aware of my privilege. I write all this from a position of ease and prosperity. Life is not a daily struggle. I have an abundance of healthy food. There are so many around the world that struggle to physically survive as global warming changes agriculture and oceans. There are those who seek the easy escape of drugs or alcohol. Refugees flee danger, seeking a new beginning and safety for their families. Mental and physical illnesses limit people. Sometimes I wonder how I dare write these words! I don't begin to understand the struggles that challenge so many. To live my life of comfort, ignoring those who struggle and suffer, is to deny the greater responsibility to all of creation. My comfort and way of life mean that I consume more of the world's resources and contribute to the depletion the world's resources and stores in which they are found. I struggle to find a way to live that is aware of both the greater need of others and my privileged situation.

Words from the prophet Micah provide direction for life. *Do justice.* Live in ways that are just and fair. Speak out against the multitude of settings that have injustice such as racism, income inequality, and violence. Black Lives Matter! And when possible, act by advocating legislation that ensures justice for all, condemning acts that belittle and demean others, and speaking out when faced with injustice. *Love kindness.* The Hebrew word *hesed* is deeper and richer than kindness and can't easily be captured in English. It is a deep, faithful covenantal caring. *Walk humbly with our God.* Be aware of God's presence in the ordinary as you go through the day.

Doing justice describes our responsibility to the greater social order. Loving-kindness tells us how we live in relationship with one another. Walking humbly with God keeps us connected to all that is holy. We need all three dimensions for our living. MB

Sub-question 2a. Is there a deep and fundamental meaning in life? Is there a Transcendent Reality that gives order to the universe and a pattern for human life?

For my thoughts are not your thoughts,
nor are your ways my ways, says the Lord.
For as the heavens are high than the earth,

So are my ways higher than your ways
and my thoughts than your thoughts.

Isaiah 55:8–9

I sometimes think we are asking questions that really have no answers. We look and see indistinct images and always we ask whether this is real or is this just my perception. When this happens, I often ask myself another question: "What lies beyond my understanding?" Is there another message as we observe the world and our place in it? Various answers have been suggested. For example, the Celts talk about "thin places" where one encounters the divine. Such places and such experiences may be elusive and unexpected. We are called to maintain an open heart and be ready to be surprised by the divine presence.

And yes, I believe there is a Transcendent Reality that gives order to the universe. It is the source of our being, a Presence who calls us into a deeper and richer state of being. I cannot capture the reality of the One who is so far beyond human understanding. At best, I can see through a mirror dimly, as the apostle Paul told those in Corinth (1 Cor 13:12). Yet I trust that which I cannot fully comprehend, knowing that I am known and understood by God.

Julian of Norwich wrote: "Truth sees God, and wisdom contemplates God, and from these two comes a third, a holy and wonderful delight in God, who is love."[7] While our human language and human imagining cannot fully comprehend God, we know that the center of God's nature is love. We live secure in that divine love, trusting God's essential nature and, as children of God, we also are called to love. "Beloved, let us love one another, because love is from God; everyone who loves is born of God and knows God" (1 John 4:7). MB

Sub-question 2b. Does it really matter whether I have a clear meaning in life as long as I manage the challenges of life? If it does matter, how do I discover my special purpose in life?

"When the Pharisees heard that he had silenced the Sadducees, they gathered together, and one of them, a lawyer, asked him a question

---

7. *Revelation of Divine Love*, from Colledge and Walsh, *Classics of Western Spirituality*, 256.

to test him. 'Teacher, which commandment in the law is the greatest?'
He said to him, 'You shall love the Lord your God with all of your
heart, and with all of your soul, and with all of your mind. This is the
greatest and first commandment. And a second is like it: 'You shall
love your neighbor as yourself.' On these two commandments hang
all the law and the prophets'."

MATTHEW 22:34–40

One question that rises to the surface in all of us has to do with the meaning of our lives. At certain moments, when life takes a twist or turn, the
question becomes important. Do we have a purpose that undergirds the
ebb and flow of family life, the range of daily activities, the social responsibilities, and the professional work we do?

It was in my undergraduate university years that the question sur-
faced for me. I wondered about a major that would prepare me for a
career. I took courses in philosophy in an era when existentialism with
all of its questions and few answers was a guiding philosophy. With my
relatively new religious faith, I faced the questions of meaning as I was
exposed to the thought of Sartre and Camus, and Kierkegaard and Bultmann, and many others.[8]

Thoughtful and kind campus ministers suggested I explore how
Jesus may have answered the questions about the meaning of life. As I
began to study the New Testament, I realized that Jesus did address the
question of meaning, although he did so in his context, first-century Palestine and Jewish teaching drawn from the Hebrew Bible. As Jesus challenged certain beliefs and practices of the Judaism of his time, he did so
by honoring the central teachings of Judaism while challenging the more
cultic and tribal dimensions that tend to creep into established religions.
He valued the Hebrew Bible and honored the law (Torah) but said that is
was given to make life better, not to unnecessarily restrict life by a set of
rules. The summary he gave on more than one occasion was the Golden
Rule: "In everything do to others as you would have them do to you, for
this is the law and prophets" (Matt 7:12).

---

8. Rudolf Bultmann is perhaps not as well known as an existentialist thinker. However, he was influenced by the German philosopher, Martin Heidegger, and used the
categories of existential philosophy in his interpretation of the New Testament. See, for
example, Bultmann's book, *Kerygma and Myth*. See as well Martin Heidegger, *Being
and Time*, and the works of Friedrich Nietzsche.

I have found this teaching the best expression of my purpose in life. I know that to mention Jesus and point to religion as a source for finding meaning does carry some risks.[9] I have tried to face the risks squarely and have struggled with the ambivalent character of religious belief and practice. Yet even in the struggle and doubt that have been ever present for me, I still find my meaning in life in my effort to be a person for others, full of love and truth.[10] DF

Sub-question: 2c. Do we have some basic responsibilities and if so, how do we integrate them into our lives?

For there shall be a sowing of peace; the vine shall yield its fruit, the ground shall give its produce, and the skies shall give their dew; and I will cause the remnant of this people to possess all these things. There are the things that you shall do: Speak the truth to one another, render in your gates judgments that are true and make for peace.

ZECHARIAH 8:12, 16

As God loves us, we are called to love God and one another. Jesus said that love of God and neighbor are the most important commandments. They summarize all of the rest of the commandments (Luke 10:25–28). We are to live in relationship with humanity and with God, acting from love, grateful for the relationships, seeking the best for others, and caring for our own wellbeing.

The Hebrew word *shalom*, often translated as peace, is helpful here. It is more than the absence of war; it is completeness, harmony, and fulfillment. *Shalom* as a life value has economic and physical implications as it seeks to create a community where there is harmony and where people find meaning in their lives. It is a gift from God and our task as well. *Shalom* involves building a community where people thrive, caring for creation, providing health care for all, and participating in the creative

9. Wilson, in his writing and in this particular book, *The Meaning of Human Existence*, argues that there is not sufficient evidence to sustain a religious outlook, and that religion is often cultic and tribal in character (147–70). Philosopher Bertrand Russell's book, *Why I Am Not A Christian*, levels a challenge to belief in Christianity, but also religious belief in general.

10. The author of the Gospel of John describes Jesus as "full of grace and truth" (John 1:14).

act of calling forth new life. We are asked to live with integrity and be aware of the larger world and its needs. We need to consider what we might do to cultivate the presence of *shalom* and what will enable us to flourish in our homes, in our communities, and in our world.

Part of working for *shalom* includes listening carefully for the divine call in one's life and sensing that God is authentically present. It doesn't demand a life of hard work and drudgery, but a life that is awake and aware of the world. *Shalom* might invite us on adventures we wouldn't seek on our own, calling forth courage and imagination. *Shalom* includes caring for the self, so that the deep peace within us might flourish and become part of the larger *shalom* God is creating. MB

Sub-question 2d. How does our career and role in life fit into our understanding of our meaning in life?

The business that veils me from the sight of your Face is the essence of unemployment even though business may be its name.[11]

RUMI

When I was struggling about making right career choices, my treasured teacher gave me two verses upon which to reflect. One was a Qur'anic verse: "Seeking only the Face of thy Sustainer Most High, that one will know peace of mind" (92:20–21). The other was the verse from Rumi quoted above.

As I meditated on the two verses, I realized that seeking God's Face is about bringing divine qualities into every endeavor of mine. Can I infuse my enterprises with a sense of the sacred and be present, aware, loving, and always remember to serve the common good? Whether I chose to be a janitor or a rocket scientist, whether I am young or old, what truly matters is that I humbly and sincerely put my heart and mind into the work and ensure that it benefits others.

Seeking Allah's Face is also about choosing a career path that is in harmony with my deepest values. If I believe in nonviolence, I cannot justify my employment in the armament industry. If I am environmentally conscious, it behooves me not to work in an organization that pollutes the planet. I cannot separate my work from my values. About Right

---

11. Rumi, *Jewels of Remembrance*, 189.

Livelihood, the Buddha said: "The hand of the dyer is subdued by the dye in which it works."[12]

What has given joy and color to my lifework is the distilled wisdom about the meaning of life shared over the years by terminally ill friends I was privileged to know. The answers are consistently the same: life is about love, kindness, awareness, patience, and service. In the different stages of our life, which the Hindu teachers classify as student, householder, retiree, and spiritual contemplative, may we bring those divine qualities into our chosen career and role in life. The teachings are simple and clear, but the practice is difficult. I have constantly endeavored and struggled to live those divine qualities in every stage of my life. The rewards are deeply fulfilling. JR

Sub-question 2e. Do you think that there is a moment or a period of time when we experience an awakening or enlightenment, perhaps a conversion to a new spirit and outlook? Does it happen a single time or is it a process?

Something missing in my heart tonight,
has made my eyes so soft,
my voice so tender,
my need for God absolutely clear.[13]

HAFIZ

In 1991, my mother fell ill and, shockingly, in seven days she died. After twenty grievous days, my father also passed away. My parents were deeply bonded as a couple. These two events shattered my world, but in the process, they also opened my heart to profound inner shifts. My life priorities rearranged themselves, and I felt a greater connection to what Sufis call "traffic and trade in the invisible realms." I did not become enlightened, but I definitely felt a greater clarity about my life and the need to connect with Spirit.

Sufis say we are all spiritual seekers, but, sadly, it takes a crisis of "health" or "wealth" to awaken us. It may be a death of a loved one, a divorce, or a sudden downturn in financial security. In our desperation

12. Smith, *World's Religions*, 108.
13. Ladinsky, *Subject Tonight Is Love*, 277.

we turn to the Source for help and consolation. We yearn to become more authentic and find greater meaning in life. For some of us, life changes forever.

In the timeline of life, it could be a singular event or a series of incidents that lead to an awakening. In a time of failure and despair, Gandhi found a verse from the Hindu scriptures that resonated deeply in him: "Truth is God." By meditating on it continuously, something awakened in him and he felt empowered and guided. For Rumi, spiritual practices taught to him by his teacher, Shams-e-Tabriz, caused his heart to burst open. Incredibly, he began to hear astonishing words of beauty and mystery from the invisible realms. In the story of the Buddha, a profound question haunted him: why would a mother give birth to a child who would eventually grow old, fall sick, and die? The impact of the question took him on a seven-year stretch for answers and, finally, after a period of contemplation, he was enlightened. In the timeline of your life, what experiences or events have contributed to your awakening? JR

Sub-question 2f. Are there stages we go through or patterns of development that increase the understanding of our meaning and purpose in life? What is the journey that leads to an increased understanding of our purpose and responsibility in life?

A stage then, we may say, is an integrated set of operational structures that constitute the thought processes of a person at a given time. Development involves the transformation of such "structures of the whole" in the direction of great internal differentiation, complexity, flexibility and stability. A stage represents a kind of balanced relationship between a knowing subject and his or her environment. In this balanced or equilibrated position the person assimilates what is to be "known" in the environment into her or his existing structures of thought. When a novelty or challenge emerges that cannot be assimilated into the present structures of knowing then, if possible, the person "accommodates", that is, generates new structures of knowing.[14]

JAMES FOWLER

14. Fowler, *Stages of Faith*, 49.

There is a wealth of research and careful writing on the general theme of human development. People such as Sigmund Freud, Carl Jung, Erik Erikson, and Jean Piaget were foundational in their writings on different dimensions of human development. Many more contemporary scholars have continued to add great insight to this broad theme. Carol Gilligan's work has been of great interest to me. Her book on women's development, *In a Different Voice*, was very perceptive regarding the differences between female and male development. On a grand scale, I have been profoundly informed by Ken Wilbur's views of the developmental structures of nearly all that exists.

There is not sufficient time and space to treat thoroughly this theme of human development, yet I want to refer briefly to the work of James Fowler on faith development. He speaks quite directly to our question. He maintains that our faith orientation is central to our understanding of our meaning and purpose of life. He suggests, when a pattern of healthy growth is present, that we go through the following stages:[15]

- We start as infants with Undifferentiated Faith, a simple innocence of trust or mistrust in those who care for us.

- In early childhood, we move into Intuitive-Projective Faith, receiving signals directly from our environment, causing us to face a range of development tasks.

- In our school years, we emerge into the stage of Mythic-Literal Faith, understanding God, for example, as like a wise and kind grandfather.

- In adolescence, we adopt a Synthetic-Conventional Faith by accepting the beliefs held by the majority of people in our culture and society.

- In young adulthood, we begin to question and shape our own beliefs and enter into the stage of Individuative-Reflective Faith.

- As we develop in healthy ways in mid-life and beyond, we may move onto the stage of Conjunctive Faith, a way of seeing, knowing, and committing to a faith that is open, growing, and changing as our knowledge increases and we begin to integrate many streams of knowledge and perspectives.

15. The pattern for growth is seldom a straight path and often one may return to an earlier stage or perhaps remain permanently in one stage such as the Synthetic-Conventional.

- In late adult life, we may grow into Universalizing Faith, although few people move to this stage, not infrequently remaining in the stage of Synthetic-Conventional Faith.[16]

As I look back upon my years of development, I find the work of Fowler and other scholars of human development to be profound and often very descriptive of my journey. Their views have increased my self-understanding, providing insights that enabled me to move toward maturity and healing. Their work has helped me to gain clarity on my purpose and responsibilities in life. DF

Sub-question 2g: How does our meaning and purpose in life take shape in responsibilities? How can I prioritize my daily and often overwhelming tasks and duties?

We urgently need to make compassion a clear, luminous and dynamic force in our polarized world. Rooted in principled determination to transcend selfishness, compassion can break down political, dogmatic, ideological and religious boundaries. Born of our deep interdependence, compassion is essential in human relationships and to a fulfilled humanity. It is the path to enlightenment, and indispensable to the creation of a just economy and a peaceful global community.[17]

THE CHARTER OF COMPASSION

A wide variety of answers have been given to the question of how our meaning and purpose in life takes shape in daily responsibilities. One common answer is that we are intelligent and have the capacity to think deeply about the human experience and the world around us. Part of this answer usually suggests that we can be self-aware and that we have a conscience. Still another related way the question has been answered is by describing humans as having consciousness or an outlook on reality. It is the ability to be aware of one's self, thoughts, feelings, actions, and environment. Building on this notion of consciousness, I would like to add

16. Fowler, *Stages of Faith*, 113. James Fowler acknowledges his dependence on the work of Levinson, *Seasons of a Man's Life.*

17. From the last paragraph of *The Charter of Compassion*, created by British religious scholar, Karen Armstrong with guidance from the Dalai Lama, 2008. It has been widely circulated and has been adopted by many cities and associations.

that because of our sensitive awareness, we are able to be compassionate. We are able to reflect on our own inner life and situation, *and* also the life and conditions of others. Compassion is that ability to identify with and feel the suffering of others; it is the inner awareness of shared suffering. It is not that we will always move toward compassion, but we are able to, and the great religious and wisdom teachers of the world have urged us to be compassionate people. It is to sense and share the calling of Mother Teresa who gave herself to the poor of India. It is to be aware of the following moral dimensions of life:

1. There is the universal golden rule, to care for others even as we would like to have others care for us.

2. It is to give up our exclusive preoccupation with our own needs and desires (not that they are unimportant) and put a high priority on the needs and desires of others.

3. It means getting involved with those who live on the margins of opportunity, education, health, wealth, and power. We have deep empathy for their suffering and commit in some form to live in solidarity with them. It is to make a caring and intelligent response to those in need.[18]

There is a risk in this question about answering it with generalities, ones that occasionally are trite and trivial. Yet these undergirding foundational principles have been helpful in guiding me. They have guided my career, family life, and social engagements; in these domains these foundational principles have taken a specific focus. For example, while my contribution was limited, I have been involved in securing peace in the midst of Northern Ireland's "troubles," engaged in interfaith understanding through a small and excellent university in Lahore, Pakistan, and lent a hand in the quest for a just peace in Israel and Palestine. DF

Sub-question 2h. Do you occasionally feel conflict between your immediate needs and desires and your sense of having a purpose in life?

18. Similar values and wording are in "The Earth Charter" published by UNESCO in March, 2000.

The Lord will fulfill his purpose for me;
Your steadfast love, O Lord, endures forever.
Do not forsake the work of your hands.

PSALM 138:8

Often, when a family crisis arises, I do less well with my work. But then I reflect on what is the real purpose in life, which is to live with integrity, and that may include responding to unplanned events. Life, for me, is always a juggling act. I can let others' demands fill my life when they say: "serve here" or "volunteer there." These are good options, but if they don't allow the space to listen to my deep inner voice, I find myself poured out and depleted. I constantly struggle keeping an equilibrium in my life, responding to family and friends, working for justice, doing the daily tasks of maintaining a home, finding time for prayer and meditation, and seeking the peace that comes when I walk in the beauty of creation.

If anything, my problem is that there are too many good things calling for my attention. And then there are the foolish distractions—too much television and preoccupation with my cell phone and computer. Maintaining a balance of being responsible and yet receiving good information and some entertainment describe my challenge of maintaining a balance in life. Not easy!

A balanced life has time for rest and renewal. In the 23rd Psalm, the Shepherd "makes me lie down in green pastures." This first year after my retirement I am learning to wait for my next invitation. My sense is that God wants me rested and renewed, and then be ready to respond to a new divine possibility. One possibility, drawing upon my years as a pastor, is to offer my service to serve as an interim pastor in a congregation this is seeking a new pastor.

I know that God's purpose for my life is in God's hands. I will not discern it or earn it by a number of good deeds or righteous living. God is at work in the midst of the complexities of our lives, calling forth goodness and new purpose. All we need to do is trust in the power of love our Creator offers. MB

Sub-question 2i. How important to you is making money, having a good job, and "getting ahead"? Is life about gaining prestige, seeking pleasure, and having power over others? Or are there other motivations that should guide us?

Do not deprive yourselves of the good things of life which God has made lawful to you, but do not transgress the bounds of what is right.

QUR'AN 5:87

We transgress the boundaries of what is right when we give the highest priority to acquiring wealth, fame, and power. It is a sign that we have let our ego dominate our life. The desires of the ego are unlimited. It is never satisfied.

Hazrat Ali said that if you give two valleys full of gold to a person, this person, driven by ego needs, will nearly always yearn for a third valley of gold. In the same vein, the Buddha said that the rain could turn to gold and still this would not quench our thirst. In another pointed metaphor, the Buddha explained that like a hunted hare we run, the pursuer of desire pursued, harried from life to life.

It is important to remember that besides having body and ego, we also possess a soul that is not obsessed with money, power, and fame. It is important to feed our body, meet our material essentials, and enjoy the good things of life, which are gifts from God. But what are we doing to nurture our soul, which is nourished by silence, prayers, music, sunsets, and laughter? May we strike a balance in satisfying both our material wants and soul needs as we aspire for a life of joy and fulfillment. Rumi reminds us that not all pleasures are the same: "Jesus was intoxicated by love of God; his donkey was drunk on barley."[19]

The Qur'an reminds us repeatedly about the need to serve God's creation. Let us remember the joy and value of accumulating good deeds in our lifetime. On the day of liberation, we will have to leave behind our wealth and titles at our palace. Friends and relatives can accompany us only up to the gravesite. But beyond that, what will take us further into those mysterious realms is the record of good deeds. JR

---

19. Barks and Moyne, *Essential Rumi*, 6.

CHAPTER 2: WHY AM I HERE?

Resources and Practices

Further Reading

1. Kathleen Cahalan, and Douglas J. Schuurman, editors, *Calling in Today's World: Voices from Eight Faith Perspective*

2. James W. Fowler, *Stages of Faith: The Psychology of Human Development and the Quest for Meaning*

3. Carol Gilligan, *In a Different Voice: Psychological Theory and Women's Development*

4. The Dalai Lama, *The Compassionate Life*

5. Jack Kornfield, *A Path with Heart: A Guide Through the Perils and Promises of Spiritual Life*

6. Brian J. Mahan, *Forgetting Ourselves on Purpose: Vocation and the Ethics of Ambition*

7. Jamal Rahman, *Spiritual Gems of Islam*

Suggested Practices

1. Share in a small group the pattern of your spiritual growth, how it got started, where you currently are, and where you would like to go. Use the questions of Chapter 2: "Why Am I Here?" as a guide for the discussion. Listen carefully and compassionately to how the others trace their spiritual growth.

2. Describe in a journal entry the pattern of your spiritual growth. Be as honest as possible, entering the positive growth, its reasons, and the challenges you are facing.

3. Discuss with a trusted friend or spiritual director as well as the small group what the next steps of growth should be and how you might get there. You may find it easier to be more complete in the your answer with a trusted friend or spiritual director.

4. As possible, take advantage of a retreat, workshop, or class that will expand your understanding of spiritual formation.

5. Share in a small group and/or in your journal your sense of vocation or calling (or lack of it) that gives your life meaning.

Foundational Question 3
What Are My Deepest Values?

Unlimited Love is the mysterious point of convergence between all worthwhile religions and is deemed the essential aspect of a presence in the universe that is infinitely higher than our own. While some view this unselfish love for all humanity as merely a human moral ideal, I view it in metaphysical terms as ultimate reality that underlies all that is, and which can transform our limited and broken lives into journeys of remarkable generous service. If Unlimited Love really does describe ultimate reality, then we need not be so surprised by people who do so much to serve humanity while claiming they are inspired by a loving energy in the universe. Unlimited Love is God's Love for us all.[1]

STEPHEN POST

THE UNLIMITED LOVE ABOUT which Stephen Post speaks has been the central core of my values and the guiding motivation of my life.[2] I have been guided in the adoption of this position by the First Letter of John in the New Testament in which the author declares: "Beloved, let us love one another, because love is from God; everyone who loves is born of God and knows God. Whoever does not love does not know God, for God is love" (1 John 4:7–8). The author of this first epistle of John also felt it was important to stress the foundational value of truth as the complement to love: "This is the message we have heard from him and proclaim to

1. Post, *Unlimited Love*, 11.
2. See my book, *Lovescapes: Mapping the Geography of Love*, in which I try to describe the many dimensions of love.

you that God is light and in God there is no darkness at all" (1 John 1:5). Light, in this statement, is a wonderful metaphor for truth or Truth in reference to God. There is another passage in the Gospel of John that affirms that Jesus came to represent and teach us about love and light. "And the Word became flesh and dwelt among us, and we have seen his glory . . . full of grace and truth" (John 1:14–15a). Grace, a word pointing to unlimited love, and light, a metaphor for truth, characterized the life and teaching of Jesus. As we follow his life and teaching we discover that his deepest values were love and truth.[3]

Across my adult years I have diligently tried to find the best ways to understand Jesus and his mission. There were many years of studying "the Christ of faith" or the ways in which the church has understood Jesus and proclaimed his message. These years of study were demanding, rich, and rewarding, but along the way I also continued to reflect on the Jesus of history. It is not that these endeavors were necessarily in opposition to each other, but they were different strategies and provided different perspectives. It is not far off to say that those engaged in New Testament scholarship have worked diligently the last two centuries to bring some clarity to these two approaches of understanding Jesus. At the end of a career engaged in this study, I have personally moved toward finding in the historical Jesus my deepest values, love in all of its many expressions, including compassion, justice, peace, and truth in all of its manifestations with an emphasis on the life of honesty, integrity, and authenticity. DF

FOUNDATIONAL QUESTION 3: WHAT ARE MY DEEPEST VALUES?

My child, do not forget my teaching,
but let your heart keep my commandments;
for length of days and years of my life
and abundant welfare they will give you.
Do not let loyalty and faithfulness forsake you;
bind them around your neck,
write them on the tablet of your heart.
So you will find favor and good repute

---

3. I have tried to provide a scholarly basis for understanding the mission of Jesus in the two books: *The Radical Teaching of Jesus* and *The Radical Invitation of Jesus.*

in the sight of God and of people.
Trust in the Lord with all your heart,
and do not rely on your own insight.
In all your ways acknowledge God,
who will make straight your paths.
Do not be wise in your own eyes;
follow the Lord, and turn away from evil
It will be healing for your flesh
and a refreshment for your body.

PROVERBS 3:1–8

Two books of the Bible help me define values. First, the book of Proverbs; it is often classified as Wisdom Literature and instructs readers on the way to live. As such, it teaches me many important values: honesty, faithfulness, gratitude, the importance of speaking carefully, kindness, humility, and the value of work. Often the proverbs contrast wise and foolish ways of living. For example: "Doing wrong is like sport to a fool, but wise conduct is pleasure to a person of understanding" (Prov 10:23). Throughout the book there is the desire to teach values to the next generation so they may live in ways that bring health to them and all creation.

Another list of values, helping me, comes from the book of Galatians. The apostle Paul writes: "By contrast, the fruit of the Spirit is love, joy, peace, patience, kindness, generosity, and self-control. There is no law against such things" (Gal 5:22–23). One may enlarge the list with values such as honesty, truth, integrity, compassion, wisdom, beauty, courage, and perseverance. And the list might go on and on. Our deepest values are those qualities that keep us closer to God's call for our lives. These values will ensure that our lives and our communities continue to thrive.

The list in Galatians is described as the fruit of the Spirit. In essence, these are not characteristics we strive for or achieve and practice in our own strength, but come as a result of the Spirit acting in our lives. They form the basis for a healthy life, lived with a sense of the holy in our midst. If we live with an awareness of the presence of the Divine, we discover that these deepest values are reflected in our relationships. There is a paradox here in that we cannot create the fruit of the Spirit by our own efforts, yet we can mold our lives so they align with the working of the Spirit. MB

FOUNDATIONAL QUESTION 3: WHAT ARE MY DEEPEST VALUES?

In the Name of God, Boundlessly Compassionate and Infinitely Merciful.[4]

THE QUR'AN

In my early childhood, my parents taught me by word and example that the core teaching of Islam is the divine attribute of compassion, and to this day compassion is the value that I most treasure and try to express in my own life. The compassionate nature of our Creator is invoked at the beginning of virtually every chapter of the Qur'an: "In the name of God, Boundlessly Compassionate and Infinitely Merciful." This invocation, called the Basmala, inspired the Prophet Muhammad to conclude that all the teachings of the Qur'an can be distilled into a message of Divine Compassion. When a Bedouin asked him about the secret inner meaning of the Basmala, the Prophet replied, "Have compassion on yourself and on others."

To expound on the astonishing power and beauty of practicing compassion in our lives, Sufi teachers use the metaphor of water in nature. They teach that water can be wonderfully soft and yielding, but over time it can also overcome the hardest granite. We also know that wherever water falls, life flourishes. Thus, the person who is gentle and merciful is not only possessed of authentic strength, but his or her compassion is life-affirming and life-bestowing.

To be compassionate with myself, I was taught to engage in self-talk with gentleness and mercy. This practice is called "Sacred Naming." From an early age I called myself "Brother Jamal." Whenever I become aware that I am being overly self-critical, I do a spiritual intervention by addressing myself as "Brother Jamal" and carrying on the conversation with mercy and sweetness. Immediately, I find that the tone, energy, and content of my self-talk shifts. In the process, lessons are learned and surprisingly, in the times of difficulties, from the womb of compassion creative solutions emerge.

To practice compassion with others, especially those who are adversarial, I was told to invoke compassionate awareness, and I needed

---

4. This invocation is called the Basmala, which opens all of the 114 Chapters in the Qur'an except one.

to learn how to distinguish between behavior and being. In dealing with those who are difficult, protect yourself and take the right action. But as you take the right action remember to keep this person's essence or divine spark in your heart. You might be upset at their behavior, but remember that their inner core is sacred. Keeping this compassionate discernment in our heart and taking the right action has the power to shift heaven and earth. JR

Sub-question 3a: Do we choose our values or do they gradually emerge in our life-experience?

My child, keep your father's commandment,
and do not forsake your mother's teaching.
Bind them upon your heart always;
tie them around your neck.

PROVERBS 6:20–21

It is not necessarily an *either/or*, but more often a *both/and*. Our deepest values begin in our childhood and the way we are raised. Yet both life experiences and maturity bring other values to the fore. As children, we are taught the values of our own family. If we are fortunate, these values include such qualities as love and respect, curiosity, kindness, and fairness. The reality is that not all children have these positive experiences. When children are treated harshly and their needs are not met, they fail to learn the values that will help them thrive.

We learn values throughout life. As we explore the damage to our earth, we come to value restraint in using the resources of creation. As we see the evidence of racism, we listen deeply to persons of color and vow to fight for justice for all people. In addition, we observe how others offer empathy and compassion, and we learn to be more caring from their example.

The world and culture around us often speak with values that may not be helpful. Advertising suggests that happiness comes in the accumulations of things. Celebrity culture honors lives that may not reflect healthy values. Even churches can bring values that are harmful. Some do not find LGBTQIA persons as beloved of God or worthy of honor and respect.

Daily experience itself teaches us values. A challenging situation may call forth courage we never knew we had. Working in a soup kitchen may help us respect those whose lives are different from our own.

As faith deepens and we understand more clearly how deeply God loves us and all of creation, our values grow stronger. We find wisdom and courage to follow God's call to love one another and honor creation. A deep spiritual relationship to the holy is the foundation of the moral life. MB

Sub-question 3b: Are there stages or patterns of growth in our moral development? If so, how would you describe them? Are they the same for all people?

In everything do to others as you would have them do to you; for this is the law and the prophets.

MATTHEW 7:12

The Golden Rule, as stated in the passage above, guided the thought and behavior of Jesus and his followers. It was one way they summarized the ethical teaching of Hebrew Bible, using the expression of "the law and the prophets" as a reference to the moral teaching it contained. The Golden Rule appears in various forms in many of the world's religions.

Lawrence Kohlberg, a faculty member at Harvard University in the latter part of the twentieth century, raised the question of how it is we develop a level of maturity that empowers us to consistently practice our ethical ideals. Drawing upon the psychological theories of human development, Kohlberg framed a developmental theory of moral growth toward maturity.[5] We might summarize Kohlberg's view in the following way. He begins by saying that there are three *levels* of moral development: pre-conventional, conventional, and post-conventional. Each of these levels has a pattern of two *stages*.

1. The pre-conventional level emerges in childhood and is based solely on the child's needs and perceptions.

---

5. His view may be found in his book, *The Philosophy of Moral Development*, published in 1981.

2. The conventional level is when moral judgments are based upon the expectations of family, society and law.

3. The post-conventional level is the period in which moral judgments are based on thoughtfully and carefully chosen personal principles of love and justice, not necessarily determined by the conventional views of society.

The pre-conventional level has the two stages:

- The first stage is the punishment-obedience orientation in which one obeys rules to avoid punishment.

- The second stage functions in terms of reward and affirmation, with the personal needs of the developing person being the primary motivation.

The conventional level, based on the approval of others, family expectations, and traditional values also has two stages:

- There is the phase of gaining acceptance and approval by one's actions, often described as the "good boy, good girl" phase.

- There is also the orientation of "law and order" with the understanding that laws and structures of order are absolute and enforced by authority.

The post-conventional level is based on experienced judgments and self-determined principles. It also has two stages:

- There is an understanding and presence of a social contract, often written and sometimes assumed, based on arranged agreements and covenants.

- It is also based on universally understood principles, such as justice and peace, which exist and are implied in the Golden Rule.

My view is that this developmental orientation is a relatively accurate general description of our moral development. Through education and a supportive and nurturing context, we can assist individuals to grow and mature and influence corporate structures to move toward the common good. His view gives me hope that through providing the right environment, we can assist individuals, associations, and even governments to improve the human condition of individuals and society. Ethical behavior can be taught and learned. DF

Sub-question 3c: What motivates us to engage in moral development? What motivates me to pursue a more mature ethical position? How much is our motivation conscious and how much is unconscious?

He is continually engaged in discovering that to be all of himself in this fluid sense is not synonymous with being evil or uncontrolled. It is instead to feel a growing pride in being a sensitive, open, realistic, an inner-directed member of the human species, adapting with courage and imagination to the complexity of the changing situation. It means taking continual steps toward being, in awareness and in expression of that which is congruent with one's total organismic reactions. To use Kierkegaard's more aesthetically satisfying terms, it means, "to be that self which one truly is." I trust that I have made it evident that this is not an easy direction to move, nor one that is ever completed. It is a continuing way of life.[6]

CARL ROGERS

As one asks the question about the origin of motivation, one is inevitably drawn into human development theory, and as the questions turn to ethics, the issue of spirituality often emerges. We engage in the process of developing a conscience and finding a moral center as we mature. There are many theories that suggest that the quest is internal, that it is built into our nature as human beings. As we mature physically and intellectually, so do we mature and develop more mature ethical standards. The theologian might argue that the developing conscience is the expression of the image of God. The biological scientist might suggest that it is a part of evolution and the product of our need to survive and continue the race. The social scientist might maintain that it is a product of interaction with our environment, present in family life, education, and social norms that influence us. Perhaps there is a trace of all of these factors, suggesting that it has both internal and external causes. Our moral compass may be a product of both conscious choices and unconscious psychic and social factors.

---

6. Rogers, *On Becoming a Person*, 181. Carl Rogers, writing many decades ago, used the masculine "he" to describe a person whether they are male or female.

What I would like to stress in this brief inquiry is how we might draw upon this range of factors, increase our understanding of them, decide to cultivate our ethical sensibilities, and choose to help create a more just and humane world. While research needs to be done and books have been and need to be written about how we move in this direction, I want to suggest three preliminary steps.

1. The first is to *learn* as much as possible about the extraordinary need for mature people who have integrity and a commitment to the welfare of others. It is a tremendously needy world. Where might I serve?

2. The second is to follow the guidance of Kierkegaard and discover who you are and then be true to yourself. This may mean some counseling and a setting in which you can *heal, grow, and be free and comfortable to become a person for others*, one who has compassion and cares for those in great need.

3. The third is to then begin to *engage* in whatever ways are possible for you to lend a hand in creating a more must and humane society and world. DF

Sub-question 3d: What guides our behavior? What are the sources we draw upon for guidance?

Consult your soul, consult your heart . . . Righteousness is what reassures your soul and heart. Sin is what wavers in your soul and puts tension in your chest, even if people approve it in their judgments again and again.[7]

SAYING OF THE PROPHET MUHAMMAD

Ultimately, what guides our behavior on important issues of our life is the voice of inner guidance. We might call it the voice of our higher self. How clearly we hear that voice is a reflection of the work we do on ourselves to diminish our ego and open our heart to divine communication.

The opinions of experts, authorities, and elders are important, but even more important is the need to find out how these opinions feel and

---

7. An-Nawawi, *An-Nawawi's Forty Hadith*, #29.

resonate inside of us. If the opinion makes us uncomfortable, we have a right to question it no matter what the cultural norms of our time dictate. This is especially true about controversial and divisive issues, e.g., abortion and euthanasia. Spiritual teachers ask Muslims to consult three primary sources of wisdom and guidance, but caution that ultimately we need to consult our heart.

The first source is the Qur'an. Muslims believe that the seventh-century revelations are divine, transmitted from Divinity to angel Gabriel to the Prophet Muhammad. Keep in mind that some of the revelations are time-specific and do not apply to the twenty-first century. Moreover, Sufi teachers humorously point out that revelations are not accompanied by footnotes! Human interpretations of the same verse can differ.

The second source is the collected sayings of the Prophet Muhammad and observation of his conduct. These are called the Hadith. Sadly, since all Hadith are based on hearsay, many are fabricated and unreliable. But it is nevertheless a valuable resource.

The third source is the wisdom of the elders, jurists, and sages. Opinions of the wise and experienced can vary and one can go shopping for the opinion closest to one's own, but there is great wisdom in their teaching.

If I look at the issue of abortion, there is no specific Qur'anic verse on this topic, but there are universal verses about the precious sanctity of life. All Muslim jurists agree on the need for abortion if the mother's life is in danger, but besides that exception there is disagreement. Those who favor abortion quote the Prophet who said that it takes 120 days for the fetus to be "ensouled." Thus, abortion in that time period is permissible. Others claim that the Hadith is fabricated and conclude that abortion amounts to murder. Eventually, I have to consult my heart for the right answer. My inner guidance tells me to be "pro-choice."

On the issue of euthanasia, I have two friends who struggled and suffered heroically with their incurable physical afflictions and chose "death with dignity." Even though the Qur'an, Hadith, and jurists say that the taking of one's own life is forbidden, my heart is fully at peace with their decision. In my heart, I realize the wisdom of Sufi sages who say that all the theologies of the world are as nothing compared to one whisper of the Beloved. JR

Sub-question 3e: What does it mean to live an ethical life? Are you a moral person? How does one know that one is a moral person?

First, by doing no harm, by avoiding evil of every kind, especially that which is most generally practiced. Secondly, by doing good: by being in every situation kind and merciful after their power; as they have opportunity, doing good of every possible sort, and as far as possible, to all. Thirdly, by attending upon all the ordinances of God.[8]

JOHN WESLEY

There are the General Rules for the ethical life established by John Wesley, founder of Methodism, and as a Methodist pastor, I am guided by this teaching. There are more details beneath each rule. For example, under doing no harm, one is to avoid the evil of slaveholding and to avoid "fighting, quarreling." My favorite prohibition is against "the using of many words in buying or selling."

The General Rules were published in 1739, and they reflect that time. While we might smile at some of the language, the three rules nevertheless provide structure for living an ethical life today. We can still apply them to the situations we face. "Do no harm and avoid evil" could urge us to be aware of the amount of fossil fuels we use and try to find ways to use less. It might suggest that we become more aware of the evil of racism and do what we can to combat that evil. Doing good is of course the comprehensive positive statement. We are to treat others with kindness and work to make the world a better place. "Attending on the ordinances of God," means to be consistent in practicing one's faith: reading the Bible and participating in a church community. In his book, *Three Simple Rules: A Wesleyan Way of Living*, Bishop Rueben Job rephrases the third rule as "stay in love with God."

Examining one's life using these three rules is one way to determine if one is acting in a way that is moral. Doing no harm, doing good, and practicing one's faith is a good outline for the moral life. We depend too upon the insights of many others to lead us into a deeper understanding of the moral life. It is important to note that what once was acceptable as an expression of a moral life in a particular time and culture, may no

8. Wesley, *General Rules*, 78–80.

longer be acceptable in our time and culture. We seek to find, then, those
values that are more universal in character and guide the human family
regardless of culture and the time in history. MB

Sub-question 3f: Is it important to honor and care for oneself while caring for others?

*That I feed the hungry, forgive an insult, and love my enemy—these
are great virtues. But what if I should discover that the poorest of
beggars and most impudent of offenders are all within me, and that
I stand in need of all the alms of my own kindness; that I myself am
the enemy who must be loved—what then?*[9]

CARL JUNG

The simple truth is that our outer relationships are a reflection of the
relationship I have with myself. If I am not loving and compassionate
with myself, I cannot truly be loving and compassionate with others. I
may learn the script of what it looks like to be outwardly affectionate
and merciful, but, as the wisdom teachers say, the varnish will not hide
the grain. Eventually, in my caring for others, I will feel inauthentic, inadequate, and incomplete. The quality of my service to others will suffer.

For this reason, Sufi teachers wisely stress the importance of being
of service to ourselves if we aspire to be of genuine help to others. When
you have challenging feelings such as anger, fear, or sadness, can you embrace them with compassion? These are simply energies begging to be
acknowledged, held, and integrated. They have an edge only because they
are separated from us. To use Carl Jung's language, when we muster courage and grace to kiss the demons and dragons within us, they transform
into a prince or princess. Our anger transforms into vitality, our fear into
mindfulness, and our sadness into great empathy for others. In this way,
we are able to be of authentic service.

If we do not do the inner work of embracing and transforming our
own difficult emotions, the dangers is that our righteous anger might
turn into revenge, and in fighting injustice, we ourselves might become
unjust. Similarly, if we do not heal our own fear and grief, when we

---

9. Jung, *Collected Works of C. G. Jung*, Vol. 14.

attempt to help those who are fearful and grief-stricken, we might ourselves be overwhelmed.

As we heal and integrate our own emotional wounds, we mature and evolve. At a certain point in time we do not have to consciously calculate how to help others. Genuine service and caring flows organically.

Consider the story of Zen Master Ryokan (d. 1831). He was once approached by his brother and asked to spend time in his household and to help his nephew who was turning incorrigibly rude and rebellious. The Master spent a few days there, but to the brother's dismay he did not say a word of admonition to the nephew. As the Master was preparing to leave, the nephew, as custom dictated, knelt to help the uncle put on his sandals. Suddenly, he looked up because he felt wetness on his forehead. Copious tears were streaming down from the uncle's eyes. In that moment, the nephew was transformed. JR

Sub-question 3g: If you believe in God, do you think we are invited to a God-centered or value-centered life rather than a self-centered life? Does belief in God make a difference?

There was a devout God-fearing monkey who made it his lifelong mission to visit neighborhood ponds to pluck the fish out of the water to save them from a watery grave.[10]

SUFI SAYING

I have lost count of the many times my teachers instructed me to meditate on this story and take to heart the critical need to expand my level of consciousness. Second only to Allah, the most repeated word in the Qur'an is *ilm* or knowledge, and the Qur'an instructs us to pray, "O God, increase my knowledge" (20:114). Thus we may infer that belief in God without higher knowledge is incomplete, and the Prophet Muhammad counsels us to seek knowledge from "cradle to grave." Even more than knowledge for its own sake, Sufi teachers ask us to move from "knowledge of tongue to knowledge of heart."

Without an expanded consciousness, our belief in God and the values that we think are God-centered can be ego-centered and actually hurt others. Over the centuries, overzealous and narrow-minded clerics and

10. Sufi Teaching Story.

missionaries of many denominations and faith traditions, in the name of God, have damaged and destroyed countless human lives in their quest to "share the good news."

Our human consciousness can never fully comprehend the enormity and mystery of God. However, we can begin to know God, say the Sufi teachers, by practicing the Divine Attributes of God, e.g., oneness, love, and compassion. A number of my close friends are atheists and agnostics who profess non-belief in God. Many of them, in my opinion, are among the most God-conscious people I know. They simply call God by a different name such as Compassion, Justice, Truth, Forgiveness, or Patience.

Whether we believe in God or not, we have to increase our consciousness if we want peace, justice, and harmony to flourish in a diverse society. The words of the golden rule articulated by the Prophet Muhammad are beautiful: "None of you has faith until he loves his brother or neighbor as he loves himself."[11] However, we cannot assume that we know what our brothers, sisters, and neighbors want and how they want to be treated.

As I write, we are making preparations in Seattle for a city-wide multi-faith summit whose topic is "Introducing the Platinum Rule: The Key to Building Community." To truly practice the golden rule, I have to advance to the platinum rule by continuously working to diminish my prejudices and connect with others on a personal level to become aware of their authentic needs and aspirations. JR

Sub-question 3h: Where do the universal values of love, integrity, and justice fit into your behavior? Is it possible for you to truly love another person (or persons) without self-interest playing a part?

May God give us light to guide us,
courage to support us,
and love to unite us,
now and evermore.

Celtic Blessing

---

11. Suhrawardy, *Sayings of Muhammad*, 1.

Love is a gift of God, poured out in abundance. I have experienced love in many ways, and it is there when I least expect it. I am often surprised that it occurs in my dealings with family, friends, and people of the community. It is in these settings, in our day-to-day life, that we have opportunities to express the value of love. There are, of course, in these settings many forms of love, from the close love of a romantic partner to the general love of humanity in its many forms.

Integrity involves being honest and having strong moral principles. A person with integrity acts in a way that is congruent with her or his values. These persons are trustworthy and we can rely on them, knowing that their words and their actions match.

Justice calls us to be aware of the needs of others and to always be fair with them. The heart of justice is fair practice. We work to see that basic needs are met for all people, and do not discriminate between them. Through the prophet Amos, God calls us to practice justice. Rather than praise and gifts, "let justice roll down like waters and righteousness like an ever-flowing stream" (Amos 5:24).

Does it really matter if self-interest plays some part in our loving of others? Love is often reciprocal, and if we find personal delight in the relationship, that does not diminish the blessings of love. Love dares us to reach beyond those we love easily in order to love those who are difficult. Jesus said, "But I say to you that listen, Love your enemies, do good to those who hate you, bless those who curse you, pray for those who abuse you" (Luke 6:27–28). Jesus calls for a more radical kind of loving that pulls us past what is comfortable and demands that we relate to all people as beloved children of God. This is never easy, but Jesus deepens our understanding of what love looks like. We work toward this, challenging ourselves to share God's love with everyone. MB

Sub-question 3i: Is there a model of an ideal person, such as Buddha, Moses, Jesus, Muhammad, Gandhi, Mary (the mother of Jesus), Fatima, Clare of Assisi, Mother Teresa, Dorothy Day, or someone you personally know that guides and motivates you?

We will have to move through a very deep valley, I believe much deeper that we can sense now, before we will be able to ascend the other side again.[12]

DIETRICH BONHOEFFER

There have been many people who have inspired and motivated me. In the earlier years of my Christian journey, I was introduced to many individuals who became models for me. As I look back to those years, one person does stand out; it was Dietrich Bonhoeffer, the young German scholar and pastor, who faced the harsh realities existing in Germany during the Second World War. He courageously and consistently modeled the virtues of faith, hope, and love in a challenging time.

He had been raised in an established family in Germany and was able to receive an excellent education. He chose to study theology and become a pastor. He studied in Tübingen University, spent time in Spain, and then returned to Berlin where he received his doctorate. He did post-doctoral study, teaching, and pastoral service in New York and London. During these years, his *faith* matured and had the essential qualities of profound theological understanding, trust in the wisdom and guidance of God, and a commitment to follow the will and way of God. While in New York, away from the tragic events of the Hitler's reign, he had to decide whether to return to Germany and become part of the resistance movement. As a person with a love for his country and deep and mature faith, he felt he must return to help his people. He returned in 1943 and formed an underground seminary, a setting in which he would reflect on the meaning of a faith community.

He went as a person of *hope*. He knew, as he got involved in the resistance movement and his opposition to Hitler's treatment of Jews, that his life would be in jeopardy. As he engaged in resistance, he and his colleagues pondered whether they should become involved in a plot to assassinate Adolf Hitler. He directly faced the realities of the conflict by engaging in an act of war even though he was a committed pacifist. He asked whether the *hope* of a better life for the German people and the Jews in particular should override his commitment to always act in peaceful ways. He participated in an attempt to assassinate Hitler. It failed, and he was arrested and placed in a concentration camp, but never lost hope.

12. Quoted but Eric Metaxas in the biography of Dietrich Bonhoeffer, *Bonhoeffer: Pastor, Martyr, Prophet, Spy*, 358.

While back in Germany, in the resistance and in the concentration camp, Bonhoeffer demonstrated his dedication to the foundational teaching that Christians are to love. He knew that there were times when to love was not simply being kind to another person, but a life commitment that is often filled with conflict and has the prophetic dimension of "speaking truth to power." He reflected in his journal about the meaning of love and how he could justify engaging in a violent act that would serve the welfare of millions of people. At the end, he became a loving pastor to those who were with him in prison. Just prior to the arrival of American soldiers, he was executed in early 1945. Dietrich Bonhoeffer became and continues to be a model for me on how to live a life based on faith, hope, and love.

CHAPTER 3: WHY AM I HERE?

Resources and Practices

Further Reading

1. Dietrich Bonhoeffer, *The Cost of Discipleship*

2. Carl W. Ernst, *Teachings of Sufism*

3. John Esposito, *Islam: The Straight Path*

4. Duncan S. Ferguson, *Lovescapes: Mapping the Geography of Love*

5. P. M. Forni, *Choosing Civility: The Twenty-Five Rules of Considerate Conduct*

6. Tana Pesso with Penor Rinpoche, *First Invite Love In: 40 Time-Tested Tools for Creating a More Compassionate Life*

7. Steven Post, *Unlimited Love: Altruism, Compassion, and Service*

8. Joseph Runzo and Nancy M. Martin, *Ethics in the World Religions*

9. Jonathan Sachs, *The Dignity of Difference: How to Avoid the Clash of Civilizations*

10. John Wesley, *Works of John Wesley*, edited by Albert C. Outler, 32 vols.

Suggested Practices

1. Attend a worship service or an event in a religious tradition that is different from your own. Be sure to observe and discern the teachings, the ethical practices, and the patterns of the community. Ask yourself how the service may have been helpful to the people in attendance and how it differed from a service in your tradition.

2. Select and read a book, such as the one by the Dalai Lama, entitled *Toward a True Kinship of Faiths: How the World's Religions Can Come Together,* about interfaith understanding and cooperation. Write down in your journal how it may be possible to learn from and collaborate with people from a different religion.

3. Volunteer to assist or at least observe a social service organization that works with troubled teenagers or people with serious addictions. Take notes on how effective their approach may be in helping these people begin to heal and find their way.

4. Select a member of your own family or in your circle of acquaintances with whom you have some tension or conflict. Begin a tangible effort to show love and compassion in a mature way that increases the chances that there may be healing in the relationship. Describe these efforts in your journal.

5. Take on an "empathy project" in which you identify a religious tradition, a political orientation, or an ethnic or national heritage that is not your own and write a brief description of why you think those who are different from you believe and act the way they do.

Foundational Question 4
Do You Believe In God?

We may, however, really begin to wonder if Christianity has not come to an end. Is it all over with belief in God? Has religion any future? Can we not have morality even without religion? Is not science sufficient? Has not religion developed out of magic? Will it not perish in the process of evolution? Is not God from the outset a projection of man (Feuerbach), opium of the people (Marx), resentment of those who have fallen short (Nietzsche), illusion of those who have remained infantile (Freud)? Has atheism not been proved and is nihilism not irrefutable? Have not even theologians finally given up proving God's existence? Or are we supposed to believe without reason?[1]

HANS KÜNG

HANS KÜNG, AN EXCEPTIONAL German theologian in the last half of the twentieth century and the early part of this century, has raised and tried to answer a fundamental question common to all of us. Is there a God, and if so, is God personal or impersonal? It is his view that "atheism today demands an account of our belief in God as it never did in the past."[2] I have in front of me approximately twenty-five books, most of them current, but many written over the last several decades that speak to this question.[3] Some attempt an answer and others suggest that the question no longer matters in that the thoughtful and educated person

1. Küng, Hans, *Does God Exist? An Answer for Today,* xxi.

2. Küng, xxii.

3. An interesting summary of some of this work may be found in the book by Terry Eagleton, *Reason, Faith, and Revolution: Reflections on the God Debate.*

today has no valid basis for belief in God. Yes, there will be over half of the world's population that will continue their belief in God because it is part of their heritage and culture and meets their needs. Yet this belief is often written off as superstition, and much of its practice tends to be local, tribal, cultic, and removed from the currents of intellectual thought in the educated world.[4]

As one who has been engaged in both worlds, the world of credible belief in God and the world of thoughtful unbelief, I have been motivated to try to find a way of belief that is defensible, valid, and a persuasive option for those who want to find a good foundation for sustaining their belief in God. Of course, as implied, belief can be sustained in cultic and sectarian ways. But my goal across the years of serving in the world of higher education and exposure to the intellectual currents of the early twenty-first century has been to help articulate a faith orientation that is not easily caricatured and can be an intellectually defensible option for thoughtful twenty-first century believers. As we answer the sub-questions of this larger foundational question, we will suggest some options for sustaining a credible and much needed orientation of faith in this critical moment of history. We will try to show how a belief in God matches the major criteria for being true. Among these criteria are:

1. We will need to be clear on what we mean by the word "God."[5] Some "gods" are not worth defending. The starting point, then, is a clear definition of what we mean by the word "God."

2. The belief in God must correspond with what we know to be true in the common sense world of our senses and current knowledge, though not limited by our current outlook and frame of reference.

3. The articulation and understanding of belief in God must be internally consistent; it must be a rational construction, one that has coherence.[6]

---

4. See Howard Bloom's work, *The God Problem: How a Godless Cosmos Creates*, written in 2012. He has put a positive spin on the loss of belief in God.

5. Several recent books have addressed the concern that the word "God" must be carefully defined. It has been understood in a variety of ways. See, for example, Aslan, *God: A Human History*; Chopra, *How to Know God*; Miles, *God: A Biography*; and *God in the Qur'an*; and Sölle, *Thinking About God*.

6. See the books by Richard Swinburne, *The Coherence of Theism* and *Faith and Reason*, both second editions.

4. We must insure that it will "work" in a healthy way in our experience, guiding us to a life of emotional health, integrity, and a dedication to building a better world.[7] DF

FOUNDATIONAL QUESTION 4:
DO YOU BELIEVE IN GOD?

The Lord is gracious and merciful,
slow to anger and abounding in steadfast love.
The Lord is good to all.
God's compassion is over all that God has made.

PSALM 145:8–9

I trust in God. The word "trust" more than "believe" expresses how I relate to God. Belief implies an acceptance of a series or list of doctrines: "I believe in God, the Father Almighty, maker of heaven and earth." This is the opening line of the Apostles' Creed. With the creeds, I find myself drawn into theological debate. For example, if we call God Father, does that mean that God is inherently masculine or does it reflect the social constructs of a human society? Belief seems to be almost exclusively intellectual; do I agree with these statements and do they make logical sense? And in our world today, belief seems connected to facts: did Jesus really walk on water? I trust in God and Jesus and have a relationship with God through Jesus, and that is enough. Brother David Steindl-Rast writes: "Faith is not first and foremost a collection of religious beliefs handed down to us by tradition. It has far more to do with that courageous trust in life that we know from our moments of breakthrough."[8]

Thus, I trust in God. God is utterly reliable in the most important ways, which is to say that God's love is absolute and ever present. I know that God sees me as beloved and that nothing that I do can ever separate me from that love. I trust in God who is so much greater than my human comprehension. Another way to phrase this point would be to say, "I give

7. There are many helpful resources in "making the case" for a trustworthy and life-giving faith. One that has helped me is Ken Wilbur's *The Religion of Tomorrow: A Vision for the Future of the Great Traditions*, published in 2017. See as well, in the Christian context, the work of Houston Smith, *The Soul of Christianity*.

8. Steindl-Rast, *Gratefulness, the Heart of Prayer*, 88.

my whole heart, my very being to God whose nature is love. This is my absolute commitment."

The verses from Psalm 145 describe some of the attributes of God, grace, mercy, love, goodness, compassion, and we could add many more. I trust God completely, feeling God's gentle mercy throughout my days. I don't worry about any belief statements or creeds, for the God I know transcends such human description, going deeper than my understanding. MB

FOUNDATIONAL QUESTION 4:
DO YOU BELIEVE IN GOD?

In the name of Him Who has no name
Who appears by whatever name you will call Him.[9]

DARA SHIKOH

I am convinced that everyone believes in God; they just use the myriad names we have for divinity.[10] Atheists simply call God by a different name: Justice, Compassion, Service, or other God-like qualities. I like the story of an atheist who told his son, "Son, there is no God." The child, who was trained to think critically, shot back, "Father, how do you know?" The father replied: "Son, you have to take it on faith."

God is Ultimate Mystery. The Qur'an says: "And if all the trees on earth were pens and the oceans were ink with seven oceans behind it to supplement it, still the Words of God would not be exhausted" (31:27). I love the insight of the Hindu sages who explain that the tongue cannot say it, but it is that by which the tongue utters; the eyes cannot see it, but it is that by which the eyes describe. How can one believe in something that is invisible and incomprehensible? Rumi observes: "The lover visible; the Beloved invisible; whose crazy idea was this?" "Have patience," says the Qur'an and explains that faith in God emerges from within, through our experiences in life.

My earliest experiences occurred when I practiced lessons taught by my parents. "God is inside and outside of us," they taught me. To "connect"

9. Sufi Master.

10. Often, those who say they don't believe in God reject the notion of a personal God who interacts in a variety of ways with human beings. But not infrequently these people acknowledge the presence of transcendence, although it may be a principle undergirding reality such as the Tao.

with God I simply had to touch my heart and say, "I love you" or focus on my heart and send out light and love. One day, while radiating inner light onto a book, I came across a poem: "I said to the almond tree, 'Sister, speak to me of God.' And the almond tree blossomed."[11] Something opened up to me; I experienced a strange sense of inner certainty about God.

Paradoxically, my faith in God grew stronger when both my parents died unexpectedly in 1991. In my grief, I was surprised to feel an inexplicable bonding with Mystery. The embrace of Mystery continues when I work with clients who have been mauled by life circumstances. They ask me never to mention in therapy the word "God." To my astonishment, by doing the prolonged work to heal their injuries, these same people, through their own volition, have become passionate devotees of God. They are living examples of the story of a Bedouin who was asked if he believed in God. He replied, "How could I not acknowledge God who has sent me hunger, made me naked and impoverished, and caused me to wander from country to country?" As he spoke, he entered a state of ecstasy.[12] JR

Sub-question 4a: Do you think there is another layer of reality beyond our scientific understanding of reality, an integral layer of reality often thought of as divine? Do you believe in a Transcendent Other or Principle, or a personal God?

Defining religion as "belief in gods" is also problematic. We tend to say that a devout Christian is religious because she believes in God, whereas a fervent Communist isn't religious, because communism has no gods. However, religion is created by humans rather than by gods, and it is defined by its social function rather than by the existence of deities. Religion is any all-encompassing story that confers superhuman legitimacy on human laws, norms and values.[13]

Yuval Noah Harari

The debate about whether there is a personal God or any god or family of gods has been with us from the beginning of human thought. We have been able to trace this debate in some detail since the development

11. Kazantzakis, *Report to Greco*.
12. Vaughan-Lee, *Traveling the Path of Love: Sayings of Sufi Masters*, 93.
13. Harari, *Homo Deus*, 182.

of writing, although archeologists have been able to provide artifacts prior to writing that point in various ways to belief in the divine.[14] Not infrequently, in the early years of human history, the debates centered on whose god was the true god, and it was often decided by a battle between tribes with different gods. In this pre-modern era, humans created gods as mythical ways of explaining the complex realities in which they lived. Often the gods were defined on a tribal basis, and they became the means of exercising power and control.[15] In time, the human imagination conceived of the possibility of there being only one true God, and perhaps the best known story of this belief is the one told in the Hebrew Bible about Abraham's trek west and the development of the Hebrew people.

The God of the Hebrew people, Yahweh, in its best expression, was understood in this way, and monotheism became a powerful force in the lives of the Hebrew people.[16] The concept of God in the early development of the Hebrew people had tribal and cultic dimensions, but also invited its followers to honor values that were more universal such as compassion and justice. As history unfolded, these values were adopted by the other Abrahamic monotheistic religions, Christianity and Islam. While these religious traditions did affirm life-giving qualities, it is important to note that these religions also carried with them the life-denying characteristics of being sectarian, controlling, exclusive, and intolerant.[17]

The defense of monotheism has taken many forms. To describe them all is beyond our scope, but let me be suggestive. There are the arguments based on experience and religious history such as the desire or need for a better life, the conception of perfection, the fact of our feeling of dependence on something "greater than ourselves," the reality of consciousness, and our expression of the selfless qualities of love and justice. These qualities, it is argued, are not necessarily the product of evolution, but hints or traces of the divine. In addition, there are the

14. See the classic work by Mircea Eliade, *From Primitives to Zen: A Thematic Sourcebook of the History of Religions.* See as well his three-volume work, *A History of Religious Ideas.* Another classic is the work by James G. Frazer, *The Golden Bough: The Roots of Religion and Folklore.*

15. See the marvelous account of the formation of gods in human consciousness by Joseph Campbell, *Oriental Mythology: The Masks of Gods.*

16. A comparable concept of the divine also existed in Persian Zoroastrianism in the same era. In is also true that the early Hebrews were not exclusively monotheistic.

17. Ferguson, *Exploring the Spirituality of the World Religions*, 10.

more philosophical arguments called physical-theological, cosmological, teleological, and ontological, all with stating points of what is and therefore what follows: things exist, therefore there must be a creator; reality consists of a cause-effect sequence, therefore there must be a first cause; there is the presence of purpose, therefore there must be an initial divine purpose; we can conceive of a perfect being, therefore we can project a God beyond us. The debate about the validity of these arguments continues, although their full defense has increasingly diminished.

A contemporary philosopher, David Bentley Hart, has simplified these arguments and made them more persuasive. He argues that there is "being" that must have come from God, consciousness that cannot be traced back to evolution, and the experience of bliss, also beyond scientific explanation.[18] DF

Sub-question 4b: Is there a spiritual dimension to our lives? If so, how do you understand it?

It's so strange to be here. The mystery never leaves you alone. Behind your image, beyond your words, above your thoughts, the silence of another world awaits. A world lives within you. No one else can bring you news of this inner world ... In order to keep our balance, we need to hold the interior and exterior, visible and the invisible, known and unknown, temporal and eternal, ancient and new, together. No one else can undertake this task for you. You are the one and only threshold of an inner world. This wholesomeness is holiness.

JOHN O' DONOHUE[19]

There is a spiritual dimension to our lives where we are connected to something that is deeper than our ordinary human existence. Here we touch that mystery that is vaster than our human understanding. Here we realize the limitations of our senses and our understanding of reality. We often have the sense that, somehow, there is an ultimate richness beyond us, a more profound holiness. There is more than the experience of our everyday lives.

18. Hart, *Experience of God.*
19. O'Donohue, *Anam Cara*, xv–xvi.

This mystery is within us as a divine spark that calls us to nurture God's presence in our lives. It flashes out with beauty and power. It is God's promise of life abundant and the assurance of holy love. It is within us that we must stop and be mindful if we are to be aware of its presence. It is beyond us as the great mystery that ties the whole cosmos together.

The spiritual dimension sustains us as we live. When we grow discouraged and frustrated, the Spirit encourages us. When we can't find our way, when we can't see any hope for the future, the Spirit whispers, "Beloved, I am here, walking with you. Together we will find a way." I think of this spiritual presence as an underground river, flowing beneath my life, always present, even when I am unaware of it. It is there, beyond my human comprehension, supporting me.

Such awareness helps me to sense the divine that is present in others. My ordinary perception is lacking. I become irritated and upset with another's views and actions. I want to judge them as less than whole. If I turn the outer perception and listen for the voice within, I sense something different. I realize that each person has the divine image and the problem is with my limited perceptions. MB

Sub-question 4c: Do you believe in prayer as a way of connecting with God, and are your prayers primarily relational or more sincere requests to find God's will for your life and aid those for whom you care?

Likewise the Spirit helps us in our weakness; for we do no know how to pray as we ought, but the very Spirit intercedes with sights too deep for words. And God, who searches the heart, knows what is the mind of the Spirit, because the Spirit intercedes for the saints according to the will of God.

ROMANS 8:26–27

Prayer is the deep connection with God. I come honestly to the One who knows me better than I know myself. Here I can express the reality I am feeling, my fears, my hopes, my questions, and my doubts. I know that I am heard.

So often, as we pray, we think we need to fill up our prayers with words. But if prayer is communication with God, we must also listen. We sit in silence with God, understanding that God, the source of life, hears our hearts' cry. We may not have the words ourselves, but as Paul wrote to the Romans, "the Spirit intercedes with sights too deep for words" (Rom 8:36). Sometimes I would like a clear answer from God, a word spoken with divine power. Often what I receive, as I sit in silence, is a quiet assurance of God's presence. Perhaps the answer I desire comes later as I watch my daily life unfold.

Prayer is not demanding what I want; it is offering my heart's desires to God. When I pray for others, I hold them in the light of God's love, trusting that God understands, and that God is at work in their lives. God is great and wiser than my understanding. While I might express my hopes and desires to God, in the end I say, "Thy will be done," trusting God alone.

Brother David Steindl-Rast writes: "Every human being knows prayer from experience. Have we not all experienced moments in which our thirsting heart found itself with surprise drinking at a fountain of meaning? . . . If what is called God means . . . the ultimate Source of Meaning, then those moments that quench the thirst of the heart are moments of prayer."[20] Thus all our living can become prayer as we sense that we are connected to our Creator and as we recognize the deep beauty of God's presence around us. "Rejoice always, pray without ceasing, give thanks in all circumstances; for this is the will of God in Christ Jesus for you" (1 Thess 5:16–18). MB

Sub-question 4d: What is the difference between spirituality and religion, and do you call upon that difference consciously in the way you seek to find your way?

And I believe that if spirituality is going to start having a real impact on the modern and postmodern world, it will have to include a fair number of these modern and postmodern facts that I am about to summarize for you. Failing to include them just makes a spiritual approach look truly dated, outmoded, and archaic, and that is one of the major reasons that religion is continuously losing ground in the modern and postmodern world—only 11 percent of northern Europe is "churched." That is only one out of ten people

---

20. Steindl-Rast, *Gratefulness, the Heart of Prayer*, 88.

have anything to do with institutional religion; nine out of ten people find it unbelievable and useless.[21]

KEN WILBUR

Over the past several years, I have had many conversations with people who say that they have given up on religion, but understand themselves as being on a spiritual pathway. Often they have asked for help and guidance in finding a spirituality that is life giving. Usually, in these conversations, there is in the background a subtle but unspoken definition of these two terms, religion and spirituality.

Religion is often understood as "a set of beliefs and practices within a community that are related to the divine. Generally these beliefs and practices include an ethical system, a form of worship, and a sustaining community."[22] But spirituality has a slightly different definition and is generally understood as "the effort to incorporate the elements of our religious traditions into our lives in a way that provides guidance in life, leading to our development as a person growing toward wholeness (holiness), insight, and responsible living."[23] In the best of circumstances, one can be a member of an organized religion and find within it a healthy spiritual pathway. Unfortunately, these circumstances do not happen for everyone who longs for a vital relationship with God or Transcendence.

One way of understanding the differences between religion and spirituality is to think about the beliefs and practices and how these terms are used to describe religious belief. Careful observation of how these terms are used will help us discern the slightly different meanings in a religious setting or a spiritual pathway. Both those who understand themselves as having a religion and those seeking a deep spirituality have a *creed* or a set of beliefs. Those in a religious tradition are often asked to accept these beliefs whereas those seeking a spiritual way may say that their beliefs are in flux and are evolving as one grows and matures. Also, those in a religious setting (church, synagogue, temple, etc.) are essentially told about the *code* of conduct that is expected. There is a set of ethical norms or rules that describe behavior for its members. Those on a spiritual pathway may say that their ethical norms or moral code is developing within them and may in some cases not meet the ethical

21. Wilbur, *Religion of Tomorrow*, 6.

22. See Ferguson, *Exploring the Spirituality of the World Religions*, 18.

23. Ferguson, *Exploring the Spirituality of the World Religions*, 18.

norms of an organized religion. Further, those in a organized religion may say that there are certain ways of worship (*cultic* norms) that honor the divine whereas the one on a spiritual pathway may find these patterns of worship less than efficacious and even tedious. They do not want to be bound by hymns that are dated and sermons that do not inform and inspire. One final category that is shared is the way the *community* in which they find common ground may differ. A religion may take the form of a corporate structure, filled with boards and committees, legal documents, constitutions, and ways of decision-making. Those who seek a spiritual way may find the organizational structure outdated and even a hindrance to personal growth.

It is great blessing to be in a religious system that is truly spiritual, yet we are living in a time of such rapid change that the gap between traditional religion and contemporary spirituality is hard to span. DF

Sub-question 4e: Where do you experience the holy? What leads you out of yourself into an encounter with the sacred?

Praying
"It doesn't have to be the blue iris, it could be
weeds in a vacant lot, or a few
small stones; just
pay attention, then patch
a few words together and don't try
to make them more elaborate, this isn't
a contest but the doorway
into thanks, and a silence in which
another voice may speak."

MARY OLIVER[24]

Mary Oliver speaks the truth of paying attention, of noticing what is right before us. The holy is beside us and we rush about too busy to see it, too preoccupied to give thanks.

I find the holy in the natural world and in the beauty that surrounds me. As the waves lap at the stone-covered beach, as the wind

24. Oliver, *Thirst*, 37.

blows through the fir trees, as the crows caw noisily, I hear the holy. In the colors of the sunset, the iridescence of the hummingbird's feathers, the flaming leaves of autumn, I see the holy. The holy is the scent of the ocean, pine, and rose. I touch holiness in the smooth rock and the fur of my cat.

The holy is present in scripture, as I read a familiar passage and see something new as a psalm speaks the truth of my day, whether it be praise and thanksgiving, or longing and lament. The Bible is a place to encounter the divine. It isn't just reading words; it is feeling the Spirit's movement between the words and my heart.

People reflect the holy in many ways. Some bring wisdom or a deep sense of compassion. Often it is easy to see the divine in people, in the laughter of a child, the kind words of a stranger, the smile of a friend. But the holy is there in everyone, even those who are difficult to love.

When I am involved with the arts, I may experience the holy. As I paint silk, I watch the dyes dance and blend, the colors growing more intense. As I sing in a choir, I cannot think of anything but the music. In these experiences, part of me steps aside as I fall into the clear delight of creation. This is holy as I touch something beyond my own control.

And I do experience the holy in worship, which often brings together much that I have mentioned: scripture, music, visual beauty, and community. God is present with us, loving and encouraging us. MB

Sub-question 4f: Should we engage with others in interfaith understanding and collaboration?

I hold that it is the duty of every cultured man or woman to read sympathetically the scriptures of the world. If we are to respect other's religions as we would have them respect our own, a friendly study of the world's religions is a sacred duty.[25]

Mahatma Gandhi was passionate about his insights that he hoped would help create and sustain harmony in multi-religious societies. He was a witness to the 1947 partition of India during which time fifteen million

---

25. Pearson, "Gandhi and the Imperative of Interfaith Dialogue." See the book by Karen Armstrong, *The Lost Art of Scripture: Rescuing the Sacred Texts* to gain a greater appreciation of the scriptures that have informed the human family.

people were tragically displaced, and over a million Hindus and Muslims died in communal rioting. He made three points:

1. It is the sacred duty of every individual to have an appreciative understanding of other people's faith traditions.

2. Every religion has truths and untruths. Revelations may be divine, but the human mind is imperfect and the human interpretation of the divine verses may be fallible.

3. If a religious extremist commits a wrong, it is better to confront the perpetrator with verses of beauty and wisdom from his or her own tradition than to condemn the religion because of the extremist's false interpretation.

As a Muslim and a US citizen living in a time of Islamophobia, Gandhi's words resonate inside of me. Given the lack of religious literacy in our country, I am painfully aware of how the entire religion of Islam is being judged by the actions of some religious and political extremists. Islam is perceived in the West as being undemocratic, violent, and misogynistic. However, through continuous interfaith work, which includes friendship, education, and collaboration on social justice projects, some of the biases are slowly eroding. At the same time, my journey in interfaith has made me realize my own biases and the critical need for me as a Muslim to have an appreciative understanding of other faiths.

Additionally, it has become amply clear to me that if I, or members of my community, do not have a sense of belonging because of suspicion and prejudice, the entire society becomes dysfunctional. A chain is only as strong as its weakest link. When one part of the body is unwell, the entire body is affected and suffers.

The work of interfaith is sometimes frowned upon because of the suspicion that this interaction and collaboration might weaken the practitioner's faith in his or own tradition. My personal experience has been the opposite. I am rooted in Islam but I find that being open to the insights and practices of other traditions, my Islamic roots have been watered and nourished. I have become not only a better Muslim, but also a more developed human being. That is why it is said that interfaith collaboration is not about conversion; it is about completion. JR

Sub-question 4g: How do we enter into interfaith dialogue?

There will be no peace among the nations without peace among the religions.

HANS KÜNG[26]

Ideally, religion should unite us all, but historically, organized religions have been used to divide. In recent times, given the rise of political and religious extremism, it is clear that interfaith dialogue is not simply a matter of etiquette and hospitality; it is a matter of survival.

The events of 9/11 brought me together with Rabbi Ted Falcon and Pastor Don Mackenzie, and we became close friends. As the Interfaith Amigos, we have crisscrossed the country and explored the process of interfaith dialogue. We have identified six stages:

1. The first stage is simply to get to know one another on a human level by sharing stories, e.g., our joys and our sorrows. The universe is made of stories, not of atoms.[27] If we interact with humility and sincerity, over time we will bond. Then, no matter how wide our theological differences, it becomes difficult to dehumanize each other.

2. In the second stage, we can talk about the core teachings of our respective traditions. Our teachings overlap, but each tradition has a special emphasis. Rabbi Ted talks about oneness, Rev. Don focuses on unconditional love, and I explain that the teaching of Islam is compassion.

3. In the third stage, we look at our holy books and discern that some verses do not conform to the core teachings. Every holy book has two kinds of verses: particular and universal. The former is in desperate need of textual and historical context; the latter are timeless, placeless, and filled with wisdom. It is imperative not to take a particular verse and advocate it as a universal verse.

4. In the fourth stage, assuming that there is now a level of trust, we are able to enter into more difficult conversations. We might compare notes about what we find difficult and awkward in our own

26. The quote is contained in the address at the Opening of the Exhibit on the World's Religions at Santa Clara University, March 31, 2005.

27. An insight from Kaufman and Herzog, *Collected Poems of Muriel Rukeyser*, 465.

traditions, e.g., exclusivity, violence, the unequal status for women, and homophobia.

5. In the fifth stage, we acknowledge that all religions are paths to a shared universal. We enrich our own path by experiencing the wisdom of other traditions. Thus, my reading of other scriptures increases my comprehension of verses in the Qur'an.

6. In the last stages, we realize that spiritual practices are critical. We simply have to do the inner work. To solve our social justice issues, we need to expand awareness, deepen compassion, and overcome biases. To heal the planet from environmental degradation, we have to overcome selfishness, greed, and apathy. JR

Sub-question 4h: How do we know what is true? As Pilate asked Jesus: "What is truth?"

God is not only the ultimate reality that the intellect and the will seek but is also the primordial reality with which all of us are always engaged in every moment of existence and consciousness, apart from which we have no experience of anything whatsoever. Or to borrow the language of Augustine, God is not only the superior summo meo—*beyond my utmost heights—but also interior* intimo meo—*more inward to me that my inmost depths. Only when one understands what such a claim means does one know what the word "God" really means, and whether it is reasonable to think that there is a reality to which that word refers and in which we should believe.*[28]

DAVID BENTLEY HART

Pilate, in our question above, is responding to Jesus during his trial. Jesus says to Pilate concerning his identity and mission: "For this I was born, and for this I came into the world, to testify to the truth. Every one who belongs to the truth listens to my voice." And then Pilate, somewhat cynically says, "What is truth?"(John 18:37–38). His cynicism prevents him from hearing and understanding the kind of truth about which Jesus is speaking. It is spiritual truth, and Dr. Hart, in our quote above, is speaking

28. Hart, *Experience of God*, 10.

about spiritual truth. He explains that spiritual truth has an internal and external form, objective and subjective components, and that the spiritual pilgrim must hold these two forms of truth in a complementary way.

Those religions that guide their followers to an understanding of and relationship with God are true to their calling when they make as clear as possible, within the confines of language and the context in which they speak, what is meant when one refers to God. God is not a thing or object in nature nor a cultural norm or ideal. God is not what we create in our own image or out of our cultural realities, but one "who is infinite fullness of being, omnipotent, omnipresent, and omniscient, from whom all things come and upon whom all things depend for every moment of their existence, without whom nothing at all could be."[29] Our way of understanding and speaking about God will be limited and approximate because God is beyond our language and concepts. But we are speaking a form of the truth when we acknowledge our limitations and point to the one who is transcendent and infinite. We speak the truth when we know that the limits of our understanding and use language that clearly states that our description of God is approximate, often cased in metaphorical language.

Jesus, in his conversation with Pilate, assumes this definition of God and includes his deep conviction that God comes to us and meets us in our experience. The God of love and light is personal and meets us in the depth of our experience. Jesus appears to be saying: "Pilate, the God of love and light can rule (reign) in our lives and bring us deep meaning and pure joy. The kingdom about which I speak is not from this world, and if it were, our roles might be reversed, but I speak about a kingdom of compassion and justice. The God who is ultimate truth is also the God of intimate truth. The God of creation is also the God of redemption, rescuing us from self-destructive ways and restoring us to lives of purpose and peace."

One might hope that at some point in his life, Pilate was able to "get it"; after all, he met the teacher filled with grace and truth. DF

Sub-question 4i? What part do faith and prayer have in cultivating a relationship with God?

Bow down and draw closer.

Qur'an 96:19

29. Hart, *Experience of God*, 7.

The best way for me (Jamal) to answer this question is to illustrate from my personal experience the relationship between faith and practice within Islam. Several times a day, Muslims bow down in adoration and draw closer, uttering words of praise and thanksgiving to God. In the final step, in a sitting position, the practitioner turns the head to the right and the left offering greetings of peace to angels who, Muslims believe, rush into spaces where God is worshiped.

The Islamic body prayer, called Salat, is derived from the Prophet Muhammad's observation of angels in prayer. In mystical experience described in the Qur'an as the Night Journey, the Prophet ascended seven levels of heaven. In that enchanting ascent, the Prophet saw angels bowing and prostrating to God while expressing praise and gratitude. From this he concluded that true prayer, in imitation of angels, consists essentially of glorifying and thanking God and using the human body to express adoration.

Muslims believe that these series of prostrations, done with humility and sincerity in the course of the day, help us let go of our attachment to ego and bring God into the center of our life. Sufi teachers say that one prostration of prayer to God frees the human from a thousand prostrations to the ego.

Over time, the body prayer builds a sense of personal intimacy with God. I love to quote the experience of my friend, Dr. Ann Holmes Redding, a popular Episcopal priest who became a Muslim without giving up her Christian tradition. In addition to her Christian practices, Dr. Redding loves to pray in the Islamic tradition because, she says, it makes her feel as though she is on a divine date with God.

A classic story about Mulla Nasruddin illustrates the practicality, majesty, and beauty of body prayers. Imprisoned for life, Mulla is near despair, but he lightens up when he hears that his spiritual teacher has received permission to visit him. Surely his teacher will slip in a concealed weapon or key to help him escape. But when the teacher arrives, all he brings is a prayer rug. Mulla is deeply disappointed and feels the need to escape, not to pray. But since he has time on his hands, he reluctantly does his body prayers, praising and thanking God by rote. He doesn't mean what he says. However, as he bows and prostrates to God over the days and weeks, he finally notices a special design in the prayer rug. It is the design of an escape route from the prison! JR

CHAPTER FOUR: DO YOU BELIEVE IN GOD?

Resources and Practices

Further Reading

1. Diana Butler Bass, *Grounded: Finding God in the World: A Spiritual Revolution*

2. James Finley, *Christian Meditation: Experiencing the Presence of God*

3. Richard J. Foster, *Streams of Living Water: Essential Practices from the Six Great Traditions of Living Water*

4. Joseph Goldstein, *Mindfulness: A Practical Guide to Awakening*

5. David Bentley Hart, *The Experience of God: Being, Consciousness, Bliss*

6. Hans Küng, *Does God Exist: An Answer for Today*

7. John O'Donohue, *Anam Cara: A Book of Celtic Wisdom*

8. Elizabeth Roberts and Elias Amidon, *Earth Prayers From Around the World Honoring the Earth*

9. David Steindl-Rast, *Gratefulness: the Heart of Prayer*

Suggested Practices

1. Select a day to be intentional about living in the present, conscious of each moment (mindfulness). As you pause and become calm, see if you can sense the presence of the divine. Be aware of the divine within you, the transcendent in the beauties of nature, the presence of love in your relationships, and your sense of being loved unconditionally by God. Say from deep in your heart, "I am truly loved."

2. In another day, in a moment of quiet reflection, begin to count the ways that you are blessed, loved, and cared for in a special way. During that day, pay special attention to the needs of others, accepting them as they are, listening to their problems and concerns without self-referencing, but staying in tune with their struggle and quest for a life of joy and peace.

3. The next time you pause to pray and contemplate, use your body in a symbolic way to express your prayerful attitude. Kneel, put your hands together, and follow the ritual order of movement as you join with others in common prayer. Make room for silence around you and inside of you.

4. Take advantage of the many books of prayers, using them to find words to express your deepest longings, your greatest fears, your deep gratitude, and your need for forgiveness, love, direction, and guidance in life. Use one of the many books of daily prayers.

5. As you have opportunity, join with others in the practice of community prayers. From time to time, join a group with different beliefs and practices from you religious tradition. Be open to learning that deep meaning is present in diverse cultures and religious traditions. Remind yourself that God speaks all of the languages of the human family, meeting people where they are.

Foundational Question 5

How Do You and How Should You Relate to Other People?

I will mention one other theological affirmation as foundational, and it is that the primary meaning of human life is to join God in the on-going processes of creation with self-giving love as our motivation, empowerment, and strategy.[1]

IT IS A COMMON practice to say that we ought to love other people. It is an easily understood suggestion. But the catch as we respond is usually how we understand the meaning of love and how it is that we can be empowered to demonstrate it. These concerns of meaning and empowerment regarding love have been central to my inner life across the many years of hearing that I should love my neighbor and act in a way toward others as I hope they might act in reference to me. As I was introduced to the Christian faith, I soon learned that Jesus put the highest priority on love as the ethical expression of my new religious orientation. I was introduced to the story in Mark's Gospel about the scribe (lawyer) who asked Jesus, "Which commandment is the first of all?" Essentially the scribe was asking what is the most important expression of belief and practice for a Jewish person of faith (and indeed for all people). The answer of Jesus, as it was later recorded, was clear and precise: "Hear, O Israel: the Lord our God, the Lord is one; you shall love the Lord your God with all of your heart, and with all of your soul, and with all of your mind, and with all of your strength.

---

1. Ferguson, *Lovescapes*, 37–38.

The second is this, 'You shall love your neighbor as yourself.' There is no commandment greater than these" (Mark 12:29–31).[2]

The conversation may have been longer than the brief summary given to us in Mark's Gospel.[3] But even as brief as it is, the two questions for which I needed answers were given. The first has to do with what Jesus meant by love. While Jesus was likely speaking Aramaic and drawing upon the Hebrew words for love, *ahab* and *hesed*, we may still discern his meaning as the logion was translated into Greek and then into English.[4] The word for love in Greek, *agape*, underlines that we are to love God and other people with our whole being (heart, soul, mind, and strength). Jesus goes on to explain that the kind of love we express to our neighbor is like the way we love ourselves, without conditions. This sort of love is without limits and seeks the welfare of those in our circle of nearness, our neighbors.

As time went along, this commandment to love God and our neighbor unconditionally expanded beyond just loving individuals (literally, our neighbor). It wasn't long before it became the standard for caring about the setting in which others lived. If we truly love all people and they are to thrive and flourish, then we will care about the context in which they live. There must be adequate education, access to a nutritional diet, suitable housing and medical care, and a social structure with a foundation of peace and justice.

This made perfect sense to me, but there was the lingering question of how I might become a more loving person. As I reflected on this concern, I noted that the love for God and neighbor were joined together, and as this insight sunk in, I realized that my love relationship with God was transforming, and that the God who is love was in the process providing the inclination, the insight, and the motivation to make me a more loving person. I pondered this insight and claimed the prayer of Saint Augustine: "Lord, ask what you will, and give me what you ask." As I nurtured my relationship with the God of love and compassion, I found myself more inclined to be a person of love and compassion. Yes, I fail at times, but remarkably the love of God forgives, restores, and re-energizes me, and I continue my learning about how to truly love others and express that love in all the ways that are available to me. My life now had a center and a direction. I discovered that nothing is more gratifying, and

2. See Lev 19:18; Deut 6:4–5.

3. It is the guidance of wisdom of Jesus to act in this way. See Bourgeault, *Wisdom of Jesus*.

4. The Hebrew word *hesed* is often translated as steadfast love.

that my heart is overflowing with gratitude to God and those who taught me that love is the heart of living the good life. DF

FOUNDATIONAL QUESTION 5: HOW DO YOU AND HOW SHOULD YOU RELATE TO OTHER PEOPLE

O Spinner, Weaver, of our lives
Your loom is love.
May we who are gathered here
be empowered by that love
to weave new patterns of Truth
and Justice into a web that is strong.[5]

Barbara Wells ten Hove

I am a weaver. I take individual threads, warp them on my loom, and weave them into something new and beautiful. Threads together form patterns of intricate loveliness. A single thread breaks easily, but the woven cloth is harder to tear. That is much like the human community. Individually, we are fine, but not very strong. And everyone has internal strength and individual beauty, but together in community we form a strong new pattern of more complex beauty. We are made to live together, sharing gifts and graces.

It hasn't always been easy for me to relate to others. I was an only child, living in a rural community where there weren't playmates. I related well with adults, but in time I had to learn how to connect with people my own age. It was an important skill for my growth and wellbeing, and I made progress in my relationships with peers during my school years. Looking back, I realized my deep need for human contact. I now know that I need to find inspiration from others beyond my own family, both to find and give support. I have also become keenly aware that I learn from those who are different from me.

It is easy to paint a rosy portrait of human relationships, but there are relationships that are harmful, even destructive. I have to admit that there are people whom I find difficult to get along with for a number of reasons. Yet even these complex relationships teach us important lesson

5. Frevert, *Welcome*, 13.

about connecting with others. There is nearly always something about our human contacts and conversations that bring understanding to us.

We are meant to live together, both in our local communities, but also in our global context. There is so much anger and destruction in the world. As we are able, we are called to provide an alternative: communities of understanding others from different cultures, empathic caring, and wise compassion—global communities that reflect God's love for all people. MB

FOUNDATIONAL QUESTION 5: HOW DO YOU AND HOW SHOULD YOU RELATE TO OTHER PEOPLE?

O humankind! We created you from a single pair of male and female persons and made you into nations and tribes that you might come to know each other.

QUR'AN 49:13

We have created some of you to be a trial for others.

QUR'AN 25:20

As the Qur'an makes clear, there is a divine reason for the marvelous diversity in humanity. It is that we may come to know each other better, to be able to connect in life-giving ways with our fellow human beings, and learn to appreciate them as manifestations of God. This process is not always easy, especially if the other person we are trying to relate to is not a member of our family, tribe, culture, or religion. In the tongue-in-cheek revelation quoted above, it appears that this unease is also part of the cosmic design. We may indeed present trials to each other, but this is part of the divine plan for learning how to overcome our prejudices and biases.

Wise elders from Asia have excellent advice for getting to know and appreciate one another, "share three cups of tea," i.e., listen, respect, and connect. To truly listen, Rumi says, we must metaphorically put our head on the other person's chest and sink into the answer. Often an enemy is simply someone to whom you have not fully listened. To cultivate respect for the other, we need to remember to distinguish between behavior and being. No matter how adversarial others may seem, their essential nature is divine; it is only their behaviors that we find objectionable. By keeping this discernment in your heart and mind, you gain the power to shift your outlook (and change "heaven and earth" as Sufis says). Then you will be able to connect with the other. And as we do, we need to keep in mind that the goal is not to change that person's values and beliefs, but to share each other's values, beliefs, and stories on a personal level. This sharing will deepen our relationship.

Once we have partaken of those three cups of tea and established a relationship, it becomes very difficult to demonize or dehumanize the other. Differences may remain, but they no longer loom as a threat. This human bonding also creates the possibility of collaborating on projects dear to both parties. This is borne out by 2017's American Muslim Poll. "About 21% of Americans who don't know a Muslim at all report favorable views of Muslims. Among those who do know a Muslim, 47% report favorable views. And for those who have a close Muslim friend, that number jumps to about 57%."[6]

The practice of sharing three cups of tea requires humility, sincerity, and persistence. Whenever I need encouragement in this endeavor, I reflect on the words of Rumi: "O God, you have created this "I" and "Us" to play a game of adoration with Yourself."[7] JR

Sub-question 5a: How important is it to have close relationships and friendships?

The key to healthy aging is relationships, relationships, relationships.[8]

GEORGE VALLIANT

The clearest message that we get from this 75-year study is this: good relationships keep us happier and healthier. Period.[9]

ROBERT WALDINGER

Drs. Valliant and Waldinger are the two most recent Directors of a unique, ongoing longitudinal study started in 1938 by Harvard University to explore factors contributing to happiness and longevity. The subjects were

---

6. Khan, "Anti-Muslim Hate," para. 10.

7. Harvey and Hanut, *Light Upon Light*, 122.

8. Mineo, "Good Genes Are Nice, but Joy Is Better."

9. Waldinger, "What Makes a Good Life?," 6:00–6:14.

mostly men selected from the predominantly male Harvard University sophomore class of 1938. Subsequently the study included disadvantaged inner-city youths, many of whom were female, who grew up in Boston neighborhoods. After tens of thousands of pages of documentation and decades of research on the physical and emotional health of the subjects, there was one overriding conclusion: the number one factor that determines our happiness and longevity is good relationships.

In the TED Talk in 2015 that went viral, Dr. Waldinger made three points:

1. Social connections make us happier and healthier, while loneliness kills.

2. It's not just the number of our relationships, but the quality that counts.

3. Good relationships protect both our bodies and our minds.

More recently, researchers at Brigham Young University and the University of North Carolina conducted a seven-year study that included women and men. Exhaustive data were examined from 148 studies that explored factors that lengthen our life span. Factor number one was again the close, dependable connections with friends and family. But, surprisingly, factor number two was "social integration" defined in this study as the amount of daily interaction with others, regardless of how strong or weak the bond. This interaction could be close connections with friends or casual chats with the teller in the bank or the cashier at the grocery store.[10] The following are some helpful suggestions gleaned from the two studies:

1. Stay socially engaged. Nurture existing relationships and cultivate new ones that enrich your life.

2. Put time and effort into reclaiming valuable relationships that may be dwindling away.

3. Let go of toxic relationships with family members. Stay connected with family members you like.

4. Take the initiative to meet regularly with friends you enjoy.

5. Greet the people you meet casually with warmth and sincerity and exchange a few words.

6. Reduce your screen time and expand your human interactions.

10. Christofferson, *Curable*, 145.

To these comments, I would add the wise words from the Qur'an: "Make room for others in your collective life; do make room; God makes room for you" (58:11).

And from Rumi: "Stay with friends who support you . . . Talk with them about sacred texts, and how you are doing, and keep your practices together."[11] JR

Sub-question 5b: What qualities or values must be present for you to have closer relationships and friendships?

Seek the company of someone the sight of whom reminds you of God, the awe of whom moves your heart, and is someone who counsels you not with the tongue of words but the tongue of deeds.[12]

IBN KHAFIF

Sufi teachers advise us to be selective about the companions we seek and choose only those who pass through the three gateways of love, trust, and truth. First, do you feel a kinship of love or affection with that person? Invite into your circle only those who move your heart. Second, do you trust the person? Select only those who "walk the walk" and whose morals and principles are not limited to words but are manifested in deeds. "Follow those who ask no reward of you and are themselves rightly guided" (Qur'an 36:21–26). Third, does this person love the truth? The Qur'an counsels us to abide with companions who, in awe of God, encourage one another in the teaching and living the truth and have patience (Qur'an 103:1–3). Similarly, the Buddha counseled members of the Sangha (community) to associate with "truth-winners," converse with them, observe their ways, and imbibe by osmosis their spirit of love and compassion.[13]

Sufi sages tell us not to be discouraged if this circle doesn't manifest healthy relationships easily in our lives. After all, the gateways are selective. Don't despair! Instead, practice the meditation in which you go to your imaginary sacred sanctuary (your "happy place" in today's parlance)

---

11. Barks, *Rumi's Little Book of Love and Laughter*, 126.

12. Attar, *Muslim Saints and Mystics*, 260.

13. Smith, *World's Religions*, 105.

where you can connect with an inner circle of companions and bask in their love.

1. Close your eyes, focus on your nostrils, and follow your breath. Enter into a state of relaxation and imagine yourself drifting into a sacred sanctuary, a place of safety, beauty, healing, and love.

2. Summon into your sanctuary an intimate circle of beings that pass the selective criteria of love, trust, and truth. They could be loved ones living or deceased, prophets or saints, historical beings, animals, elements of nature, anyone your heart desires.

3. Allow yourself to be cherished, nurtured, and nourished by these companions. It is in their nature to love you. Spend time here as you surrender into the tenderness and compassion they hold for you.

4. When it is time to come into present awareness, say good-bye to each member of your circle. Receive their thanks and blessings.

Practiced regularly, this meditation can refresh the lonely soul and, in good time, may cause an external circle of companions to become present for you. JR

Sub-question 5c: How much do you value having a loving family? Or miss haveing a family? What does a family look like? How can we choose our family? How do we deal with unhealthy relationships within families?

Better is a neighbor who is nearby, than kindred who are far away.

Proverbs 27:10b

Then his mother and his brothers came; and standing outside, they sent to him and called him. A crowd was sitting around him; and they said to him, "Your mother and your brothers and sisters are outside, asking for you." And he replied, "Who are my mother and my brothers?" And looking at those who sat around him, he said, "Here are my mother and my brothers! Whoever does the will of God is my brother and sister and mother."

Mark 3:31–35

We often think of families in idealized terms and imagine them as an ideal base of support. Jesus' words suggest that family relationships are more complicated and do not always match our ideal. Jesus invites us to expand our definition of family.

There are so many forms of families: couples without children, parents with children, single parents, grandparents raising children, and same-gender couples. At their best, all can reflect God's realm of life and love. But it is seldom easy. Relationships between people take understanding, work, and energy. In addition, families and their needs change over time: caring for small children is different than parenting teenagers. Illness and eldercare present challenges to families. Poverty, racism, unemployment, and other struggles make family life difficult.

I consider myself as fortunate. I was blessed with a loving family and, for the most part, enjoyed raising my own children. I knew sleepless nights with worries about my children: their health and their happiness, their growth and education, and their ability to function well in the world. Like my own upbringing, my parenting of my children wasn't perfect: I worked at being a "good-enough" mother and struggled to figure out exactly what that might look like.

My own family has changed over the last two years. Our niece, a single mother, gave birth to a son. They live nearby and spend every weekend with us. My husband and I provide a day of childcare each week. We delight in this new and surprising role and are learning again about all the energy it takes to deal with a toddler. Grandmary, Gruncle, mother, and child form a family. We are there for each other and that relationship deepens and enriches our life. But I am aware that not all families are healthy! There are relationships within families that are harmful rather than nurturing. When this happens, it may be wise to form a family from friends and neighbors that will support and encourage you.

Jesus encouraged those in the crowd to expand their concept of family. It wasn't just his mother, brothers, and sisters that formed his family. His family was made up of "whoever does the will of God." We need family, but that family isn't limited to our biological relatives. Family is larger than that and centered in God's love. MB

Sub-question 5d: Is love and sharing life at a deep and true level with others important to you?

Alone we can do so little; together we can do so much.[14]

HELEN KELLER

I often need a sounding board in my life; someone I can talk with as I try to sort out my own life and someone who can help me understand the broader situation in the world. I need their stories and their viewpoints that enlarge my understanding of reality. When I am struggling to come to a decision, it helps me to talk it over with a friend. Sometimes, I will have the answer already, hidden deep inside me. I won't find that answer until the presence of another draws it out of me. I need others to challenge my own limited viewpoint and to offer other ways of seeing reality. As I listen to another's story, I am carried to an experience different from my own and gain a perspective that is new to me.

There is a blessing from those who have known me for years and who share memories with me. I don't have to explain everything. These friends know me well enough to understand. There is also a blessing from new friends who enlarge my understanding and who invite me to share my life as I listen to theirs. It takes time to build trust necessary for deep sharing. A true friend doesn't betray something said in confidence. Over time, we learn which individuals have insights that are deep and helpful. And we learn who can be completely trusted.

It is important to keep broadening my connections with people. What may begin as a casual relationship may lead to profound and deep levels of close friendship. I need to be open to those whose views and experiences challenge my own. A deep relationship asks me to listen carefully and to open myself to another's experience. It calls me to be vulnerable and to reveal parts of myself that I try to keep hidden. *Yes*, love and sharing life at a deep and true level with others is very important to me. MB

14. Lash, *Helen and Teacher*, 489.

Sub-question 5e: Are love, compassion, empathy, and caring the heart of living wisely and well? If not, what is?

The Way that Jesus taught is radical, both in the sense of its rising from the deepest taproot of his tradition and in its scandalous upending of the foundational assumptions on which an entire system of oppression was based. It offered a radical understanding of an extravagantly loving God and how such a God could be known; it promoted a radical sense of human dignity and a capacity for emboldened and abundant life; and it cultivated an ethic of radical care that extended not only to loved ones, neighbors, and strangers but also to enemies, opponents, and oppressors. This path of Jesus—summed up as loving God with every dimension of our being, cultivating an authentic love for ourselves, and loving our neighbors as ourselves—was, at its core, a way of radical compassion.[15]

FRANK ROGERS, JR.

I look back across the ways that my faith journey has gone, starting in my high school years with a fairly naïve and a relatively orthodox expression of Christianity. However, the experience of the university and graduate school years and the general complexity of life created questions for me about my understanding of Christian faith, one that was somewhat conservative in its interpretation of Christian beliefs and practices. The graduate school years, after nearly five years of active campus ministry, were especially filled with these questions, yet there was also an emerging faith orientation within me that could celebrate questions and new ways of "putting faith together." As the years passed, primarily in teaching at the university level, I began to be comfortable with a good measure of humility about faith questions and in particular the ways of understanding God.

I discovered that my thoughts about faith were foundational and helpful, but were approximate and symbolic pointers to the "ground of being." I still used traditional Christian language, but began to realize the metaphorical character of this language. My journey became less stressful and more healing, and I began to have a sense of peace about being on a faith journey. I took comfort in my tradition but did not make it

15. Rogers, *Way of Jesus*, 13.

absolute and exclusive, and I continued to grow and learn about other religious traditions. Perhaps the most important factor in this growth was the understanding and full acceptance of the love of God as expressed in the life and teaching of Jesus. I continue to chase down questions that come to the surface in the study of religion in its many manifestations and struggle to understand the complex world in which I live. But I have a good measure of peace in this process. I rest in the love of God, yet often change the linen on this bed of rest.

My answer to the sub-question, "are love, compassion, empathy, and caring the heart of living wisely and well?" is a firm yes. There is of course the need for the expansion of my answer and many subtle nuances in its full expression. Space does not permit the book-length description of my yes, but let me suggest three foundational directions:

1. Love, compassion, empathy, and caring (and there are other related terms)[16] have given my life *meaning and purpose*, integrating the many aspects of my faith formation and providing a path toward maturity and health. Love in its many dimensions has put my life together and given it an integrated center. I have "miles to go before I sleep" but I sense I have chosen the right path.

2. With love as the center of my identity, I have begun *to see each day as an endeavor to listen with empathy, help those who struggle, and support a range of programs and initiatives designed to improve the life of others*. Even with my many limitations of knowledge and ability, I can endeavor, even in the smallest ways, to be one who loves. Do my needs and limitations get in the way? Of course, but daily I set out be a loving person.

3. I know that that I am also called by my commitment to love individuals, yes, but to extend my vision and *help alleviate those conditions in the world that cause suffering*. And there is so much pain and hardship in nearly every corner of the earth. I have learned that "the world is the theatre of love."[17] DF

16. See my book, *Lovescapes*, chapter 2.
17. Kashmiri Proverb.

Sub-question 5f: What kinds of people do you enjoy the most? How do you stretch yourself to encounter and understand others whose life situations are different from yours?

Love is patient; love is kind; love is not envious or boastful or arrogant or rude. It does not insist on its own way; it is not irritable or resentful; it does not rejoice in wrongdoing, but rejoices in the truth. It bears all things, believes all things, hopes all things, endures all things.

1 CORINTHIANS 13:4–7

Paul, the first-century missionary and thoughtful interpreter of the new religion that was to be called Christianity, often sent letters to the churches he had founded. He arrived in Corinth about 50 CE and ministered to the new converts for nearly two years. As he left, his ministry continued with them, even from a distance by sending thoughtful letters. He addresses a range of concerns, one of which was the unbridled sexual orgies common in the city. He was also concerned about the divisions and conflicts that arose in this new community of faith. His letters provide guidance to them and express the hope that they might reach a level of unity on certain subjects and engage in their mission of welcoming new converts and nurturing the faith of all the members.

After speaking about some of these ethical and rancorous concerns in his first letter, he says, "let me show you a more excellent way." It was a Way that helped the Corinthians and will help us answer our question of how we get along with and enjoy others who are different from us. Paul says that the "way" can be summed up in the word "love" or in his use of Greek, *agape*, best understood as unconditional and unlimited love. He explains what the way is as follows:

1. He initially emphasizes the positive and says that love is *patient and kind*. As we associate with people daily in our family, in our work, and in the rounds of life, we bring the attribute of patience. We need to be patient with the joys and concerns of others. We allow them to be who they are and to speak about their lives, sometimes complaining and expressing frustration, grievance, and worry, and other times showing a measure of happiness because they are content with their pattern and events of life. We listen with acceptance rather than judgment, express empathy, demonstrate tangible care,

and do not interrupt with constant self-referencing. These are the contours of patience and kindness. We then act as it is appropriate and offer to assist them in tangible ways as they speak about their needs and concerns. I enjoy people who are patient and kind with me, and I find it deeply gratifying to express patience and kindness to others and help them along the way.

2. I don't find it as easy when I meet those who are arrogant, rude, irritable, or resentful. There are times, especially if I am tired or anxious, that I may want to avoid rude people and just be with those who offer wise care for me. I know there are cases when I have inadvertently been arrogant or rude and shown a measure of irritation and been resentful. Yet I sense that love is the heart of my identity; my faith in the God of love and light has given me a new attitude that empowers me to show loving behavior to those in need. I discard my arrogance and rude behavior.

3. With this outlook, I then engage in loving relationship with others for the long haul, knowing that change comes gradually. I take no comfort in wrongdoing and focus on what is true to my deepest values of love and compassion. With the DNA of love, I am able to bear all things, believe I am on the right path, hope in God's grace, and endure the hardships along the way because I know that "love never ends." Love is the greatest of the values that undergird my life. DF

Sub-question 5g: What kinds of people are hardest for you to love (to care about)? Is there any prejudice in you against others who are different from you? How do you open yourself to understand their perspective?

Will you commit to lewdness such as no people in creation ever committed before you? For you come in lust to men in preference to women. No, you are indeed a people transgressing beyond bounds.

Qur'an 7:80–81

Come to know the other.

Qur'an 49:13

I want to answer these questions by focusing on a specific and complex subject, and I trust that the experience I describe will be helpful in providing insight about how to deal with those who are different from us. As a young Muslim, I was taught that homosexuality is an abominable sin, and so I naturally felt that gays and lesbians needed to be *healed* in order to be in a saving relationship with God. Several years ago, when a Muslim couple brought their teenage gay son for therapy, I applied all my fervor and Sufi techniques to heal him and return him to the straight path. The young man wept and told me many sorrowful things: for example, he told me that his mother wanted to commit suicide because of his orientation; his father wanted to relocate the family to another state; and he did not want to be gay but could not help himself. I heard him, but did not listen. I was too focused on my techniques and prayers for healing.

After several months, the teenager told me that he felt closeness to God, but his same-sex attraction had not changed. His disappointed parents took him to several well-known teachers and healers in Muslim countries, but in a few weeks they returned. To my amazement, the parents had completely changed, not because the change therapies had *cured* their son, but because they had driven him to attempt suicide. This shocked the parents into reconciling with the truth that their son was born with a same-sex orientation. They explained to me that interpretations of the verses on diversity celebrated in the Qur'an, over time and with higher consciousness, must evolve to include everyone, including those with a different sexual orientation.

The parent's new attitude changed my own prejudice, and with a more open mind and heart, I began reading avidly on the subject and talking with homosexual people. One of them gave me a book to read entitled *American Grace*, which explained how homophobic Christians had softened their attitudes over time.[18] These Christians had been friends with coworkers and neighbors without realizing that some of them were gay. When political and social conditions made it easier for gays to disclose their sexual orientation, their heterosexual friends' moral judgments became less rigid and harsh. Personal relationships of mutual respect and affection had already been established. This phenomenon, called a "bridge model" in the book, didn't change the words of scripture, but something more important occurred: attitudes shifted. Our understanding of Scripture is often shaped by social relationships. JR

18. Putnam and Campbell, *American Grace*.

Sub-question 5h: How should we deal with relationships that are unhealthy and possibly harmful to us?

Do you have the patience to wait
till your mind settles and the water is clear?
Can you remain unmoving
till the right action arises by itself?

He who stands on tiptoe doesn't stand firm.
He who rushes ahead doesn't go far.
He who tries to shine dims his own light.[19]

Tao Te Ching, 15, 25

I would like to think that I can get along with almost everyone, but when I meet another person whose behavior is filled with anger and harsh judgment, I discover that I get uncomfortable and don't easily continue in the relationship. In particular, the behavior that is hardest for me to endure is when I am attacked and harshly judged. It touches me at the tender point of my insecurity and lack of self-regard. I feel threatened and not infrequently I turn on myself and let go of a more realistic and healthy self-image. I also resist the behavior if it is an attack on those whom I love and those who are victims of injustice, war, and poverty. Perhaps there is a personal lesson to be learned, a thread of truth in the harsh judgment of another. And there may even be a thread of self-righteousness when I sense there is extreme prejudice toward a group or class of people in another's comment; I know that I am not totally free of all aspects of prejudice and discrimination.

As Lao Tzu suggests in the quote above, the first place to go in addressing an unhealthy relationship and one that may be harmful is to mindfulness, pausing to center oneself and to be sure that you have a good understanding of what is actually happening in the relationship. I once worked in a setting in which two of the people on my team had applied for the senior position that I had accepted. They were good and gifted people, but they did watch me closely and occasionally were critical of my leadership and work. It was hard for me in a new setting, especially one in which two others who reported to me were more experienced in some aspects of the work we did. I suffered some when I sensed their lack of support, and I knew that there were times when my behavior and

19. Quoted by John Templeton in *Agape Love*, 70.

senior level leadership were not ideal. As time went along, I didn't ever reach the point of full confidence and excellent service in my role, but I did slow down, let my "mud" settle and the water clear, and as I did, some right actions arose. Pausing, pondering, centering, and practicing mindfulness did help. I tried to take the high road.

And part of the high road was to honor them, respect their experience and judgment, and move away from my desire, intensified by not feeling accepted, to be thought of us experienced and wise. I learned that honoring them and making sure others knew of their experience and good judgment was the right direction. It was more healthy for me, lessened the tensions with them, and the product was higher quality work by all of us. It is not that I all of sudden was totally at peace, but the direction we took together became a way for us to work in a more healthy manner. While I was not always successful, I did try to stand on the high ground, and when I did, I become a better leader and the work we engaged in together was much improved.

I have applied the lessons learned in this difficult appointment to other aspects of my life and wide range of relationships that I have had across the years. I pause, center, and focus on the realities of the situation. I am not always free of hurt and insecurity, but I do better when I am mindful and humble about my part in the larger mission. DF

Sub-question 5i: How do we build communities of meaning and purpose?

Belonging can be thought of as a longing to be. Being is our capacity to find our deeper purpose in all that we do. It is the capacity to be present and discover authenticity and whole selves. This is often thought of as an individual capacity, but it is also a community capacity. Community is the container with which our longing is to be fulfilled.[20]

PETER BLOCK

I've struggled with this question since my retirement from the ministry. When I was working, the church formed an important community of meaning and purpose. There were challenges, of course. No community

20. Block, *Community*, xix.

has been without its challenges. But I was part of a community of faith that worked to deepen our relationship with God and that cared for one another and the larger world. In my very first year of ministry, I discovered that entering a sanctuary filled with people of faith brought joy and meaning. I might be depressed, or worried about my sermon, but the very presence of these people and the relationships that we shared drew me into a healthier and deeper faith. I'm struggling now in retirement. When I go to church, my relationship with other church members is different. I'm not their pastor. I listen more often instead of speaking that was inherent in my role as a pastor. Now, this is not bad. It is just different, and I am trying to find my own meaning and purpose in this new role.

I do need to be part of a larger community and involved with other people. And yet this is my "fallow" year when I step back from responsibilities and listen for God's next call. So instead of volunteering, I am taking some of the art classes I never had as a child, and I find that as well as the skills learned, I enjoy being with other students. I participate is some small spiritual growth groups. When I leave the house, I try to intentionally connect with those I meet at the library or the store. This year it takes a bit more work to be with others, but I need the energy and wisdom that that they bring to my life.

Our world needs communities with a sense of purpose and meaning. We gather around so many topics: care for our planet, concern for the most vulnerable, learning and sharing knowledge, political issues, peace, and the arts. We work and learn together. I think of singing in a choir: there many voices create a new beauty, individuals gather around a common purpose. We support each other musically and personally. That's just one example; there are many other communities of meaning and purpose. MB

CHAPTER 5: HOW DO YOU AND SHOULD YOU RELATE TO OTHER PEOPLE?

Resources and Practices

Further Reading

1. Peter Block, *Community: The Structures of Belonging*
2. The Dalai Lama, *How to Expand Love*

3. Thich Nhat Hahn, *How to Love*

4. Andrew Harvey and Eryk Hanut, *Light Upon Light: Inspirations from Rumi*

5. Johann Hari, *Lost Connections: Uncovering the Real Causes of Depression—and the Unexpected Solutions*

6. Robert D. Putnam and David Campbell, *American Grace: How Religion Divides and Unites Us*

7. Frank Rogers Jr., *The Way of Jesus: Compassion in Practice*

Suggested Practices

1. Seek out a new friend, a person whom you have noticed, perhaps admired and respected, by introducing yourself and suggesting, as they have time, if you might meet and get acquainted, perhaps have coffee and conversation.

2. Evaluate those organizations in which you belong, perhaps at work or where you live, and assess their value. Do you learn in them, find friends, and a role that is gratifying? Do they contribute to your wellbeing?

3. Take a close look at your family, its structure, and whether it is a supportive and nurturing set of relationships. In what ways do you find love and support and in what ways do you wish it were different?

4. Find an organization that has a purpose about which you care, but one in which you have had no involvement. Attend one of their meetings, meet new people, and see if there is a way you might contribute to their purpose and goals.

5. Begin a journal in which you write assessments of your relationships (family, friends, colleagues at work, and strangers with whom you would like to get acquainted). Write about your feelings, both positive and negative, and how you might make changes that increase the quality of your friendships and the joy that comes from honest and caring relationships.

Foundational Question 6
How Should I Take Care of Myself?

In those days Jesus came from Nazareth of Galilee and was baptized by John in the Jordon. And just as he was coming up out of the water, he saw the heavens torn apart (open) and the Spirit descending like a dove on him. And a voice came from heaven, "You are my Son, the Beloved; and with you I am well-pleased." And the Spirit immediately drove (led) him out into the wilderness.

MARK 1:9–12

ACROSS MY ADULT YEARS, I have been especially conscious of how I prepared myself for a good life, one that was healthy and filled with a measure of inner peace, loving relationships, and responsible work. I am grateful, as I look back, that these were the primary components of my adult years. Yes, wrong choices and mistakes were made, causing a measure of suffering and a step backward, but even these challenges contributed to my maturity. I gained insight on how I should and could take better care of myself. As I thought about this most important task of self-care, I realized I needed both a *firm foundation and sustaining practices.*

A major influence in my development was the somewhat brief although clear and compelling account of the way that Jesus prepared himself for his life work. He had a firm foundation and cultivated sustaining practices. What were the primary elements of his foundation? His life circumstances were not ideal, and we should not overly idealize them. For example, Nazareth, where he grew up, was a small village with a good measure of poverty and few external resources such as schools as we know them today. Yet there was likely a small synagogue in the region, serving as a school, a place of learning about faith, and a setting for worship. From all accounts, he had a very supportive family life, and his marvelous mother has been honored as much as any woman in history. At a fairly young age, he joined his steady and mature father, who was a carpenter, and perhaps took over the business at a fairly early age when his father died. At about thirty years of age, Jesus sensed a deep and profound calling, one growing out of the influence of his family and his religious beliefs. His foundation prepared him to become a teacher, a healer, and a prophet.

He knew that to be faithful to his calling, he needed to take care of himself and be prepared for the challenges of his vocation. As a first step, *he went to a trustworthy friend for guidance.* He traveled south to spend time with his cousin, John the Baptist, and to learn how in his tradition a prophet could contribute to the common good and the spiritual life of the people. A first step for us, as we seek maturity and an undergirding spiritual life, is to use trusted and caring friends who love us and give us counsel. As I look back on my growth, the positive influence of spiritual leaders and friends with more experience and a loving presence were exceptionally helpful to me as I sought maturity and a healthy and meaningful life.

A second step in my movement toward maturity and spiritual direction was a series of retreats and conferences, and then the three years of seminary training, followed by post-graduate study. Not everyone must go to seminary, of course, but time apart in quiet reflection focusing on intentional spiritual growth can be life-changing. As Jesus did in the wilderness, I also faced the challenges that might have drawn me away from my vocation as a pastor and teacher. Over fifty years later, I still use the beliefs and practices that were cultivated in conferences, retreats, and time devoted to study and the steady use of sustaining practices.

A third step for Jesus was a focused act of dedication. Jesus, while with John, used the method within the Jewish tradition of baptism for an act of dedicating one's life to the will and way of God. Many religious people, even from as far away as Jerusalem, were coming into the rural region of the Jordon River to John for baptism, an act that was understood in different ways, as it is in our several traditions. But one understanding, common to the many different interpretations and methods, is that it is sacrament, a sacred moment in which we dedicate (or be dedicated as a child) to a truly spiritual life. Jesus sensed in his baptism that God both heard and honored this act of dedication. In his heart of hearts, he heard the voice of God affirming his commitment: "You are my son, the Beloved, and with you I am well-pleased." He was ready. DF

FOUNDATIONAL QUESTION 6: HOW SHOULD I TAKE CARE OF MYSELF?

For it was you who formed my inward parts;
You knit me together in my mother's womb.
I praise you, for I am fearfully and wonderfully made.
Wonderful are your works; that I know well.

PSALM 139:13–14

We are fearfully and wonderfully made, part of God's gift to the world. William Brown translated Psalm 139:14, "I praise you, for I am exquisitely awesome. Wonderful are your works; that I know quite well."[1] God created us in God's own wisdom, so we reflect the divine presence, and God saw everything that God made, and indeed, it was very good.[2] When we realize how wonderful and how precious we are, we can cherish God's gift. We don't take our health and wellbeing for granted, but care for ourselves wisely, honoring God as we do so.

I used that translation, "I am exquisitely awesome" in a sermon I preached on Psalm 139. We had unannounced guests that Sunday—from a camp for differently-abled adults including folks in wheelchairs, with a sign-language interpreter to assist them. How powerful and how true it was to tell them that each one is exquisitely awesome! "Exquisitely awesome" does not mean perfectly healthy or beautiful or capable. "Exquisitely awesome" simply means created in God's image, reflecting God's creative act in our living. God loves diversity and humanity reflects that variety. You are exquisitely awesome because God made you the way you are.

We care for ourselves so that we might better share God's love with all of creation. There are many aspects to the task of taking good care of ourselves. We care for our physical bodies, considering diet, exercise, and regular medical care. We care for our emotional selves, reaching out for help when we need it, finding practices that nourish our emotional wellbeing, and building communities of care and trust. We care for the spiritual dimension of our lives, finding ways to touch that fire within that connects us with the holy.

1. Brown, *Seeing the Psalms*, 211.
2. Gen 1:31.

None of us is perfect. We all have limits of some kind or another. Even so, we need to discover *our* unique gifts and nurture them with practice. We need to find our deep passion and use it to help others.

We know too well the dangers that result when we do not practice wise self-care. Neglect is the context in which burnout happens; it occurs when we are so busy that we fail to consider carefully the impact of our words and actions and where damage to others happens.

Care for yourself. You are God's gift to the world. You are "exquisitely awesome." MB

FOUNDATIONAL QUESTION 6: HOW SHOULD I TAKE CARE OF MYSELF?

Value the worth of five things before they are replaced by the other five conditions: value your youthfulness before old age arrives, value health before sickness strikes, value your wealth before you become needy, value peacefulness before hardship comes, and value life before death arrives.[3]

Saying of The Prophet Muhammad

As I enter into the last quarter of my life, I marvel at how quickly time has passed. Recognizing how much I have aged physically over the years, I resonate with the Taoist saying that autumn is inevitable and, when it arises, no leaf is spared because of its beauty, no flower because of its fragrance. I have been a procrastinator all of my life, but the dawning realization that change is inevitable and time is precious inspires me to stop putting off what needs to be said and done in my remaining years. The time is now and the place is here, I tell myself.

I also remind myself daily that my body is a divine gift. It is the temple of my soul. Besides yoga exercises and healthy eating, I aspire to walk daily so that I can remain healthy for as long as possible. Close to my place of work is a small lake and I often conduct my meetings while walking and talking around the lake.

The resource of material wealth is important especially in times of need. But I know from my own experience that truly great wealth lies in the close relationships and circles of friendship I have cultivated over the decades. In periods of difficulty, including financial stress, family and

3. Fadiman and Frager, *Essential Sufism*, 90.

friends have been extraordinarily gracious and generous in their assistance. The value of these relationships is priceless.

To achieve contentment in the cycle of life's ups and downs, we need to practice mindfulness at all times and learn to be grateful for our blessings. I often meditate on a teaching story about a monk who had a terrible toothache that made him feel miserable. "If only this toothache would pass, I'd be so happy," he said to himself. And then he had an "Aha!" moment. Turning to his fellow monks, who were also acting unhappy because of various difficulties, he asked if they too had a bad toothache. "No" they replied. The monk continued: "Then why are you unhappy? Don't you realize that this very moment is a non-tooth-ache moment?" How easily we take our blessings for granted. One of the best practices of good self-care is to wake up to our blessings and to be grateful for all the non-toothache moments in our lives.

Even more important in the area of self-care is the advice that my parents taught me from an early age: Be compassionate with yourself. Don't avoid or delay difficult tasks, take action when necessary, speak out when it is called for, but always remember to treat yourself with mercy and gentleness. This last piece of advice has served me best of all in my journey of self-care. JR

Sub-question 6a: How do we develop and mature? How important is our environment in either nurturing or limiting our growth toward maturity?

Over the years I have developed a picture of what the [human being] living humanly is like. This individual is a [person] who understands, values, and develops one's body, finding it beautiful and useful; one who is real and honest to and about oneself and others; one who is willing to take risks, to be creative, to manifest competence, to change when the situation calls for it, and to find ways to accommodate to what is new and different, keeping that part of the old that is still useful and discarding what is not. When you add all this up, you have a physically healthy, mentally alert, feeling, loving, playful, authentic, creative, productive human being.[4]

Virginia Satir

4. Satir, *Peoplemaking*, 2–3. Note: I have slightly altered Virginia Satir's language making it inclusive, but not changing her meaning.

Across the last century and into our current one, many people from different perspectives have attempted to describe the dimensions of human development. Freud, for example, focused on psychosexual development and Jean Piaget focused on cognitive and language development. A contemporary scholar, Robert M. Sapolsky, describes our development in biological categories.[5] I get some help and insight when answering our question from Erik Erikson (1902–1994), influenced by Freud, but using development stages more rooted in development psychology.[6]

Erikson, acknowledging the great variation of developmental patterns in different ages and cultures, suggests eight stages of human growth and development.[7]

1. There is the infant, from birth to sometime between twelve and eighteen months, who has the needs of nourishment and security and will learn in this stage either *trust or basic mistrust*, depending upon the care one receives from parents.

2. There is the small child, ages eighteen months to three years, who needs to learn about the body's needs and physical skills such as walking and grasping and who develops either *autonomy* or *shame and doubt* if they are not learned.

3. There is the stage of three to six years in which the child becomes more dependent or self-sufficient and will face the developmental challenge of learning *initiative in mastering skills* or *feeling guilt if the skills are not learned.*

4. From six to twelve years, the challenge is between the feeling of *industry or inferiority*, as the child learns new skills, but risks in this challenge the feelings of failure and incompetence.

5. In adolescence, there is the increased importance of peer relationships and the developmental challenge of *identity versus role confusion*. The young person must begin to achieve a sense of identity in occupation, gender roles, politics, and religion or remain confused about essential identity.

6. In young adulthood, the challenge is successfully developing love relationships, with the developmental crisis being *intimacy or isolation*.

---

5. See Sapolsky, *Behave*.

6. See Erikson, *Identity*, for his description of human development.

7. I used his categories in describing how we learn how to love and the place of faith in my book, *Lovescapes*, 123.

7. In middle adulthood, each adult must find good ways to make a contribution to society and support the next generation. The developmental crisis is between *successful accomplishment* and *stagnation*.

8. In late adulthood, there must be the culmination of a sense of acceptance of oneself and the sense of fulfillment, so the developmental challenge is between *ego integrity* and *despair*.

Our pathways will differ greatly depending on our biology, our parents, our place in the family, our environment, and the values of our time and place in history. These influences and their respective importance have been treated extensively in the literature of human development. As I read through this literature and have experienced so much of what it describes, I find myself moving toward self-understanding and a measure of maturity and inner peace by affirming the following summary observations:

1. My health and maturity have been influenced by the caregivers I had in life. But I have had to grow beyond their influence to be free to view the world and my place in it not from their perspective and unmet needs, but from contemporary and more life-giving perspectives.

2. I have had to make clear choices along the way, some in the early stages of life, but later I made more independent and intentional choices that have lead to a greater degree of self-fulfillment and responsible living.

3. As I have grown and developed across the years, I have increased my capacity to be a more loving and compassionate person, a clear goal of my life.

4. Yes, biology, genetics, family, culture, time and place in history, but I also say yes to freedom and wise choices. DF

Sub-question 6b: How do we find a measure of peace, joy, and happiness?

But I have so much to be grateful for. Imagine what could have happened to me if I had been on a donkey.

One day the Mulla discovered that his donkey (his helper, companion, and source of livelihood) had disappeared. The entire village searched far and wide, but to no avail. The donkey was simply gone. In the evening, the villagers found the Mulla on his knees in the town square, raising his hands toward heaven and exclaiming, "Thank you, Allah!" "Mulla," they asked, "don't you realize that your donkey is gone forever?" "I know, I know," replied the Mulla, "but I have so much to be grateful for! Imagine what could have happened to me if I had been on the donkey!"[8]

Embedded in this classic story is the insight that when we manage to offer gratitude to Spirit even in times of affliction, we are giving thanks for unknown blessings already on their way. The Prophet Muhammad taught us to praise God in both good and bad times. When things were going well, he would say: "Praise be to God whose grace brings all goodness to perfection." In times of difficulty he also said, "Praise be to God," and would simply add, "under all conditions."

We live in a world of opposites. We value peace and joy because we have also experienced their opposites, anxiety and sorrow. To attain what Buddhists call equanimity in our world of opposites, we have to accept and embrace the ten thousand joys as well as the ten thousand sorrows in our lives. If we are able to do this, metaphorically we are placed in the center of the wheel of life. The wheel goes up and down, the essential experience of our lives, but the center is unperturbed.

This brings to mind a Sufi story by the thirteenth-century sage, Attar. A powerful monarch was exhausted by the unpredictable ebb and flow of fortunes, and he yearned for inner peace. He begged the court sages for words of wisdom that would protect him from being overly exultant and prideful in times of victory and save him from falling into the depths of depression in times of failure. After much reflection, the sages presented him with a ruby ring on which were inscribed the four words: "This too will pass."

How does one explain the beauty and power of gratitude? The Qur'an offers an insight: "Everything which dwells in the earth and heavens extolls the limitless glory of God" (59:1). When we offer our thanks and praise, we are connecting and celebrating with the universal cosmic vibration. Our personal vibrations are uplifted and we feel exalted. If we continue our practice in times of despair, we are graced with a sense of hope and possibility. Therefore, as often as possible in my daily life, I

---

8. Rahman, *Sacred Laughter of the Sufis*, 77.

touch my heart and express gratitude for things small and large. For me, gratitude is the overarching practice to create and sustain serenity and happiness in life. JR

Sub-question 6c: How do we manage fear, insecurity, anger, and sadness?

"It is He who has created for you (the faculties) of hearing, sight, feeling, and understanding; little thanks it is you give!"

QUR'AN 23:78

"That is He who grants us laughter and tears."

QUR'AN 53:43

Sufi teachers explain that feelings, happy or sad, come from God. They are all sacred. Difficult feelings such as anxiety, anger, fear, and sadness have an edge to them because we sense that we are separated from them and they often are caused by factors in our external environment. We feel them intensely and they are begging to be acknowledged, embraced, healed, and integrated. There is a special technique called "Sacred Holding" that acknowledges the challenging feelings and embraces them with tenderness and compassion. Not only do the hard feelings soften, but also once integrated, they become a valuable source of self-knowledge, empowerment, and blessing. For help with integration, we can turn to the practice of Sacred Holding, a six-step process:

1. In a state of meditation, give yourself permission to fully experience your difficult feelings. Do this little by little with mercy for yourself.

2. Ask yourself, "Where do I hold this feeling in my body?" Feelings have a resting place, and we experience them in the physical body: the heart, throat, solar plexus, and the belly. Patiently direct your consciousness to locating the site of what is called "physical holding."

3. Once you have located the feelings as sensations in the physical body, acknowledge them with your consciousness. You can use Sacred Naming to talk to yourself: "Dear Heart, I am sorry for what you are experiencing; allow me to support you as you grapple with this difficulty." Hold your sensations with the tender embrace of

your soul. If the sensations move to another location, move your attention to that place. There is no need to fix or analyze the sensations. Simply be present with the holding as long as you want. The Qur'an has a beautiful metaphor for this light of gentle awareness to soften and transmute: it is akin to "the dawn as it breathes away the darkness" (Qur'an 81:18).

4. Lovingly direct some questions to the center of sensations in your body: "Do you have a message for me?" Simply listen. Be attentive and respectful, even if you hear nothing.

5. Ask tenderly, "How may I befriend you? How may I love you and integrate you?" Again, listen carefully.

6. Be intentional about allowing your breath to flow through that physical locus of your feelings as you inhale and exhale. Allow the Divine Breath to caress that focal point. Little by little, you will experience healing, integration, and transformation of the difficult feelings. JR

Sub-question 6d: Are there stages or levels in our journey toward wholeness? What might they be? Is this journey linear or meandering?

To discuss the problems connected with the stages of human development is an exciting task, for it means nothing less than unfolding a picture of the psychic life in its entirety from cradle to grave.[9]

CARL G. JUNG

The literature on the stages of human development is extensive and somewhat varied. As I have moved through this literature, I have found it to be enlightening, providing me with frames of reference for self-understanding and growth toward wholeness. I did introduce one view in the entry 6a, that of Erik Erikson, and I want to draw upon it and other views such as those of Jean Piaget (cognitive development), Lawrence Kohlberg (moral development), and James Fowler (faith development) and share

---

9. Jung, *Modern Man in Search of a Soul*, 95.

a sort of summary of my growth, underlining my belief that there are stages of growth toward wholeness.[10]

I have discovered that I live in a society and world that invite unhealthy patterns of living. I occasionally suffer from insecurity, the fear that I am not prepared to cope with the very real challenges of contemporary life. I often feel paralyzing guilt as I reflect on the ways that I have failed. And there are times when I am overcome with anxiety as I worry about the future. The materialistic culture in which I live promises (and lies about it) relief if I earn more money, buy a fancy car, have an elegant house, take a vacation, and gain some control or power over others to satisfy my needs. Feeling tension, I sometimes find it easy to eat comfort food or drink the second glass of wine that gives me instant gratification. I later go to bed worrying about my diet and the demands of life; sleep does not come, and I am not able to get the rest I need. I do some self-reflection and sense I need to exercise and take good care of myself. But, on occasion, I rationalize that I am too busy or too tired.

Often I do step back, assess my condition, and decide to make some changes. As I look back on this repetitive behavior, I realize there have been and continues to be pathways to health and wholeness. Our lives are complex, we face different challenges, and it is therefore difficult to find just one pattern of recovery that works for everyone. So I share a pattern of life that has been helpful to me as I seek to become a more authentic, healthy, compassionate, and mature person. A *first step is to face our situation honestly*, and we often need the help and guidance of others who are wise and love us dearly in order to see it. It is possible for us to realize that we need to seek new patterns of life.

A *second step is to cultivate a positive attitude toward change.* It may take a while, in part because we have long established unhealthy habits and values that have become integral to our way of living. It is not easy to give them up, and we are good at denial and rationalizing why change is unnecessary. My experience has been that I need others to help me see my need for change and to expose myself to the range of options available to help me facilitate change.

The third step, of course, *is to change my behavior.* By learning more about the mystery and art of living, I will be able to find new patterns of behavior.[11] We need to learn the contours of healthy living, gain an

---

10. The summary is partially based on James Fowler's outline in *Stages of Faith*, 52. Fowler, of course, focuses on the place of religious faith in our development.

11. See Tippett, *Becoming Wise: An Inquiry into the Mystery and Art of Living.*

understanding of our situation, and then use our accumulated wisdom to take tangible steps toward the healthy life.

So, in answer to our questions, we might say there is movement through stages of development, although it is not always direct and linear. Both nature (our given makeup) and nurture (our environment) play a part. Wholeness, or the integration of physical health, emotional maturity, full cognitive development, and a thoughtful faith will look somewhat different for each person, but it is very gratifying when these aspects of our lives mature and coalesce and we achieve integration and a life of peace and purpose. DF

Sub-question 6e: Do you have a strong sense of self-worth and a good self-image? How do you deal with self-doubt? Are you able to see yourself clearly?

Care about people's approval and you become their prisoner.[12]
Choose your jailors with care and deliberation.

ORAL TRADITIONAL SUFI SAYING

It seems to be a law of nature that we humans need others' approval in order to love ourselves. Whenever we meet someone, says the poet Hafiz, we plead, "Please love me! Please love me!" We do this silently, of course, or else the person to whom it is expressed might call the police or the "psych ward." Because of this need for approval, our self-perception is often informed by the feedback we receive from others. We often forget that "beauty is in the eye of the beholder" and that our true beauty is a matter between our feelings and our higher self. It is this higher self whose wisdom we must learn to trust.

I cannot claim that I had a good self-image growing up. I was a painfully shy child, overly sensitive and lacking confidence. The opinions of others mattered greatly to me, and I was overly eager to please everyone. Fortunately, my wise and loving parents recognized my difficulty and taught me an insight that changed my life forever. "Whosoever's approval we seek becomes our slave master," they said, and they encouraged me to meditate on that insight repeatedly. After many weeks of meditation, I realized that the antidote to my psychological imprisonment lay in the

12. Mitchell, *Tao Te Ching*, 9.

Sufi saying, "Choose your jailors with care and deliberation." Slowly, over time, I was able to choose my higher self to be my "jailor."

The operant words are "slowly, over time." Again, I bless my parents for teaching me the value of working "little by little" and assuring me that eventually my efforts would be rewarded by a quantum leap. But it is an extended process, just as a twig develops in imperceptible stages to break into a flowering bud. The key is to persist in spiritual practices that encourage good self-care, such as compassionate self-talk, "sacred holding" of difficult feelings, and frequent repetition of a positive mantra to stay centered and grounded throughout the day.

An inescapable influence on self-image is the culture of our environment. As a brown man, I have encountered racial bias in both South Asia and the West, and this discrimination weighs on the spirit. My self-esteem was nourished, I believe, by my parents' teachings about approval and abiding spiritual practices. Also, the friendships and community that I have built over the years have been invaluable in helping my spirit to be fairly untroubled in this regard. The exquisite kindness and fierce protection of friends have immeasurably softened any insecurities and fear I experience because of racial discrimination. To this day my knees are scraped with prayers of gratitude for the gift of such wise and loving parents, and for the added blessing of so many friends and fellow travelers. Alhamdulilah! (God be praised!) JR

Sub-question 6f: Am I making good progress in my journey toward health and wholeness? For example, do I take good care of myself with diet, sleep patterns, and exercise?

You cause the grass to grow for the cattle,
and plants for people to use,
to bring for food from the earth,
and wine to gladden the human heart,
oil to make the face shine,
and bread to strengthen the human heart.

PSALM 104:14–15

If I am truthful, my answer to this question must be yes and no. I try to eat well. I find that membership in a CSA (Consumer Supported

Agriculture) means that for much of the year a box of vegetables arrives weekly. Several things happen here: 1. I support my neighbors. 2. My food is not shipped across country. 3. The freshly harvested food has a higher nutritional content, and 4. We simply eat more vegetables. These are the gifts of God. There is delight as food gladdens the heart and makes us beautiful and strong.

> I will both lie down and sleep in peace;
> For you alone, O Lord, make me lie down in safety. (Ps 4:8)

I am fortunate that it is easy for me to sleep, and I am grateful for God's gift of rest. Worries can keep me awake and fretting, and then I remember that over and over Jesus told us not to worry, but to trust God.

> Those who wait for the Lard shall renew their strength,
> They shall run and not be weary,
> They shall walk and not faint. (Isa 40:31)

Here is where I fail more often. I'd rather sit with a book, or sew, or paint, or work on the computer than go out and walk. I'm working on this challenge.

Right now, I am in good health with only the normal limits that aging brings. I am aware that even my best efforts cannot keep me from disease or accidents. The reality is that most lives include times of physical suffering and pain. I try to live in ways that encourage physical health and hope to face times of illness and hurt with courage and a cheerful spirit. MB

Sub-question 6g: What means or methods are helping me continue to grow and deepen?

For the first person did not know wisdom fully,
nor will the lost one fathom her.
For her thoughts are more abundant than the seas,
and her counsel deeper than the great abyss.

SIRACH 24:28–29

We are always growing, always learning, for wisdom is vaster than human comprehension and invites us on a continuing journey of exploration. There is always something more to learn, something more to understand. The previous question focuses on physical health: diet, sleep, and exercise. But there is mental, emotional, and spiritual health as well.

I've always been a reader. As a tiny child, I wanted to be read as well as the adults around me. I greeted people who came to visit by pushing a book at them, insisting that they read to me. Learning to read opened a vast universe of ideas and experiences. I read for many reasons. A novel takes me into a different world. I read poetry that evokes a deep and sometimes terrible beauty. Nonfiction provides me with new information. And all genres seem to invite me to wonder at the craft of the writer.

There are of course many other ways to learn: lectures, television, movies, travel, and conversation. And, of course, some things are learned best by doing. Don't just tell me how to do something; show me how to do it and watch as I try it for myself. Then let me practice and develop a new skill.

I continue to work to develop spiritual practices that sustain my relationship with God. Regular worship is important as I gather in a community to sing and pray. There are many personal spiritual practices I draw on: journaling, reading the Bible and other spiritual books, contemplative prayer, walking a labyrinth, conversation with friends, and praying the Psalms. I don't do all of those every day, but these are part of the rich resources that keep me connected to the Holy. I try to spend some time in prayer as I begin the day. As I prepare for bed, I consider what gifts the day has brought me and offer a prayer of gratitude. MB

Sub-question 6h: On occasion, we need to take care of the deeper patterns or feelings in our sub- or unconscious life. How much do you feel influenced by them and how do we access those patterns that may harm us and heal them?

This kind of disturbance of memory suffices for the obsessional neurosis; in hysteria it is different. This latter neurosis is usually characterized by amnesias on a grand scale. As a rule the analysis of each single hysterical symptom leads to a whole chain of impressions, which upon their return may be literally described as having been hitherto forgotten.[13]

SIGMUND FREUD

Space does not allow a full-blown treatment of Sigmund Freud's theory of psychoanalysis. Nor does it easily fit under the category of wisdom. In the field of psychotherapy, his views have been debated extensively with many rejecting his basic approach and others using it with some revision. What lives on in our contemporary understanding of the human psyche because of Freud is that there are forgotten events and dimensions of our lives that are unconscious, many of which impact our mental health. It is this larger more general insight that we want briefly to address and view through the lens of wisdom.

We are wise to acknowledge that there have been experiences in our lives, often in our childhood, that have had a negative influence on our growth toward maturity and peace of mind. Some of these experiences we remember, and we know that working through these hurtful and harmful experiences can bring some relief from depression and fear and lead to health and wholeness. There is also a measure of emancipation as we gain insight on what happened, why it happened, and the way that it influences our lives. As Freud reminds us in the quote above, we may remember the way our father has damaged us by his harsh judgment of our behavior and even physical punishment. We can reflect on whether we were accepted and loved, or in many cases, rejected and abused.

It is not uncommon to carry feelings of rejection and abuse, but not be able to fully recall what attitudes and actions of our past, often as children, have created deep feelings of depression, anxiety, and low

13. Freud, *General Introduction to Psychoanalysis*, 294.

self-esteem. One part of the therapeutic strategy of Freud and contemporary therapists who have updated Freud, is that the recovery and understanding of those damaging abuses can be liberating and lead to a more healthy process of self-actualization. In our time, we are learning about how many women were sexually abused as children or in the workplace. We are also aware of how violent action in war has traumatized so many people. There has been some relief and help in the #MeToo Movement for women who have been abused and now have more freedom to speak about their abuse without shame or guilt. We know people and hear about others who in violent wars now have what is called Post-Traumatic Stress Disorder, and patterns of healing have been developed.

What does wisdom suggest for those of us who suffer from the harmful behavior of others whether in the present or the past? How do we access this pain and find healing if we have pushed these feelings about actions and patterns of harm below the surface into our unconscious mind?

1. First, we should get help, yes from friends and wise people in our circle of acquaintances, but also from those with *special training*.

2. There are also *support groups* that can be extremely helpful. Joining with others, as, for example, in the way it is done by Alcoholics Anonymous, gives the assurance that you are not alone and that progress can be made.

3. And, of course, if those who have harmed us are still alive and available, there may be wisdom in *having a conversation with them*. These conversations can be very difficult and may easily become counter-productive if it just becomes a time of exchanging angry accusations. Almost inevitably there will be some denial and defensiveness. But with the help of another person who has excellent interpersonal skills and some distance and is trusted by both parties, it can become a time of release and reconciliation.

4. Others I have known have used writing in a *journal* about the abusive behavior and resulting feelings. This process can be liberating as well.

The way to health may not be easy, but gaining understanding and insight can be healing, emancipating, and life giving. DF

Sub-question 6i: How do you relax? Do you have hobbies or like to play games? Do the arts help you express your deepest self?

In an aesthetic experience, in the creation of contemplation of a work of art, the psychological conscience is able to attain some of its highest and most perfect fulfillments. Art enables us to find ourselves and lose ourselves at the same time. The mind that responds to the intellectual and spiritual values that lie hidden in a poem, a painting, or a piece of music, discovers a spiritual vitality that lifts it above the itself, takes it out of itself, and makes it present to itself on a level of being that it did not know it could ever achieve.[14]

Thomas Merton

There are so many things I enjoy, but I find that the arts are most meaningful to my life. My experience of the arts has been richly rewarding in many ways. Sometimes I am a creator, whether it is weaving cloth, sewing a quilt, writing a poem, or making a collage. Other times I participate with others in the arts: singing in a choir or reading poetry. And then I experience the art that others create: visiting an art gallery, listening to a concert, watching a play or a movie, or reading any well-crafted writing.

"Art enables us to find ourselves and to lose ourselves at the same time," wrote Thomas Merton. Art takes a certain concentration that carries us beyond rational thought to an encounter with color, shape, form, and sound. When I go to choir practice, I have to set aside my ordinary concerns as the notes and rhythms demand my full attention. I listen to my voice alongside the others as we seek to express what the composer intended. I lose myself as I find myself in the singing.

Art has the power to keep me centered. This fall I spent a week at a silk painting workshop. I left home discouraged, feeling depressed that I was no longer working as a pastor. As the week progressed, I found that the depression dissipated. I lost myself in the rich colors, watching how the dyes transformed the silk, interacting with each other in new ways. I practiced my own skills and experimented to see what would happen. I found a deep delight as I worked beside others to learn and grow. I lost myself in the work and found new truths about who I am as one who creates.

14. Merton, *No Man Is an Island*, 34–35.

I need to find time to create. My young son expressed it well years ago. I must have been crankier than usual because he turned to me and said, "Mom, you need to sew." He was right. He knew that if I took the time to sew or quilt, I would relax and be a happier mother.

I returned to my weaving loom this week. It takes concentration and thinking to prepare the loom, but as the shuttle moves back and forth between the warp threads, creating a pattern of beauty I enter a quiet, centered place, not unlike prayer. Art asks for my physical, emotional, mental, and spiritual presence. God is with me as I weave. MB

CHAPTER 6: HOW SHOULD I TAKE CARE OF MYSELF?

Resources and Practices

Further Reading

1. Nathaniel Branden, *Honoring the Self: Self-Esteem and Personal Transformation*

2. William Brown, *Seeing the Psalms: A Theology of Metaphor*

3. Erik Erickson, *Identity: Youth and Crisis*

4. James Fadiman and Robert Frager, *Essential Sufism*

5. Thomas Merton, *No Man Is an Island*

6. Virginia Satir, *Peoplemaking*

Suggested Practices

1. Give attention to the practice of meditation. Essentially it is a time of pause, focusing on the present, and engaging in mindfulness. There are several kinds and approaches to meditation. Get some help, find one that works for you, and build in some time in your schedule to meditate. It is awakening and healing.

2. Find time to reflect and ponder about any changes you would like to make to you life. Seek guidance from caring friends and begin to make the changes that are your highest priorities.

3. Speak with a friend or a counselor (a good listener who will not self-reference) about your deepest fears and most painful emotions. Identifying them and articulating their cause is part of the healing process.

4. Journal about both what you would like to become as a person and what you think might prevent you from achieving these goals.

5. In your journal and in conversation with a trusted friend or counselor, speak about what brings you the greatest joy and deepest satisfaction.

6. Continue your reading about "the journey of life" and stay involved with an organization and a small group of people that focus on improving your life.

Foundational Question 7

How Important Is It for Me to Belong to Groups and Organizations and Have a Supportive Community?

Expanding and strengthening our social bonds beyond the immediate mother-child and pair-bond relationships to wider kin and community was an important cultural step for our species, and its origins are likely to be in the social dependency of mothers, the pooling of childcare, and the maternal pursuit and maintenance of cooperative networks.[1]

GAIA VINCE

LIKE NEARLY ALL OF us in our advanced and contemporary cultures, I live in an environment of interacting groups, organizations, and family structures. As I write in the time of the 2020 elections in the United States and the coronavirus pandemic, I realize how collective bodies of people have a profound influence on my life. I care deeply about how our society is governed. And of course I want my family to be safe from illness and provided with excellent health care. Gaia Vince, a British science writer, traces these levels of interdependence back to human origins and how they evolved in a rich variety of ways through to the present. She gives us a thoughtful overview in her recent book of the biological and cultural evolution of humans and how human groupings have sustained the human family.

Our question takes us beyond a scientific and cultural understanding by asking how the groups and organizations in our contemporary

1. Vince, *Transcendence*, 48.

setting both sustain us and in some cases harm us. As l look back over the decades of my life, I can name the dozens of groups that have shaped and sustained me, from the family into which I was born, the schools I attended, the cities and states in which the family lived, the profession I chose, and to the complex variety of economic and political structures I had to navigate. In some measure, I am who I am because of all of these associations. Grateful to many of them, harmed by some of them, and sustained by more than I can name or explain, like all people, I have evolved because of them. As I get in touch with this vast array or organizations and their profound influence, I find myself reflecting on how I might help some of them become more intentionally engaged in creating an environment that makes us better and happier human beings.

I want to support those associations with the clear purpose of helping to create a more just and humane world. I wish I had the influence of the United Nations and the power and influence of the President of the United States to impact global infrastructure and create a more empathic civilization.[2] I do not have that influence, but I can be guided by certain values and participate in groups that have comparable values. I can have some influence on those with positive goals in the region in which I live. And, in some cases, I can help sustain those that are working beyond my region to wider sections of my society and the world. I would summarize these values in the following way:[3]

1. I would begin with *love and compassion*, the way of caring deeply about the welfare of others and by taking positive action to relieve suffering in all of its diabolical forms.

2. I would stress the need for a commitment to *truth and authentic living*. I will support groups that speak about and address what really is happening, and, as a member of the association, always try to be one who has integrity and lives in harmony with the values that are foundational for the group. Good happens when we are people of integrity.

3. I would stress the need for *justice*, knowing that human welfare, and indeed the welfare of all living creatures and the fate of the earth,

2. See Jeremy Rifkin's book, *The Empathic Civilization: The Race to Global Consciousness in a World in Crisis.*

3. I am fully and painfully aware that each of these values needs book-length development.

depend on being treated fairly by the law and having fair access to and distribution of resources.

4. I would give my heart and soul for a more *peaceful* world, one in which justice prevails and one in which deep human conflicts are resolved by diplomacy rather than violence. DF

FOUNDATIONAL QUESTION 7: HOW IMPORTANT IS IT FOR ME TO BELONG TO GROUPS AND ORGANIZATIONS AND HAVE A SUPPORTIVE COMMUNITY?

In you, O Lord, I take refuge;
let me never be put to shame.
In your righteousness deliver me and rescue me,
Incline your ear to me and save me.
Be to me a rock of refuge,
a strong fortress, to save me,
for you are my rock and fortress.

PSALM 71:1–2

I'm writing this short essay during the COVID-19 pandemic, a time when we are asked to stay home and practice social distancing. Stanford psychologist, Jamil Zaki, says: "Social distancing is vital to slowing the spread of COVID-19, but it also pushes against human beings' fundamental needs for connections with one another. Especially during difficult times, people feel an urge to commiserate, to comfort, and to be comforted by each other. Experiences show that the support of loved ones softens our response to stress."[4] He reframes our language to claim our need for community even when we are apart: "We should think of this time as 'physical distancing' to emphasize that we can remain socially connected even while being apart. In fact, I encourage all of us to practice 'distant socializing.'"[5]

The longing for community is strong and real. Currently we are cut off from even the causal community of people we meet and see in the grocery store, the library, and the playground. My calendar is empty;

4. De Witte, "Instead of Social Distancing Practice," para. 5.
5. De Witte, "Instead of Social Distancing Practice," para. 8.

all the meetings are cancelled. Using Dr. Zaki's term, we recognize that distant socializing takes effort. We need to rethink how we reach out and connect with other people in these new circumstances. Instead of sitting down for a cup of tea, we are able to talk with our neighbors outside in the garden. Instead of gathering for worship, we attend a religious service via computer. Many pastors find that they are learning new skills to produce worship videos.[6] And there are some special gifts in this strange time. For example, I connected via online worship with friends that are geographically far from me.

By the time you are reading this book, this time of worry over the COVID-19 virus may be in the past. What did we learn from this experience of "distancing" that we have carried into the future? What did we learn from the experience that is now integral to my life? I know that what I learned is that I cherish our social connections even more deeply, for we now know how much we miss them. MB

FOUNDATIONAL QUESTION 7: HOW IMPORTANT IS IT FOR ME TO BELONG TO GROUPS AND ORGANIZATIONS AND HAVE A SUPPORTIVE COMMUNITY?

A wall standing alone is useless
but put three or four walls together,
and they'll support a roof and keep
the grain dry and safe.[7]

Rumi

I have lived as a minority person in Christian countries for most of my life, and I have occasionally experienced the sting of discrimination. As a student in London in the late sixties, I experienced so much racial bias that my spirit was dampened and I longed for a sense of belonging and dignity. Eagerly I sought the company of other minority people so that together we could share our concerns and support each other in the less-than-welcoming society.

Discomfort turned to terror the night I encountered a menacing group of skinheads in the London subway. Being small and light on my

---

6. del Rosario considers the impact of this in "What If Online Worship Lasts."

7. Barks and Moyne, *Essential Rumi*, 246.

feet, I was able to outrun them, but afterward I realized that I had come very close to being badly hurt. Because of that personal experience of visceral fear, I now empathize with the dread felt by religious and racial minorities during periods of social unrest, and I understand the instinct to seek safety in groups of one's own "kind." The support to be found among my own group is very important. From these experiences I came to realize that it is also essential that I spend my life building communities that offer sanctuary and psychological and spiritual wellbeing. It became for me a calling.

Newly fearful for my physical safety and eager to leave the toxic environment in England, I grabbed an opportunity to study at the University of Oregon. In my first week there, I joined the Foreign Student Organization. Later, as its President, I worked tirelessly to see that foreign students were treated with dignity and their needs were heard and addressed by the University authorities and state Legislature.

Many years later, now in Seattle, my life took a bold and unconventional turn; I began working full-time with a pair of close friends and we devoted ourselves to the creation of an interfaith group called the Circle of Love. For seven years we participated weekly in creative worship services in different people's homes, set up educational classes on religion and spirituality, and initiated interfaith events in the community.

Through an astonishing turn of events in 1999, our group was gifted with an historic church building that needed a congregation. Overjoyed that we had become a congregation and reeling with disbelief, we chose the name "Interfaith Community Sanctuary" and dedicated our work to fostering understanding, peace, and harmony between the world's religions. Then came the events of 9/11 and the birth of Interfaith Amigos. For two decades, along with Rabbi Ted Falcon and Pastor Don Mackenzie, I have traveled across the country to share a message of inclusivity. We have learned that it is important to build walls, not with the goal to separate, but to join together and create sanctuaries of friendship, hope, and interfaith understanding. JR

Sub-question 7a: Do the groups and associations you have sustain you, guide you, and motivate you?

It is possible that the next Buddha will not take the form of an individual. The next Buddha may take the form of a community, a

community practicing understanding and loving kindness, a community practicing mindful living. And the practice can be carried out as a group, as a city, as a nation.[8]

THICH NAT HANH

For the past few decades, my heart's desire has been to help create and live in a community that celebrates diversity, furthers spiritual maturity, and engages in acts of social service. On all counts, my associations with the Interfaith Community Sanctuary (ICS) and the Interfaith Amigos have been deeply fulfilling.

The tight-knit community of ICS, some two hundred members, is amazingly diverse. We include people who call themselves spiritual but not religious, people with dimensions of several religions in their outlook, (e.g., a Jew who also practices Buddhism and a Christian who is also a Muslim), secular humanists, Wiccans, atheists, agnostics, and people like me who are rooted in one tradition but open to the wisdom of other traditions. We are proof that religions may differ in form, yet are similar in essence. As the Sufis say, "The branches of a tree sway differently in the wind but are connected at the roots."[9] And Sufis affirm, "When I and you are absent, I have no idea if this is a mosque, synagogue, church, or temple."[10]

What bonds our diverse community together is not theology but abiding personal friendships, spiritual practices, religious literacy, and working together on service projects. Another key factor is the sincere endeavor of the leadership to be non-hierarchical. By universal agreement, the powers of board members are limited so that ego and self-interest don't become factors in decision-making. Members of the congregation offer valuable advice, attend monthly meetings, and are empowered to vote against recommendations of the board. When conflicts do arrive, elders and mutual friends immediately intervene with discussions, prayers, and practices.

I have a deep desire for this community to be engaged in social service, and I am very pleased, even amazed, that ICS provides support of two projects dear to the hearts of my family. One is a school for girls

8. An extract from a talk given by Thich Nat Hanh on the Day of Mindfulness at the Spirit Rock Center in Woodacre, California, in October, 1993.

9. Loizzo et al., *Advances in Contemplative Psychotherapy*, 76.

10. Shabestari, from the Persian classic *The Secret Rose Garden*, quoted in Cranmer-Byng et al., *Wisdom of the East*, 65.

and women, and another is a medical clinic in our ancestral village in Bangladesh. The amount raised, hundreds of thousands of dollars, by the congregation over several years is mind-boggling and points to the power of goodwill, creativity, and group collaboration.

With my Interfaith Amigos, I continue to learn about the power of friendship, trust, and vulnerability. Through our intimate conversations and learning from one another, we realize that religious disputes, if looked at carefully, are often rooted in illusion and vanity. Over time, any sense of personal competition among us has evolved into the joyfulness of collaboration. Little by little, we have grown to find delight and meaning in supporting and uplifting one another. Our mission is to find creative ways to celebrate one another's festivals and rituals, articulate our beliefs with understanding, show compassion, and have the courage to face the areas where our religions go astray and carefully interpret sacred texts in ways that serve the common good. JR

Sub-question 7b: Are there any risks and disadvantages in joining groups and associations? Are there ways to help organizations overcome their limitations and be more consistent with their stated goals?

Pluralism is not diversity alone but energetic engagement with diversity because mere diversity without real encounter and relationship will yield increasing tension in our society.[11]

THOMAS FRIEDMAN

In 2019, our progressive and pluralistic ICS invited a couple of diehard supporters of President Trump to speak to our congregation. The program rattled the nerves of at least a half a dozen congregants. They advised me to never again invite people like those who came because their views are "poisonous" and their comments disturbed the harmony of our close-knit community.

As I pondered their remarks, I realized the truth of Noam Chomsky's insight that, "If we don't believe in freedom of expression for people we

11. Pluralism Project of Harvard University, quoted by Thomas Friedman in *Thank You for Being Late*, 344.

despise, we don't believe in it at all."[12] If we live and speak only with members of our own tribe, we begin to live in a bubble. In and of themselves, bubbles are not bad. They may give members a sense of security, belonging, and vision and are therefore useful. But if we have little or no interaction with others who are different, our bubbles slowly develop an inevitable sense of superiority, such as the "holier than thou" and "I am right and you are wrong" attitudes that exclusive religious sects can exhibit.

So the question is, how can we venture out of the safety of our preferred group to connect with members of other groups, especially those that support values and points of view with which we disagree? This is a question often posed to the Interfaith Amigos, and what follows is what we usually advise: Ask the other, "Is there anything I can tell you that would help change your mind?" If that person is honest, the answer is usually "No." Then tell the other person respectfully and honestly that there is nothing he or she could say that would change your mind either. And then say, "But it would be noble in God's eyes to work together on a service project, such as one that helps the marginalized." This approach can be very helpful in bursting those two unfriendly bubbles.

After the event of 9/11, I persisted in connecting with two evangelical Christians who were blatantly Islamophobic. In spite of their repeated rebuffs, I persevered. Over time, we developed a relationship. Slowly, their suspicions and biases softened, and they lost their fears and harsh opposition to Islam and Muslims. I changed as well. My heart was touched by the sweetness of friendship among their members and their authentic dedication to social justice concerns. My biases gave way to a deeper understanding of the other, and I now welcome opportunities for us to work together to serve marginalized peoples. JR

Sub-question 7c: What is our part in belonging to a supportive community? Is it easy for you to take the initiative and join a group or association of people?

"If there is among you anyone in need, a member of your community in any of your towns within the land that the Lord your God is giving you, do no be hard-hearted or tight-fisted toward your needy neighbor.

12. From the 1992 documentary film that explores the political life and ideas of Noam Chomsky, titled *Manufacturing Consent: Noam Chomsky and the Media*. See Achbar and Wintonick, *Manufacturing Consent*.

You should rather open your hand, willingly lending enough to meet the need, whatever it may be . . . Give liberally and be ungrudging when you do so, for on this account the Lord God will bless you in all your work and in all that you undertake. Since there will never cease to be some in need on the earth, I therefore command you, 'Open your hand to the poor and needy neighbor in your land.'"

DEUTERONOMY 15:7–8, 10–11

Throughout the Bible, there is the call to care for the vulnerable within a community. This command has special urgency in the Hebrew Bible. The message is clear! We are responsible for the wellbeing of all. We need to support one another.

There are many forms of supportive communities in our world today, often with a specific purpose or cause. Some groups focus on environmental issues or political action. Other groups gather around interests or hobbies. Years ago, Steve (my husband) and I liked to go to a bakery for breakfast on Saturday morning. There were other regulars there, and over the years we became a community, catching up with each other nearly every week. It was an important supportive interaction for us. I have fond memories of these conversations.

Our question is: What is our part in belonging to a supportive community? First, we need to show up and be present for one another. Then we need to behave in ways that keep the community healthy, using our best group and interpersonal skills. We listen with empathy, whether it is to listen to the choir director who has challenges or to resist the temptation to dominate the discussion and continually self-reference. The wellbeing of the whole and every member is important. Is there good morale in the group? If not, how might I improve the health of the whole group? Is each member finding the support they need? If not, how might I reach out to this person and listen with empathy? And we need to be especially sensitive to the way individual gifts and differences are honored and celebrated.

It can be hard to enter a new group. If the group has been meeting for some time, you may feel a little like you are an outsider. You may not fully understand the relationships that are already there or know for sure just how to act. I find it helps to be a bit of an anthropologist at first. Try to observe the customs and dynamics of the group, listen to the stories, discern the role of various people in the group, and then assess and learn where and how you might fit in.

It is also the case that sometimes a certain group may not meet our needs for any number of reasons. If this happens, it may be wise to step aside and see if other groups would be a better fit for us. When I find a group where I feel valued, where I am learning, and where I encounter other perspectives, I then commit to it and find good ways to fit into the rhythm of the group. The bottom line is that we need each other. We need to feel heard and understood by those who share our experiences and perspectives. We often learn from those who are different from us. It is worth the effort to find and be part of supportive communities. MB

Sub-question 7d: How do we balance being alone and being with others?

In the stillness of the quiet, if we listen, we can hear the whisper of the heart giving strength to weakness, courage to fear, hope to despair.[13]

HOWARD THURMAN

Finding the right of balance between being with others and having time alone has been a constant struggle for me. There are times when I long for quiet space to work alone. I drop back from obligations and say no to requests. I then realize I am lonely and that I need the companionship of others. So I connect again with others, often getting so busy with them and then find that I have little time for myself. It becomes a somewhat difficult dance in my life: finding time to work alone and yet connecting with community. I hear the soft and comforting music of working alone, and at other times, I want to get on the dance floor with others and waltz.

I need time alone to work creatively. I open myself to the mystery of solitude and pay attention to what is happening inside of me. I lose myself, forgetting my own situation, as I am challenged by shape and color, texture and form. When I don't have this time of contemplation and exploration, I become anxious and feel stressed.

Yet I know I need to be with others. I learn so much as I listen, and deep down I know it helps to interact with people. Two things happen when this occurs: 1. I clarify my own thoughts as I express myself

13. Thurman, *Meditations of the Heart*, 95–96.

to someone else. And 2. I gain insight from another's perspective. Deep down, I know it is good to connect with other people, to listen to their stories, and to try to understand their perspective. It opens my world and carries me away from my own self-preoccupied views.

As I move from time apart to time together, I recognize that different people react differently to the common environment. For example, extroverts gain energy when they are with others and introverts need quiet to recharge following time in a group. For most of us, we need both social interaction and quiet time apart. Finding that balance is one of life's challenges. MB

Sub-question 7e: Do you think of yourself as an introvert or an extrovert? How do you discern the difference?

People are different in fundamental ways. They want different things: they have different motives, purposes, aims, values, needs, drives, impulses, urges. Nothing is more fundamental than that. They believe differently: they think, cognize, conceptualize, perceive, understand, comprehend, and cogitate differently, And of course, manners of acting and emoting, governed as they are by wants and beliefs, follow suit and differ radically among people.[14]

As we meet and associate with others in our various groups, we soon discover that not everyone in the groups has the same sensitivity and temperament as we do. At times, these circumstances can be quite disconcerting. For example, I often think my sense of the length of the discussion and my suggestions for moving on are sound. Yet others have not always affirmed my sense of timing or my suggestions and points of view. They need time to talk. Over time, I have made peace with the reality that we are different. I have been tremendously helped by a variety of psychological tools that identify different characteristics and patterns of feeling, thinking, and acting. One of them, the Myers-Briggs Type Indicator (MBTI), supplemented by the Keirsey Temperament Sorter, has been especially helpful for me because it has given some categories for understanding personality types and why I feel the way I do in groups. The MBTI suggests four contrasting personality types: 1. Extroversion

14. Keirsey and Bates, *Please Understand Me*, 2.

or introversion; 2. Sensing or intuition; 3. Thinking or feeling; 4. Judging or perceiving. Sixteen patterns emerge as these characteristics interact. Each of us may be understood and described by letters representing the categories. For example, I tend to be an INTJ.[15] I want to focus on the first descriptive category as a way of responding to our question.[16]

I think of myself as primarily an introvert, and as I have been tested, using a scale of 1–10 with 1 being almost exclusively an introvert and 10 being almost exclusively an extrovert, I learn that I am a 6 on the introvert side and a 4 on the extrovert side. Because much of my work as a teacher and minister over the years of my career has involved working with others, I have learned to be more out-going. One psychologist who administered the test called me an introvert who has become a professional extrovert.

As an introvert, I do tend to think about what I should say rather than immediately joining a conversation or discussion as would an extrovert. Often I am more of a listener, although in certain roles, I am called upon to speak. As I leave settings in which I am called upon to speak, I am ready to return home to enjoy the peace and quiet it brings, whereas the extrovert might wish to still be engaged in conversation. I like social occasions, but prefer small ones and do better in them when I have a clear role and function. I do need to recharge after these occasions, and I reflect on my natural shyness, sometimes wishing I enjoyed these gatherings as much as my extroverted wife.

I have been in leadership roles and have found ways to be a constructive extrovert. In planning and decision-making settings, I find that my best contributions come from anticipation and planning. I have done the background reading, letting its point of view sift and sort and become constructive contemplation that leads to better planning. I am also ready to hear the views of others and able to integrate these views into a larger picture describing a course of action. I have found that this style of leadership can be very helpful, although on occasion, I somewhat passively let the group decision prevail.

Perhaps the greatest gift to me with my introverted temperament is that I have learned to listen carefully and to respond to the views of others with understanding and empathy. People often feel heard and sense that their role in decision-making is valued. I wish I could say that this

15. N is the letter used for Intuition.

16. See as well Oswald and Kroeger, *Personality Types and Religious Leadership*, and Chester and Norrisey, *Prayer and Temperament*.

awareness and style in organizational settings were always present, but, unfortunately, I have had to grow and continue to mature in my interaction with others. I still make mistakes of being too quiet or even frustrated because my view did not prevail, but by being aware of my style, I have helped some groups to find their way into the future. I am learning to accept who I am and my role with groups and associations. DF

Sub-question 7f: Do you feel like you belong when you are in groups or do you often feel left out? Do you feel energized by being in groups or do you feel tired when the time with others is over?

When ink joins with a pen, then the blank paper can say something. Rushes and reeds must be woven to be useful as a mat. If there weren't interlaced, the wind would blow them away. Like that God paired up creatures and gave them friendship.[17]

RUMI

I enjoy working in groups because the interweaving of ideas from members leads to creative solutions. However, for me, inspiration and creativity can flow only in an environment of friendship and trust. Without some previous bonding with the others in the group, I feel withdrawn and reluctant to express myself fully.

Although I am basically shy, I genuinely enjoy cultivating friendships with people. One of my joys in life is meeting friends regularly to have meaningful conversation over food and beverages. It feels as if I am warming my hands at the central fire on a wintry day. Group meetings energize me if there is kinship of spirit among us because of friendship.

Too often in the past I have attended monthly board meetings of prestigious organizations where I had little or no human connection with the members. I accepted their invitation to be on the board only because it lent prestige to my work. For them, my presence as a Muslim fulfilled their need for diversity. To justify my position, I strained to say something wise or impressive. It felt artificial and inauthentic. I now understand the wisdom of the Sufi teachers who advise us to take a risk and let go of the

17. Barks and Moyne, *Essential Rumi*, 246.

personality masks we wear in our roles in life. Such a release is liberating, and the truth is that our real face is the most beautiful.

I have had occasion to withdraw from spiritual groups even though their vision of working for unity appealed to me. The meetings were remarkably formal. There was much quibbling and sniping among the members about expenditures and a constant focus on fundraising. The work was important but I felt unfulfilled. I was expending my time and energy on the wrong concerns. It brought to mind the words of Tagore: "While God waits for His temple to be built of love, man brings stones."[18]

Why is it, then, that I enjoy all aspects of the monthly meetings of our Guiding Council of ICS,[19] even when the issues are often dry and mundane? Partly, of course, it is because we are all friends sharing a common vision, and our process is non-hierarchical. Even more, I believe that ultimately it is because we practice the art of making sacred our ordinary moments. A discussion about how much to raise the salary of the gardener and janitor becomes interlaced with heartfelt prayers, compassion, balance, laughter, and reflection on the golden rule. The discussion nourishes and delights my soul and leads to wise and practical decisions. JR

Sub-question 7g: Do you like yourself the way that you are or would you like to develop better social skills? What ways are available to you to improve your interpersonal and social skills?

Six months into her new, independent life, Katie Bishop was fifteen pounds heavier and truly miserable. She didn't just feel fat, she felt ugly. And after an unpleasant run-in at the home office and a spat with one of her neighbors, she was even beginning to wonder if she would ever be socially acceptable outside the little town that had made her feel so trapped.[20]

We have known people like Katie who have had trouble finding their way into improving their interpersonal skills and participating in a constructive way in groups. At times, we have had some of her feelings and

18. Tagore, *Fireflies*, 47.
19. Interfaith Community Sanctuary.
20. Cacioppo and Patrick, *Loneliness*, 1.

identified with others who have had a similar experience. She had left her family and the setting in which she grew up in order to get away from her small town that she saw as having limitations, preventing her from realizing her potential in a career and a life that would bring joy and gratification. Yet her new setting was just as difficult. I learn from her brief story that she was overly dependent upon external circumstances, not that they are unimportant, but was miserable because she did not have the inner resources to find happiness in either setting, her original home or the location of her new job.

I want to look more deeply into her situation, that of others with similar problems and my own experience of moving into adulthood. My foundational starting point is that I am persuaded that true love is at the heart of human fulfillment, and that we often suffer in nearly all situations if there is the lack of love. The love about which I speak is rooted in self-love and the love we share with others. The word love, as we use it, can have a wide variety of meanings, often summarized in three Greek words: 1. *agape* that is unlimited and unconditional love; *eros* that is the love and attraction that is drawn out of us by the beauty and richness of the object of love; and *philia* that is the love felt and given among friends.[21] These various forms of love were missing in Katie's life. She did not bring the presence of love in its several forms to her circumstances. What she needed, regardless of her location, was unlimited and unconditional self-love. She did not recognize that fully accepting oneself is the first step in finding a fulfilling life. It was Jesus who said that we are to love our neighbor as we love ourselves, and we often miss the part about loving ourselves. And without the unconditional acceptance of ourselves, we are unable to love others and establish good friendships and appreciate the grandeur, subtly, and beauty that surrounds us. I agree with the Irish poet, John O'Donohue, that "You are sent here to learn to love and to receive love."[22]

There are ways to begin learning how to love in a deep and profound way and to experience the joy and fulfillment that comes from the experience of love. Time and space does not allow a full description of learning how to love, but four steps are a beginning:

1. Seek the help of a counselor and good friends that will, by their empathy, help you to cultivate self-acceptance and self-love.

21. See my book, *Lovescapes*, 41–44.
22. O'Donohue, *Anam Cara*, 27.

2. As you are with friends, be conscious of the way that love can be expressed, by affirming them, by tangibly helping them, and by being open to receive their love.

3. Get involved in classes on self-understanding, human relationships, the cultivation of interpersonal skills, and read widely about the "lovescape" in which we live.[23]

4. And remember, "For God so loved the world . . ." You are part of this world and truly loved by God. DF

Sub-question 7h: What is the difference between a healthy group or association and an unhealthy group or association?

In the love of persons, then, people bestow value upon one another over and above their individual or objective value. The reciprocity of love occurs when each participant receives bestowed value while bestowing it upon the other. Reciprocity has always been recognized as a desired outcome of love. Since it need not occur, however, I define the lover as the one who bestows value, and the beloved the one who receives it.[24]

IRVING SINGER

A healthy group is one that values its members and has policies and objectives that seek the welfare of those whom they serve. They achieve this mission in many ways; I will stress five: 1. The group trains and empowers its members to serve the mission of the organization. 2. The leadership of the group guides its members and keeps them informed about the progress of the organization; they sense that they belong. 3. The leadership of the group has ways of encouraging all the members of the group with reports and involvement in shaping the future of the organization. 4. The group has policies and practices that enable its members to flourish and mature. 5. The group provides guidance and practices that sustain the

---

23. There are endless books. One basic book for the cultivation of loving behavior and interpersonal skills is Goleman's, *Emotional Intelligence: Why It Can Matter More Than IQ.*

24. Singer, *Nature of Love*, 6.

individual, encouraging a positive outlook and the ability to sustain the individual in times of difficulty and challenge.[25]

An unhealthy group has many characteristics that are almost opposite of those listed as positive. They are: 1. The group tends to be over-controlling of its members and limits them from participation in the shaping of the larger vision of the organization. 2. The group tends to be overly ideological, blindly committed to one exclusive way of believing and functioning, and tends to resist change. 3. The leadership of the group tends to confine its members to one responsibility and does not allow its members to understand the way sub-groups function collaboratively to implement the mission. 4. Such a group often becomes overly zealous, even fanatical in their outlook, a mode that is often damaging to its members; they fire those who dare to disagree. 5. The result is a group experience that is filled with fear, mistrust, and intolerance. In short, the members of the group do not feel valued (loved), low morale occurs, people leave, and the organization, which on paper may have a respectable vision and mission, fails to achieve its goals because those who belong to the group or work for the company do not find fulfillment in their work.

In a healthy group, members begin to value and love themselves, value and love others in their circle of acquaintances, find work that values them and gives them a sense of belonging and ownership, and have a sense of fulfillment in making a contribution to the common good. DF

Sub-question 7i: What difference do groups or associations make in individual lives, in the community, and in the world?

Never doubt that a small group of thoughtful, committed citizens can change the world. Indeed, it's the only thing that ever has.[26]

MARGARET MEAD

Margaret Mead's well-known quote reflects the power that groups have to make a difference in serving the common good. Many of the major positive changes to society were powered by efforts of ordinary people.

---

25. Ferguson, *Exploring the Spirituality of the World Religions*, 10.
26. Lutkehaus, *Margaret Mead*, 95–96.

For example, people without power and status led the suffrage movement and the civil rights movement, yet their efforts changed our world.

I've seen this effort of ordinary people working to create positive change produce results at the local level as well. Years ago, I observed a few teachers in our small town who saw a need for a food bank. They recognized that children were hungry, and therefore could not easily focus their attention on the lessons at school. There was a food bank in the next town, ten miles way, but the reality was that it was difficult for those using public transit to travel even that short distance. There was opposition to the teachers' initiative to create a local food bank for the families of the children, but on February 14, 2002, the food bank opened, and it is still serving the community today.

On an individual level, twelve-step organizations, like Alcoholics Anonymous, have helped thousands change their lives and gain control over their addiction. Many other examples could be listed such as programs for struggling teenagers and homeless people, programs started at the church I recently served.

In the midst of the COVID-19 pandemic, we have the opportunity to change the situation in which we live, and indeed to aid the whole world by slowing the spread of the disease. So we stay at home as much as possible, washing our hands and sanitizing surfaces. It is a strange way to help one another in that we don't encounter them day to day and see the results. But we help by remaining in our homes, careful not to spread the virus!

It is so important to stress that we do have the power to change the world. We do so by helping others, by engaging with others to address community concerns, and by caring for our world with ecological sensitivity; we change the planet on which we live. What we do matters! The way we live each day can make a difference. This can include activities such as avoiding the use of plastics, using mass transit, writing letters to the editor, donating to agencies that serve others, volunteering to clean the beach, or working at the food bank. These efforts give meaning to our lives. We recognize the deep web of relationship that connects us. Faced with the needs of our world, we acknowledge that we cannot care for every situation, but we can help in some way. MB

CHAPTER 7: HOW IMPORTANT IS IT FOR ME TO BELONG TO GROUPS, ORGANIZATIONS, AND HAVE A SUPPORTIVE COMMUNITY?

Resources and Practices

Further Reading

1. John T. Cacioppo and William Patrick, *Loneliness: Human Nature and the Need for Social Connection*

2. Daniel Goleman, *Emotional Intelligence*

3. David Keirsey and Marilyn Bates, *Please Understand Me: Character and Temperament Types*

4. Irving Singer, *The Nature of Love*, 4 vols.

5. Rabindranath Tagore, *Fireflies*

6. Gaia Vince, *Transcendence: How Humans Evolved Through Fire, Language, Beauty, and Time*

Suggested Practices

1. Assess the value of the groups to which you belong and ask yourself whether they contribute to your sense of purpose in life, your health and wellbeing, and your enjoyment and satisfaction. Rank them on a scale of one to ten with ten being almost perfect.

2. If you do not belong to or participate in groups or associations, find one that matches your values, your interests, and your needs for connection. Get involved and then determine if you made a good judgment about the group's capacity to increase your fulfillment.

3. Review the range of organizations whose work impacts you. For example, review the governments of your state and your region (county or city). Are they doing a good job, making your life better, and responding to your needs, the needs of your family, and the people in your community?

4. If you are in a religious community, ask whether your spiritual needs are being met by this spiritual center. Are you receiving

guidance and inspiration to cultivate a life-giving and mature spirituality? What ways might you contribute to the mission of this religious community?

Foundational Queston 8

Why Do I Suffer and Why Is There So Much Evil and Suffering in the World?

One day the heavenly beings came to present themselves before the Lord, and the Accuser also came among them to present himself before the Lord. The Lord said to the Accuser, "Where have you come from?" The Accuser answered the Lord, "From going to and fro on the earth, and from walking up and down on it." The Lord said to the Accuser, "Have you considered my servant Job? There is no one like him on the earth, a blameless and upright man who fears God and turns away from evil. He still persists with integrity, although you have incited me against him, to destroy him for no reason."

Job 2:1–3

Many have read and heard about the story of Job; it is a profound and subtle answer to our question about why we suffer. The story begins with a conversation between the Lord and the Accuser.[1] The Accuser says that those who live an upright life will turn away from the Lord when they experience deep suffering, asking why the Lord would cause or allow it. The Lord replies: "Have you considered my servant Job?" In response, the Accuser causes Job to suffer with the loss of his wealth and status, his family, and his health (covered with sores). Friends arrive with the answer that surely Job is getting what he deserves because of his wickedness. Job pleads his innocence and says that he has maintained his integrity and his deep faith in God. In time, Job partially weakens and

---

1. Often the word "Accuser" is translated as Satan.

questions whether his faith in God has merit. He ponders the question of why God would allow such suffering. A wise person (Elihu) says: "But in this you are not right. I will answer you: God is greater than any mortal" (Job 33:12). God's ways are beyond your understanding. Job listens and yet begins to question the justice of God.

A dialogue begins between the Lord and Job, with the Lord asking Job, "Where were you when I laid the foundation of the earth? Tell me, if you have understanding" (Job 38:4). Job is humbled and accepts that he does not fully understand. His friends are humbled as well, Job's fortunes are restored, and Job is able to look back across his life, endorse the wisdom that comes with experience, and live in peace in his last years.

The story does not give us a simple answer to the problem of suffering, yet suggests an outlook and attitude toward our suffering.[2] The outlook is that we are not always fully able to understand all the reasons why we suffer and why others suffer as well. There is an element of mystery, although it is true that we all bring some suffering on to ourselves. We learn how to have humility in reference to this profound existential question, and then keep our faith in God and live in a godly way. This becomes our lifelong attitude or spirit about the challenges of life. Friends may try to help us, but often don't fully understand. Even the wise Elihu who counsels faith and integrity may sound a little too pious and not touch us at the deepest level. Job's answer is to do the very best we can and learn how to live with the suffering we have. In time, justice will prevail and life will get better.[3] DF

FOUNDATIONAL QUESTION 8: WHY DO I SUFFER, AND WHY IS THERE SO MUCH EVIL AND SUFFERING IN THE WORLD?

Suffering arises from attachment to desires in the created world.

SECOND NOBLE TRUTH OF BUDDHISM

2. For a thoughtful treatment of the problem of evil from a Christian perspective, see Hick, *Evil and the God of Love.*

3. Some have said that the story of Job and its equivalent in other ancient literature probably should not have included the restoration of Job's good fortune. The real answer is to wisely and bravely accept what comes our way. The debate between the two points of view, accepting our suffering with wisdom and courage, or hoping that it is only a time of testing and that our suffering will cease, should continue. Pondering this question is the way of wisdom.

And in everything we have created opposites so that you might bear in mind
that God alone is One.

QUR'AN 51:49

All of us carry hidden scars and pain in our hearts. Sufi musicians sing
the words of an anonymous poet: "Tears are colorless. Thank God! Oth-
erwise, my pillow would betray the secrets of my heart." Some suffering is
inevitable in our lives. "Into each life some rain must fall" goes the common saying. But why is this so? The reasons are many and various. For
one thing, we live in a world of duality in which that falling rain can be
either a blessing or a curse. When it falls gently, it nurtures and sustains
life on our planet. But when it comes in torrents, it can destroy life and
cause terrible losses for those who live in flooded and washed out areas.
We like to call these events "acts of God" and we ask why God allows
them. The answer to this question is wrapped up in mystery.

We humans, too, are dual in nature, embodying both divine essence
and what the Qur'an calls a "slinking whisperer" that tempts us to pursue
our own pleasures without regard for the needs of others. Egged on by
that whisperer, we have laid waste to the earth in greedy pursuit of riches,
thereby causing environmental destruction, war, and untold human suffering. It is not up to God to directly intervene and prevent us from behaving
badly. According to the Qur'an, it is up to each of us to raise our consciousness and grow into more mature human beings so that we can refuse the
suggestions of the slinking whisperer and listen to our better angels.

On a personal level we ask with some urgency: "Why do I suffer?"
Often our suffering happens because I'm attached to the idea that what
happens in our lives should be other than it is. We are not content, and
our discontent occurs when we humans forget that everything in the created world is impermanent. Change is bound to occur in our lives. When
that happens and it doesn't go our way, we feel disappointed, frustrated,
and saddened. We suffer. The antidote, the sages tell us, is to focus on
essence, not form; on substance, not appearance; on permanent values,
not passing occurrences. This insight may be particularly helpful when
loved ones die or we have difficulty in a relationship. The loved one is not
entirely gone or estranged; his or her essence is still in your heart.

Suffering can lead to emotional and spiritual growth. God turns us
from one feeling to another, says Rumi, so that we have two wings with
which to fly. The more deeply sorrow carves into our being, says the poet

Kahlil Gibran, the more joy our being can contain. But there are limits to this positive outlook. For those living in intractable pain or poverty, or whose lives have been upended by war and disease, it would be cruel to suggest that they should somehow "grow" from their suffering. Instead of asking why God allows such wretchedness, perhaps we should ask ourselves how we can let God use our hands and feet to help in the healing of this suffering world. JR

FOUNDATIONAL QUESTION 8: WHY DO I SUFFER AND WHY IS THERE SO MUCH EVIL AND SUFFERING IN THE WORLD?

Anyone who has had even the briefest introduction to Buddhist teaching is familiar with its starting point: the inescapable truth that existence entails suffering.[4]

JACK KORNFIELD

Why there is the presence of so much evil and suffering is one of the most profound and vexing questions with which humans struggle. Deep inside, we long for a world of peace and security where all people thrive. We long for shalom. Shalom is a Hebrew word that means more than peace among conflicting groups and the absence of violence. The presence of shalom brings completeness, wholeness, peace, and harmony, and all that people need to flourish. Yet there is much in our world that resists the blessings of shalom. All around us, we see violence in all of its forms: greed, manipulation, racism, and warfare.

Some suffering comes from things we are unable to control such as earthquakes, tornados, and pandemics. We can take steps that reduce the intensity of this kind of suffering, as, for example, by building structures that will withstand earthquakes. Likewise, we can do some things to avoid illness, perhaps with vaccines, but we cannot avoid it altogether. COVID-19 has happened. These kind of occurrences cause suffering, although they are not what we generally call evil.

Evil is when there is the intention to harm and cause discomfort and suffering. Evil resides in the human community on both a personal and a societal level. I confess that I struggle with the problem of this kind of evil

---

4. Kornfield, *Wise Heart*, 241.

in the world. Why is there so much violence and greed? Why do humans abuse others? Yet they do. Evil is real, and I have experienced it. There are forces that work against goodness and indeed life itself.

I do not believe that God is the source of evil. Theologian R. Kendall Soulen said: "Christian faith is about confidence that God's power is able to help us withstand evil, even when we don't understand it."[5] Jesus gave us the prayer that asks, "Deliver us from evil." That is asking God to help us withstand evil, and it indirectly goes against any sense that God creates evil and imposes it on us.

So in the face of suffering, we rightly ask, "How can I help? What can I do to ease the world's pain? Where might I be a bridge over troubled water?" These questions are the response of faith. We trust that God is present in places of suffering and loss, and we know that God works through human agents to bring healing and hope. We stand ready to help.

Finally, there is the suffering of grief and loss. Our lives are finite; all of us will die. Death is not evil, but is part of creation and part of the great cycle of life. We are invited to die with dignity and gratitude. MB

Sub-question 8a: How do I cope when I feel discouraged and depressed?

Hear my prayer, O Lord;
Let my cry come to you.
Do not hide your face from me
in the day of my distress.
Incline your ear to me;
Answer me speedily in the day when I call.

PSALM 102:1–2

I often turn to the Psalms to help me cope with difficulties in my life, particularly the psalms of lament. Here in Psalm 102, I see that God hears our struggles, and that we don't always need to be or pretend to be happy just because God love us. God hears and accepts our anger and our frustration, our pain, and our complaints. The lament psalms give me permission to be fully myself and to admit my anger and sadness.

---

5. Soulen, "Christian Theology of the Problem of Evil," 1:43–53.

I discovered this when my first semester of seminary was almost over. My husband was told that the company was closing his office and he would be laid off. We had sold our home near Seattle and moved across the country so that I could attend seminary and train for a career in ministry. We needed my husband's income to pay the mortgage and pay for our two school-aged sons. In Psalm 35, I found language for my anger and pain. It asks God for deliverance from enemies. The corporation that laid my husband off was my enemy, and I prayed the psalm:

> Contend, O Lord, with those who contend with me;
> fight against those who fight against me!
> Let them be put to shame and dishonor
> who seek after my life.
> Let them be turned back and confounded
> who devise evil against me. (Ps 35: 1, 4)

This psalm helped me to express feelings I wanted to deny. It allowed me to pour out my negative feelings before God. It's a longer story than can be told here, but literally, at the last moment, my husband found a new job.

The reading of and reflection on these marvelously honest psalms is one way I cope when discouraged and depressed. In addition, there are many ways in which I find guidance and comfort: walks in nature, conversation with family and friends, singing in the choir, and weaving or spinning. And there are times in our lives when it is important to turn to a counselor or a therapist to find the healing we need. Our hurt feelings may go very deep and be more than we can manage alone, and getting some professional help is a fine resource. I have learned that it is important to honestly face my hurt and anger and find appropriate ways to understand it and let it heal. MB

Sub-question 8b: How do you find the strength and energy to engage with the serious issues facing the world? What difference can you make? How can you deal with your own limited efforts?

Thus says the Lord: Do not let the wise boast in in their wisdom, do not let the mighty boast in their might, do not let the wealthy boast in their wealth; but let those who boast boast in this, that they

understand and know me, that I am the Lord; I act with steadfast
love, justice, and righteousness in the earth, for in these things I
delight, says the Lord.

JEREMIAH 9:23–24

It is easy and all too common to be overwhelmed. There is so much suffering in our world: disease, hunger, racism, income inequality, and violence. Violence plagues nations, neighborhoods and homes, robbing people of security and peace. Global warming threatens creation itself. Reading the paper or listening to the news brings the world's pain before us. And I often ask myself: "What can one person do?" If these problems were simple, they would likely have been solved long ago. The problems we face are in fact extraordinarily complex and seriously threatening, and it is very difficult to find good solutions.

As I ponder these challenges, I remember that it is not all up to me. It is not my effort that will create God's realm of justice and peace. It is God, working through many individuals, that will bring us toward a world of healing and hope, where all people flourish and where the earth and its creatures will find fullness of life.

Yes, our human efforts are needed, but God is the primary actor. We don't create the new order; God working through us brings forth the new creation. Therefore, I do what I can to align my being with God's purpose. If we are created in the image of God and have within us the Spirit of God, we can partner with God and act with steadfast love, justice, and righteousness.

I look for things I can do. For example, I don't use a clothes dryer but hang the laundry out—a small effort to stop global warming. And the accumulation of small efforts makes a difference. Daily, I work to treat others with respect and caring. I vote for leaders who express values that are compassionate and just and lead to the common good.

I have learned to refuse to let the world's problems overwhelm me. The news media are full of stories of problems and disasters, but the thousands of acts of kindness that occur each moment don't often get mentioned. All around the world people are working to make a better life for children.

I let the beauty of the world heal me. I walk to the beach, look out at the water, and watch as the sun slips below the horizon. It is vast and grand, and I sense that I am very small. Yet I am a part of this larger amazing creation, connected to all that is and an integral part of the family of God. MB

Sub-question 8c: Is it possible to change these conditions? What conditions can be changed and what are the conditions that are nearly impossible to change?

Thus says the Lord of hosts: Even though it seems impossible to the remnant of this people in these days, should it also seem impossible to me, says the Lord of hosts?

Zechariah 8:6

Jesus looked at them and said, "For mortals it is impossible, but not for God; for God all things are possible."

Mark 10:27

I do think more solutions to our problems are possible than we might imagine. To say no too easily or quickly to possibility is to deny the chance for improvement. To say yes to possibility is to acknowledge that God is at work in the world with us and invites us to join in creating a more just and humane world.

I grew up near a paper mill in the fifties and sixties. At that time there was little effort to improve the environment. Effluent from the mill was poured directly into the river, and chimneys belched toxic fumes. Over the years the company worked to reduce the pollution of air and water, but the efforts were not adequate. As a child I was horrified as I looked at the pictures of children with polio living in iron lungs. At that time, Jonas Salk, Albert Sabin, and other scientists developed the vaccine so that polio no longer threatened the lives of children.

The problem that is even more difficult to solve than climate change and disease is how we change the cruelty of humans toward one another. To my mind, this is the deepest evil. But even in this context, there are signs of hope. We do see the presence and evidence of our "better angels." The ending of apartheid in South Africa along with the efforts of the Truth and Reconciliation Commission are outstanding examples.

As persons of faith, we are called to be open to the movement of the God's Spirit, and that Spirit may beckon us to work for things that seem impossible. And often our efforts seem to do little. But gradually, though the dedication and sacrifice of many good and gifted people, these harmful conditions begin to change. To say that something is impossible to change is to deny the reality of God's work in the world. MB

Sub-question 8d: On a grand scale, will humankind survive given the threats to our earth home? Or, as Einstein asked, "Is the earth friendly?" How do we find the strength to cope and to help people deal with the problems we all face with global warming?

The world now has the technologies and financial resources to stabilize climate, eradicate poverty, stabilize population, restore the economy's natural support systems, and above all, restore hope . . . We can calculate the costs of changes needed to move our twenty-first century civilization off the decline-and-collapse path and onto a path that will sustain civilization.[6]

Lester Brown

As I write we are in the middle of the coronavirus pandemic, and the questions about human survival and personal survival force their way into our minds and hearts. The Governor of New York, Andrew Cuomo, is projecting that over two hundred thousand people will catch the disease in his state.[7] As I write, the problems are very severe all around the globe. Over five hundred thousand people have died, and nearly ten million people have become infected by the disease. And if the coronavirus pandemic weren't so central to everyone's concerns at this moment, we would likely be focusing our attention on a similar projection, that there is a comparable threat to human life because of global warming and climate change.

Good and gifted people, regional and national government officials, and those with enormous wealth are stepping up to assist. Yet there are also many government officials, many private corporations, and whole countries that "don't get it" or are unable to respond because of the lack of influence and resources. As we learn about these conditions, we are motivated to find ways to survive and thrive. We do live in a world on

---

6. Brown, *World on the Edge*, 198.

7. It has now far surpassed this number, and other states such as Florida, California, and Texas have exceeded this number as well. At this point in time, it appears to be out of control in the United States.

the edge, are facing "the fate of the earth,"[8] and our inadequate systems of global management may lead to "collapse."[9]

There are ways to overcome the severe problems we face. The resources and global infrastructure are present and available, but it will take an informed and common effort to find our way into a more secure future.[10] The issues are complex and beyond the scope of a short essay; so what I would like to do is to suggest some fundamental values and principles that should guide us as we seek solutions.[11] I will begin with values and focus on just three, although many more might be listed:

1. The first is that we must truly *value the planet*, its inhabitants, its resources, and its systems. It is our reality and our home, and we must care for it in wise ways.

2. Second, we must *value all of life*, human life (of course), all sentient creatures that suffer, and indeed all that lives in the natural world. It is a primary way of caring for our earth home.

3. Third, we must *value our scientific understanding, our vast economic resources, and our adequate natural resources* and use them in small, large, and global ways to design and create an empathic civilization that is compassionate and seeks justice.

The principles that should guide us in this endeavor are numerous, and again I'll just focus on three:

1. We will need to move beyond thinking only of our welfare, our needs, and our future and begin to think and function less competitively and more collaboratively. We now understand that the earth is small, and that we are intimately connected across the globe. We need to think *globally*, as challenging as this perspective is for some people.[12]

8. See Jonathan Schell's book, *The Fate of the Earth*.

9. See Jared Diamond's research in his books, "*Collapse: How Societies Choose to Fail or Succeed* and *The Third Chimpanzee: The Evolution and Future of the Human Animal*.

10. In reference to have the financial resources to resolve our economic problems, see Jeffry D. Sachs, *Common Wealth: Economics for a Crowded Planet*.

11. The list of suggestions could easily be expanded, and indeed, each one deserves a book length development. My list is just a starting point.

12. I find it almost alarming that our current federal government is moving away from a global perspective and is almost exclusively concerned with national concerns.

2. We will need to be better *informed* about the issues, what it is that we face, and then find the best strategies for a secure future.

3. We will need to find *ways to make change* that appreciate different cultures, different states of development, different governmental systems, and different religious outlooks, and yet is sufficiently agile to create a more just and humane world. DF

Sub-question 8e: How should we address the challenges of climate change and global warming? How do we create a more equitable economy? How should we deal with violence, both international and personal?

The atmosphere is thin enough that we are capable of changing its composition. Indeed, the Earth's atmosphere is so thin that we have the capacity to dramatically alter the composition of some of its basic molecular components. In particular, we have vastly increased the amount of carbon dioxide—the most important of the greenhouse gases.[13]

AL GORE

We should be grateful to Al Gore, a former Vice President of the United States, for his informed and dedicated efforts to address the profound problems of climate change and global warming. He has given his life to solving these problems and has wisely informed the citizens of the United States, and indeed many parts of the world, about the consequences we face if we don't address this critical threat. There is an abundance of information about the many components of global warming. Kate Davies, referring to it as the "global eco-social crisis," lists the following dimensions of the crisis:[14]

1. Climate disruption: For example, we are already experiencing heat waves, droughts, floods, hurricanes, tornadoes, and wildfires, rising sea levels, ocean acidification, and reduced food production. Global temperatures are rising faster than the earlier predictions.

13. Gore, *Inconvenient Truth*, 24–35.
14. Davies, *Intrinsic Hope*, 4–6.

2. Water scarcity: About seven hundred million people living in forty-three countries suffer from water scarcity.

3. Species extinction: Approximately a quarter of all mammalian species are likely to become extinct in the next twenty-five years.

4. Pollution: It is present in many forms in nearly all of our neighborhoods.

5. Environmental injustice: Environmental deterioration is widespread and those unable to cope are often ignored and the most threatened.

6. Population growth and consumerism: The population is already near eight billion and moving rapidly toward ten billion people. And a high percentage of people continue to believe that happiness consists in the abundance of things possessed; they have a way of life that is addicted to buying and throwing away objects when used.

Interwoven with the challenge of climate change is an economy in the United States that continues to favor the wealthy and severely handicaps those with limited or no income. The gap between the rich and poor staggers the imagination. Given these problems, as one might expect, there is increasing violence at the international, national, and regional levels.

How do we address these overwhelming problems? There are few easy answers, although thoughtful and resourceful efforts are being proposed and are underway.[15] Again, our approach is the way that wisdom guides us, not the articulation of detailed plans (not that we don't need them). The following ideals should guide us:[16]

1. Create an earth community with ecological integrity

2. Create an earth community of care and respect for all people

3. Create a global culture of social and economic justice

4. Create a global context of participatory governance, nonviolence, and peace.

---

15. For example, see the book by Michael Lerner, *Revolutionary Love: A Political Manifesto to Heal and Transform the World.*

16. See my book, *The Radical Teaching of Jesus,* in which I list four broad-based goals expressed in the document "The Earth Charter" prepared by the Earth Charter International Secretariat, based in San Jose, Costa Rica (*Radical Teaching of Jesus,* 217–18).

We must find ways of turning these ideals into fundamental social change with compassion-driven programs that benefit our families, communities, nations, and the world. DF

Sub-question 8f: What are the other threats we face, and how do we find the strength and energy to engage with these challenges? What difference can you make?

First step: invite friends, neighbors, fellow students if you are an educational institution, co-workers, co-retirees, or members of your civic or political or religious organization to join a study group.[17]

MICHAEL LERNER

I want to respond to this question in a personal way, focusing on the unrest we feel inside of ourselves as we get a realistic appraisal of the overwhelming problems that threaten us. I want to suggest that working with others on these problems is a way that brings us a measure of peace, and, of course, a modest way to make a difference. I occasionally feel discouraged by the challenges we face, wonder how I might help solve some of these problems, and have learned that connecting with others is essential for finding some answers.

Johann Hart, in his recent book entitled *Lost Connections: Uncovering the Real Causes of Depression—and the Unexpected Solutions* makes the case that positive connections are essential to overcoming depression and finding a life of meaning and fulfillment. His focus, as the title suggests, is more about depression than discouragement, but what he suggests will help us to overcome our discouragement before it becomes pathological depression. Let me briefly summarize his thesis. First, he maintains that many people in our society (and other societies as well) have become "disconnected." They are not engaged in meaningful work, have few if any positive relationships, lack sustaining values, do not have status or respect, fail to appreciate the beauty and grandeur of nature, and are therefore without hope and a secure future.[18]

---

17. Lerner, *Revolutionary Love*, 225.

18. Hart's point in the book is that one overcomes depression by making one's environment positive rather than attempting to overcome depression with pharmaceuticals.

He lists the connections (reconnections in many cases) that empower people and enable them to flourish. They are:

1. Reconnect with people, perhaps with family and certainly those one encounters day-to-day in groups.

2. Reconnect with the social groups and associations that value you and your contribution.

3. Recover and reclaim the foundational values that have guided your life.

4. Seek your meaningful work in a setting that values your skills and wisdom.

5. Find ways to experience joy and happiness (and in so doing overcome self-addiction and self-preoccupation).

6. Acknowledge and overcome any childhood trauma that may still be deeply troubling.

7. Set personal goals that will lead you into a gratifying future.

Getting involved in groups and with other people who are engaged in a variety of ways to solve the critical problems we face will not only lead to partial and regional solutions to the problems, but will assist us in overcoming our discouragement and depression. We will be encouraged and inspired by other people, engage in meaningful work, and find ways to express and act on our values. We will find a measure of inner peace as we move away from self-addiction and engage in the quest to find solutions to our problems. We can find a measure of comfort and gratification by making progress in our quest for the common good. DF

Sub-question 8g: What harsh truths about yourself do you prefer to ignore? How do you appease your conscience about these truths?

There is not an animal on earth, nor a bird that flies on wings, but forms part of communities like you.

QUR'AN 6:38

If slaughter houses had glass walls we'd all be vegetarians.[19]

Paul McCartney

Of many human failings, the one I would most like to ignore is that I sometimes indulge my desire for meat and poultry even though it means that animals must die to serve my gustatory pleasure. For many years I appeased my conscience by telling myself that Muslim butchers make a swift swipe of the blade and simultaneously recite Qur'anic verses so that the animal feels little or no pain, and then the meat is blessed by citing verses of Holy Scripture. My connection to eating the flesh of another living being was limited to buying a neat package from the market and at best thanking the animals for their sustenance at the table by saying grace.

But then, several years ago, I forced myself to witness the slaughter of cows in my ancestral village of Bangladesh. As each animal was dragged, quivering and kicking to its execution site, I saw how desperately it tried to escape and how its eyes bulged with fear. No matter that its death would occur with one swift swipe of the blade and be blessed with Qur'anic verses; I saw with my own eyes the cruelty of the slaughter. Since that time I have watched several documentaries on slaughterhouses and have talked to people who work in those settings. I have also been inspired by the celebrated animal rights activist, Temple Grandin, and I am now convinced that the killing of animals for our conditioned craving is not only a monumental ethical issue, but a sort of litmus test measuring the state of human consciousness.

At the same time, I am aware of the power of generational conditioning. I have stopped eating beef, but I still indulge in chicken from time to time. It is so difficult to liberate oneself from slavish adherence to cultures and habits. For those of us who crave the taste of meat, but quail at the thought of killing animals, it is heartening to know that many wealthy organizations and meat businesses are pouring money into the creation of meat substitutes based on vegetables and even animal cells cultured in the laboratory.

As I slowly but surely overcome my own addiction to meat, I try to encourage others to do the same by reminding them of the Qur'anic verse that animals have communities like our own. The Prophet Muhammad rarely ate meat and pointedly warned the community about addiction to meat. The Qur'an talks about the practice of distributing meat to the

19. "'Glass Walls' with Paul McCartney," 00:05–07.

poor during the Islamic festival called Eid al-Adha, but explains: "It is not their meat nor their blood that reaches Allah: it is your piety that reaches Him" (22:37). As we evolve, may we express our piety by giving alms rather than meat to the poor, and by treating animals as the sentient beings they are. JR

Sub-question 8h: Do you ever wonder why God allows evil and suffering?

Be a lamp, a lifeboat, or a ladder. Help someone's soul heal.[20]

RUMI

I remember asking my parents this very question when I was young, and my father responded with a story. There was a pious person who travelled widely in search of knowledge and wisdom. Everywhere he went, he witnessed the extreme suffering of the marginalized people and injustices perpetrated on the vulnerable. One night, in deep anguish, he broke down and cried out: "God, how can you allow this? I beg you, please do something." That same evening, Spirit appeared to him in a vision and spoke: "Beloved one, I did something. I created you." The real question, my father explained, is simply this: "In the face of evil and suffering, what am I doing to help?" He also gave me a saying of the Prophet Muhammad to reflect on: "Whoever amongst you sees an evil, let him change it with his hand. If he is unable to do so, then with his tongue, and if he is not able to do so, then with his heart, and this is the weakest form of faith."[21]

My mother also offered me a remarkable insight. The Qur'an tells us that God assembled all of unborn humanity before sending us to earth and asked: "Am I not your Sustainer?" Exhilarated at hearing God's voice, humanity shouted in unison: "Yes! We testify." Then, according to Islamic legend, God directed us to a huge cosmic tree and pointed to various-sized packages hanging on the branches. These were packages of suffering, God said, and we had to choose a package before descending to earth. The nobler souls chose the larger packages so that others would suffer less. The point of this story, according to my mother, is that when someone is afflicted with enormous suffering, my response should be less

20. Breton and Largent, *Love, Soul and Freedom*, 329.
21. An-Nawawi, *An-Nawawi's Forty Hadith*, #34.

about pondering the mystery of suffering and more about offering help with utmost gratitude in my heart.

As I write, we are in the pandemic of the coronavirus. All kinds of spiritual theories abound, among them is that the virus is ordained by God to punish us for our misdeeds. I don't accept this view. It is not my place to play the role of God nor do I think that God would ever punish us by inflicting disease. The teachings of my parents inspire me to simply help those in dire need with gratitude and great humility. If I do ponder on these bewildering times, it is to awaken to insights that will help me make changes in my attitudes and lifestyle and contribute to a better world, post-coronavirus. JR

Sub-question 8i: Do you have answers or ways of explaining why evil and suffering exist?

We are what we think. All that we are arises with our thoughts. With our thoughts we make the world. Speak or act with an impure mind and trouble will follow you as the wheel follows the ox that draws the cart . . . Speak or act with a pure mind and happiness will follow you, as your shadow, unshakable.[22]

THE BUDDHA

There is no one-size-fits-all explanation for the existence of evil and suffering, but one approach is to recognize the extraordinary power of our own thoughts, both positive and negative, in reference to suffering. In a very real sense, our thoughts chisel and sculpt our destiny. Rumi says that if your thought is a rose, you are a rose garden; if it is a thorn, you are fuel for the bath stove.

Negative thoughts, if they are unresolved or unrestrained, can lead to negative and difficult feelings such as hate and frustration, which if we are unmindful, give rise to what Sufis call "negative imaginary scenarios." If these are allowed to fester, the imaginary scenarios can overwhelm us and manifest in our daily lives. In times of unrelenting anger, pain, and helplessness, "it's not that the eyes grow blind but hearts grow blind" (Qur'an 22:46). We end up saying and doing terrible things.

---

22. Byrom, *Dhammapada*, 1–2.

We might argue that these negative scenarios exist only in the imaginative realm and should not pose any dangers in the real world. But the scientific truth is that the subconscious does not differentiate between the real and imagined, fact or fiction. In any case, every thing in the universe is interconnected. What we think, feel, and visualize in one realm, mysteriously affects the other realm.

Depending on your belief system, there is another reason why we have to be careful with our thoughts. According to the Qur'an (114:4), the invisible world is inhabited by both positive and negative energies: positive energies who whisper loving thoughts and clear guidance and a "slinking whisperer" who tempts us to go astray. These opposing forces awaken our power of choice between good and evil. The energies of Satan are quite intense: "By Thy Glory I shall certainly cause them all to rebel and go astray," he announced to God (Qur'an 38:82), and "I shall assault them from before them and behind them, from their right and left" (Qur'an 7:17).

In Sufism, it is paramount spiritual practice to do a spiritual intervention the moment one becomes aware of any unchecked negative thought, feeling, or imaginary scenario swirling in the mind. I was taught to say, "Letting go! Letting go!" and "Tauba! Tauba!" The word *tauba* implies forgiveness and an intention to turn to God for help from the guiles of the slinking whisperer. God assures us that we have many allies in the mysterious realms: "Remember, you implored the assistance of your Sustainer, and God answered you: 'I will assist you with a thousand of the angels ranks on ranks'" (Qur'an 8:9). JR

CHAPTER 8: WHY DO I SUFFER AND WHY IS THERE EVIL AND SUFFERING IN THE WORLD?

Resources and Practices

Further Reading

1. The book of Job

2. An-Nawawi, *Forty Hadith*

3. Coleman Barks and John Moyne, *The Essential Rumi*

4. Lester R. Brown, *World on Edge: How to Prevent Environmental and Economic Collapse*

5. Kate Davies, *Intrinsic Hope: Living Courageously in Troubled Times*

6. Jared Diamond, *Collapse: How Societies Choose to Fail or Succeed*

7. Al Gore, *An Inconvenient Truth: The Planetary Emergency of Global Warming and What We Can Do about It*

8. Michael Lerner, *Revolutionary Love: A Political Manifesto to Heal and Transform the World*

9. Jeffrey Sachs, *Common Wealth: Economics for a Crowded Planet*

10. Jonathan Schell, *The Fate of the Earth*

11. David Wallace-Wells, *The Uninhabitable Earth: Life After Warming*

Suggested Practices

1. The issues and problems that threaten us are complex. Plan to select a few books and begin to inform yourself about the challenges that we are facing in the future and how we might cope.

2. Decide which issue may seem the most important and urgent for you and explore how you might make a contribution to solving the severe problem you have chosen.

3. Be sure to join with others, possibly in an already established organization that engages in solving the problem that is of most concern to you.

4. Begin to "tidy up" your own life in reference to habits and practices that contribute to the problem. Take tangible steps.

5. Explore ways to influence public policy in reference to the issue for which you have the greatest concern. Seek government support for the concern.

Foundational Question 9

How Do I Help to Create a More Just, Peaceful, and Humane Society and World?

The President in Washington sends word that he wishes to buy our land. But how can you buy or sell the sky? The land? If we do not own the freshness of the air and the sparkle of the water, how can you buy them?

Every part of the earth is sacred to my people. Every shining pine needle, every sandy shore, every mist in the dark woods, every meadow, every humming insect. All are holy in the memory and experience of my people.

We know the sap which courses through the trees as we know the blood that courses through our veins. We are part of the earth and it is part of us. The perfumed flowers are our sisters. The bear, the deer, the great eagle, these are our brothers. The rocky crests, the dew in the meadow, the body heat of the pony, and humans, all belong to the same family.[1]

CHIEF SEATTLE

WE ARE LIVING IN a very troublesome time, adjusting to the coronavirus pandemic and to the serious threats to the environment because of global warming. Many are unemployed and without access to food.

---

1. There are several versions of this letter; this one is from a speech he gave in 1854. Seattle, of course, is his Anglicized name from his Duwamish tribe, spelled closer to Si'ahi and pronounced as Sealth or See-ahth.

These challenges have made for a historical moment not unlike the Great Depression, given the serious threat to the wellbeing of so many. What added to the strain and stress was the apparent incompetence of those in the federal government as they attempted to respond to COVID-19 and to achieve the best balance between having the safety precautions in place because of the pandemic and the need to restart the economy. Daily there were confusing statements from the White House and a failure to provide guidance to the nation. On occasion, the quest to find good solutions was handicapped by the insertion of political differences and which level of government should take responsibility. Yes, leadership must come from the states and regions of the country and, in fact, many states have responded wisely. But a comprehensive federal response was not been fully developed and implemented.

Contemporary solutions, based on the most recent science, must be used in our response to the virus and to the challenges to the environment. Chief Seattle did not have the benefit of modern science to deal with the problems of illness and climate change and might affirm that he didn't need them. What he and so many of his people had, going beyond science, was wisdom and compassion. His letter to President Washington continues:[2]

1. The shining water that moves in the streams and the rivers is not just water, but the blood of our ancestors. If we sell you our land, you must remember that it is sacred.

2. The rivers are our brothers [and sisters]. They quench our thirst. They carry our canoes and feed our children.

3. If we sell you our land, remember that the air is precious to us and that the air shares its spirit with all that it supports.

4. Will you teach your children what we have taught our children? That the earth is our mother? What befalls the earth befalls all the children of the earth.

5. This we know: the earth does not belong to us, but we belong to the earth. All things are connected like the blood unites us all.

6. One thing we know: Our God is also your God. The earth is precious to God and to harm the earth is to heap contempt on its creator.

7. We love this earth as a newborn loves its mother's heartbeat. So, if we sell you this land, love it as we have loved it. Care for it, as we

2. I am leaving out some of the letter and have added the numbers for clarity.

have cared for it. Hold in your mind the memory of the land, as it is when you receive it. Preserve the land for all children, and love it, as God loves us.

8. One thing we know-there is only one God. No one, red or white, can be apart. We *are* all brothers [and sisters] after all.

We need a modern-day Chief Seattle. DF

FOUNDATIONAL QUESTION 9: HOW DO I HELP TO CREATE A MORE JUST, PEACEFUL, AND HUMANE SOCIETY AND WORLD?

Please forgive the trespass of your servant; for the Lord will certainly make my lord a sure house, because my lord is fighting the battles of the Lord; and evil shall not be found in you as long as you live.

(1 SAMUEL 25:28)

Abigail, the wife of Nabal, is one of my favorite biblical heroines. She is married to a foolish man (whose name means "fool"). Young David and his followers have been protecting Nabal's flocks and shepherds, but when they asked him to come for a feast, Nabal refused. David and his men vowed revenge. Hearing of this, Abigail loaded donkeys with two hundred loaves, wine, grain, raisins, figs, and five dressed sheep. If Nabal wouldn't invite David to the feast, Abigail would bring the feast to them. Abigail bowed low before David, and with an eloquent speech, convinced him not to seek revenge.

In general, in the ancient world, women did not decide who should or shouldn't come to a feast. But Abigail had the wisdom to understand the implications of the situation and the courage to step between two angry men. She used the gift of hospitality to reconcile and reduce the hostility.

Now most of us don't stand between two parties that are vowing to destroy each other. But we do face situations where we might speak out and counsel restraint. We have opportunities to use our own wisdom to evaluate a situation. We need to speak up and act when we recognize injustice and possible violence. In other words, we use what we have, and know that often "silence is violence." Abigail gathered the food she had and brought it to a group of angry men. She spoke words of truth that assured them that they were valued. She risked the anger and displeasure of her husband to do what she felt was right. We too can dare to acknowledge injustice and speak truth to justice, as we speak words of healing and peace. MB

FOUNDATIONAL QUESTION 9: HOW DO I CREATE A MORE JUST, PEACEFJUL, AND HUMANE SOCIETY AND WORLD?

Haven't we made a pair of eyes for him? And a tongue and a pair of lips? And shown him the two ways? But he has not quickened along the path that is steep. And what will explain to you what the steep path is? The freeing of one who is enslaved, or the giving of food in time of need to the orphan with claims of relationship, or to the helpless, lowly one in the dust.

QUR'AN 90:8–16

Sufi teachers point out that it is highly significant that the first injunction on the steep path to foster justice and peace is the freeing of one who is enslaved. This is both a literal and a metaphorical call to make lasting and structural improvements within oneself and in society. In order to free myself from slavery of the ego, I make constant efforts to overcome my negative traits such as prejudice, greed, and selfishness. Simultaneously, I endeavor to deepen my positive qualities of awareness and compassion. The work is difficult and I falter often, but I am convinced that without enduring inner work by all of us who care, we will never change the root cause of social injustice and degradation of the planet.

It is important to emphasize that the ego is an instrument of the soul. Our task is not to destroy the ego, but to tame and transform it. I often audit my progress of taming and transforming the ego by asking myself: (a) how I treat those who offer me no material advantage; and (b) how I treat those over whom I have power.

To be freed from the slavery of the economic system dominated by mega corporations, I, with my family and members of our interfaith community, have made a conscious decision to be fully aware of our motivation and where we spend our dollars. Too often, the very institutions we habitually criticize are the ones we unconsciously support with our hard-earned money. We now deposit our money in local banks, buy from socially conscious stores, and invest in selected institutions. For us, this behavior is a moral issue. At the same time, I have to be very mindful not to lapse into self-righteousness. Many agree with this ethical stand but are forced, because of their sparse resources, to buy from places that may not be socially conscious, but offer the lowest prices.

At the Interfaith Community Sanctuary, we have taken the words of the Buddha to heart: "However many holy words you read, however many you speak, what good will they do you if you do not act upon them."[3] Thus, to give one example, rather than simply talking about the presence and risks of patriarchy, we have taken action to respect the feminine. Traditionally, it has been the unquestioned prerogative of men to lead Islamic worship services. At ICS, for the last few years, women deliver the sermon and lead prayers to a mixed congregation of men and women on Muslim holy day of Friday. And recently, we decided that all weekly Sunday Interfaith worship services include a ritual that honors the feminine qualities of the divine.

Our freedom and joy, we believe, lies in the sprouting and proliferation of grass roots circles that focus on spiritual education and serving creation. The interaction among these groups will bring positive and lasting changes in society. JR

Sub-question 9a: What responsibility do we have to make a better world, and in particular, what role do the arts have in creating a better world?

But let justice roll down like waters and righteousness like an ever-flowing stream.

Amos 5:24

The artist serves humanity by feeding its hungry spirit in as real a sense as if he fed its hungry bodies.[4]

Sylvia Shaw Judson

---

3. Byrom, *Dhammapada*, 5.
4. Bryans, *Full Circle*, 8.

The Bible tells us over and over again that we have a responsibility to make a better world. In Genesis, God placed the human in the garden, "to till it and keep it" (Gen 2:15). The Ten Commandments provide a structure for humanity to live in right relationship with God and community (Exod 20:17; Deut 5:1–13) Through the prophets, God reminded the people that even more than proper worship, God wants justice and righteousness in and for all people (Amos 5:34; Mic 6:8; Isa 1:16–17). Jesus taught that the law is summarized as the love of God and the love of one's neighbors (Matt 22:37–40). There is a particular concern for those who have little: the widow and the orphan, the alien or sojourner, and the sick and the hungry. God calls humanity to work for justice and righteousness for all people.

The arts are part of what the world needs. They touch the spirit, drawing us beyond ourselves and awakening the spiritual within. Even scripture itself is art, as words create meaning in ways that are both beautiful and evoke a more profound meaning and way of life. The music of Bach, the paintings of Van Gogh, the plays of Shakespeare, the poetry of Mary Oliver, and so many other artists and arts draw us into a deeper reality, connecting us with something beyond ourselves. The arts open us up to sacred truth beyond our understanding. Madeleine L'Engle wrote: "When the words mean even more than the writer knew they meant, then the writer has been listening."[5] The artist connects to the holy, listens for the word of grace and truth, and expresses that encounter in beautiful ways. We need the arts. MB

Sub-question 9b: Do you occasionally feel helpless and unable to change situations that cause suffering and damage to our earth home and those who live in it? For example, do you sometimes wonder what you might do to help erase the lingering and very present prejudice against minorities in our country?

It's a wonder I haven't abandoned all my ideals, they seem so absurd and impractical. Yet I cling to them because I still believe, in spite of everything, that people are truly good at heart. It's utterly impossible for me to build my life on a foundation of chaos, suffering, and death. I see the world being slowly transformed into a wilderness, I hear the

5. L'Engle, *Walking on Water*, 22.

approaching thunder that, one day, will destroy us too, and I feel the
suffering of millions. And yet, when I look up at the sky, I somehow
feel that everything will change for the better, that this cruelty too
will end, that peace and tranquility will return once more. In the
meantime, I must hold on to my ideals. Perhaps the day will come
when I'll be able to realize them![6]

ANNE FRANK

The Holocaust was one of the most violent and evil events in human history, causing incredible suffering and loss. Prejudice against Jews, as well as homosexuals, Roma (Gypsies), Poles, Soviet prisoners of war, and persons with disabilities drove the Nazi regime to persecute and kill. In the midst of this genocide, Anne Frank, a young Jewish girl, wrote her thoughts as she hid from the Nazis. This passage from her diary is a profound witness to the power of hope in the midst of utter despair. She recognized the reality that drove her family to the attic: "I feel the suffering of millions," yet dared to proclaim, "I somehow feel that everything will change for the better, that this cruelty too will end."

Anne is an example for all of us. Yes, of course, we feel helpless against the overwhelming problems and struggles of the world. When so many suffer, what can we do? It is so easy to slip into despair and apathy. What difference will it make if I do anything? And for that matter, what good is my small effort, when the evil is so great? At times the news is filled with descriptions of acts of violence toward people of color. Prejudice and racism have dominated so long. The voices proclaiming the value of whites are loud and constant. Violence and racism are deep within our culture. The legacy of slavery and the genocide of indigenous peoples are ours. We hear jokes about dumb Indians and see police killing innocent African Americans.

As a white woman, I acknowledge the racism that is deep within me and with my culture. It is far too easy to dismiss persons of different races and cultures and to fail to treat them as equal. It is far too easy to assume that I am not racist. In reality, I am steeped in a racist culture and have absorbed the perspective even as I struggle to overcome such perspectives. I need to pay attention to the voices of those who are different from my own, to read books written by people of color, to speak up against the

---

6. Frank, *Diary of a Young Girl*, 333.

casual remarks of others, and to guard my own tongue and thoughts so that I resist the racism that is deep within me. I want to respect all people as God's beloved, but I recognize patterns of thought and behavior within me that do not do this. MB

Sub-question 9c: Do you really care, or do you think we are here just to satisfy our own needs and desires?

It is He who made you His representatives on earth.

QUR'AN 6:165

Greater indeed than the creation of man is the creation of the heavens and earth; yet most men do not understand.

QUR'AN 40:57

I believe that the primary failing common to most humanity is our heartless abuse and exploitation of Mother Nature. We have catered to our selfish needs and have not been worthy stewards of the earth, nor have we valued the primal and pristine sacredness of nature. It has taken the crisis of a deteriorating environment to slow down our exploitation and awaken us to the wondrous beauty of nature and the life-giving nourishment that Mother Earth offer us endlessly and selflessly. We are realizing belatedly that we are incredibly bonded with nature and that, if our planet cannot breathe and thrive, we humans will suffocate and perish.

This is not new information. A scientific adviser during the Carter administration (1977–81) made a remarkable observation that gets to the root of our predicament: "I used to think that the top environmental problems were biodiversity loss, ecosystem collapse, and climate change. I thought that with thirty years of good science we could address these problems. But I was wrong. The top environmental problems are selfishness, greed, and apathy."[7]

What will heal our environmental crisis at a core level? We have to take responsibility and expand our consciousness. If we can learn to focus less on material acquisitions and find fulfillment in the simple joys

---

7. Curwood, "'We Scientists Don't Know How To Do That,'" para. 3.

of life, we can relieve some of the brutal pressure that 7.8 billion people are placing on the environment.

What else can we do to make lasting changes? In our simple community, we have committed ourselves to three simple practices:

1. In our daily prayers, we place the planet in our hearts and ask forgiveness for our neglect and desecration. In the course of the day, we send light and love to elements of nature.

2. We initiate and support a number of programs and projects that restore harmony, balance, and love in nature. For example, we have collaborated with other organizations to plant trees, which are so necessary to the air we breath. For us, the planting of a tree is almost an act of worship and we often repeat the words of the Prophet Muhammad: "Even if you fear that the Last Day has arrived, plant the sapling you hold in your hand."[8]

3. We spend meditative time in nature to connect with what the Qur'an calls "Signs of God" or what mystics describe as "Glow of Presence." This deepens our love and reverence for nature. Occasionally, we recite poetry in a circle. Just recently, the words of a Zen master resonated in me as I lay in the grass and listened to a friend: "Sitting quietly, doing nothing, spring comes and the grass grows."[9] JR

Sub-question 9d: Are there threats to our liberal democracy and, if so, what are they?

Anything which keeps a politician humble is healthy for democracy.
Irish Blessing

If we are to guard against ignorance and remain free, it is the responsibility of every American to be informed.
Thomas Jefferson

Throughout the course of human history, the primary obstacles to good governance have been arrogance and ignorance of the type we are seeing

8. Hadith from Nasr, *Heart of Islam*, no. 143.
9. Basho, "Spring."

in the United States today. In my opinion, ego-driven leaders and a section of the electorate that is willfully uninformed threaten the foundations of our liberal democracy.

These same threats corrupted the Islamic empire when it was a dominant power in the Middle Ages. To awaken the people, sages invoked a fictional character, the thirteenth-century Mulla, who was a village idiot and a sage rolled into one, and used him to convey profound truths through stories of humor. For example, to poke fun at pompous monarchs' fondness for lofty titles such as "God Exalted" or "God Beloved," they told the story about a monarch who hired the Mulla to craft a succinct and meaningful title. After much reflection, the Mulla penned, "God Forbid!"

Fear is a timeworn way of manipulating a population in order to divide and rule. To point out the folly of this tactic, elders told the story of a mother who brought her incorrigible son to the Mulla. "Please," she pleaded, "I have tried everything. Put some fear in his heart." The Mulla contorted his face, let out deep growls and commanded the boy to listen to his mother. He looked and sounded so fearsome that the mother fainted and the Mulla rushed out of the room. When the mother regained consciousness, she berated the Mulla: "I asked you to frighten my son, not me." The Mulla replied, "Madam, when you invoke fear, it consumes everyone. Fear has no favorites. Did you not notice that I myself got so scared that I had to leave the room?"

Often when people do not believe in themselves, they abandon the use of their own discernment and listen unquestioningly to so-called authorities. They are like Mulla's wife, who summoned a doctor because the Mulla was gravely ill. "Madam, I regret to inform you that your husband has expired," the doctor said to the weeping woman. But the Mulla was alive and feebly protested, "I am alive! I am alive!" "Quiet!" the wife retorted, "Don't argue with the doctors!"

I want to add one more story to illustrate about how we abandon critical thinking. A dispute arose in the community: "What is more useful, the Sun or the Moon?" They consulted the Mulla. After much thought, the Mulla opined: "In the daytime, we already have light and so the Sun is redundant. At night, it is dark, and the radiance of the Moon is helpful. Thus we need the Moon more than the Sun."

Alas, we learn from history that we do not learn from history.[10] The Islamic empire has since collapsed, but the tales repeated in the bazaars are extraordinarily relevant to our own situation now. JR

Sub-question 9e: What is the role of education and political leadership in the government to guide us to a more just, peaceful, and secure human future?

Education is the acquisition of the art of the utilization of knowledge ... This is not an easy doctrine to apply, but a very hard one. It contains within itself the problem of keeping knowledge alive, of preventing it from becoming inert, which is the central problem of education.[11]

ALFRED NORTH WHITEHEAD

Until philosophers are kings, the kings and the princes of the world have the spirit and power of philosophy, and political greatness and wisdom are met in one, and those commoner natures stand aside, cities will never have rest from their evils, nor, nor the human race, as I believe, and then only will this our State have a possibility of life and behold the light of day.[12]

PLATO

Some of the world's greatest minds over the course of history have articulated answers to this fundamental question. And, in most cases, their answers have included both the type of education required and the essential wisdom and character of political leadership. Alfred North Whitehead (1861–1947) was a professor in Ireland and England in the early part of his career and then went on to finish his career as Professor of Philosophy at Harvard University. He was persuaded upon reflection on the educational systems in both Europe and the United States that the aim of education is to provide students with an education that will lead to a better life for students and the citizens of the state and guide political leaders in the formation of a just and humane society. He was aware that educational institutions all too

10. Mills, *Power Elite*, 23.

11. Whitehead, *Aims of Education*, 16–17.

12. Plato, *Resp.* 5.

easily become isolated and elite groups of intellectuals that enjoy the search for truth, but do not address the ways that profound and systematic knowledge is part of the foundation of a democratic society. It was certainly not the case the Professor Whitehead stressed only practical knowledge or that he in any way disdained profound research in all fields. Rather, he stressed that the ideal state must be guided by truth and knowledge; ignorance is the great enemy of the democratic order.

If he were alive today, he might counsel the current government of the United States to give more attention to advance science in addressing COVID-19 rather than being driven by political aspirations. As a thoughtful scholar in ethics and religious studies, he would also have counseled the current government to be guided by those values that are universal in scope and compassionate in character.

Professor Whitehead was very influenced by Plato and once said that all modern philosophy is but a footnote to Plato's ideas. Plato consistently wrote in the form of a dialogue between thoughtful participants who were guided in their thinking by one of Plato's teachers, Socrates. In his great work in political studies, the *Republic*, Plato, using Socrates as a spokesperson, argued that the best government should be led by a well-informed person whose education was comprehensive in scope, a philosopher.[13] He maintained that the ideal leader of the government should be a "philosopher king." Such a person would have a broad range of knowledge, be a person of integrity and one who would guide the affairs of state in a way that would insure justice and a good life for the citizens.[14]

As we address the global coronavirus pandemic and face the challenge of climate change, there are may who are grateful that most of our educational systems, from kindergarten to post-graduate studies, do provide an education that prepares students for a meaningful and fulfilled life. But, at the present time, many of us are disillusioned by the lack of leadership by our federal government and wish that the leadership was committed to the truth, had integrity, insured justice, and was wise and experienced. Yet we do not lose hope, living faithfully by our ideals of compassion, truth, and justice. DF

13. The philosopher in Plato's time was not bound by the current understanding that philosophy is a narrow field in the university's curriculum, but a broad-based knowledge guided by wisdom.

14. There has been some criticism of Plato in that he did not always argue for the rights of women (he might have said "philosopher queen"), and did not directly address all the issues of slavery. But his extraordinary wisdom endures.

Sub-question 9f: What approach to education should we take? How would you rate your education?

My child, keep my words
and store up my commandments with you;
keep my commandments and live,
keep my teachings as the apple of your eye;
bind them on your fingers,
write them on the tablet of your heart.
Say to wisdom, "You are my sister,"
And call insight your intimate friend.

PROVERBS 7:14

Learning has come easily to me, so school was always a place I wanted to be. I felt affirmed in my learning. My mother was a teacher, and education was highly valued in my home. It was expected that I would go to college. I've spent much of my life in school—over twenty-five years at least. I've had some amazing teachers who encouraged me to explore, who challenged me to go deeper, and who were wonderful companions on my journey of learning.

In terms of education, I had many advantages. English was spoken in my home. People spent hours reading to me. I'm told that as a child I greeted family members as they came in with the demand: "a book! a book!" When I got to school, I read about Dick and Jane, who looked much as I did.

How does education reach children with different backgrounds? Children come from homes speaking languages other than English. Other children have learning disabilities. There are so many learning styles: some learn from reading, others need to hear, others need to move and be active, and some children thrive in noisy situations and others need quiet to concentrate. The challenge for education is to find ways to teach each individual, providing the resources the child needs to flourish. Teachers work with limited resources. They don't have the time to spend with each particular student, adapting the curriculum to the individual. There is no one-size-fits-all approach, and the best teachers see the different needs and work to teach in a manner that provides what each student needs.

As much as the content and the teaching styles are important, I think I have been most influenced by the relationship between student and teacher. I learned from a teacher's understanding of and enthusiasm for a subject. As the teacher began to know me better, they inspired me and challenged me in many ways. I am so grateful for the remarkable care and gifts of so many of my teachers. MB

Sub-question 9g: Are you satisfied with our type of government?

That here we highly resolve that the dead shall not have died in vain, that this nation, under God, shall have a new birth of freedom; and that the government of the people, by the people, and for the people shall not perish from the earth.[15]

ABRAHAM LINCOLN

Freedom, or Free Democracy, is something very different and much more difficult to achieve. It is a balance between popular will and individual rights. It is a civilized society that tries to establish diversity through the guarantee of civil liberties.[16]

JACQUES BARZUN

I am very satisfied with our democratic form of government and was educated in a way that taught me to honor it. As a child, I was taught that a government of the people, by the people, and for the people was the best form of government and that we must make sure that it "shall not perish from the earth." I still deeply believe in this form of government. However, I am currently disillusioned by the reality that this way of governing our affairs is being challenged, ironically by the very office that was established to preserve and implement it. In the fifth grade, I was asked to memorize the Gettysburg Address and recite it in front of the class. I did so with naivety, but also with firm conviction. I am now more keenly aware that the preservation of this form of government is difficult,

15. Lincoln, Gettysburg Address, Nov. 19, 1863. See https://rmc.library.cornell. edu/gettysburg/good_cause/transcript.htm.

16. Barzun, *Of Human Freedom*, 19.

and that thoughtful people in different ages and cultures will attempt to implement a democracy in a variety of ways. In fact, a democracy builds in the option of interpretation and negotiating differences of opinion.

I fear that we have a federal government, and of course a few cases of state and regional governments, which are removing the option of proposing alternative points of view about how we resolve our problems and ensure justice for all. At the federal level, I sense that we are moving toward a government that does not honor debate and opposing views. Many of those serving in federal government who have dared to challenge President Trump and his insistence on governing in a way that serves his desire to be re-elected are consistently fired. In addition, there are many who are seeking equal rights for minority populations and advocating for those who are living on the margins, but find that the government consistently acts on behalf of the wealthy and privileged classes.

At this time of writing, I look forward to the time of election, hoping that there will be change and new leadership. I want the democracy that I learned about as a young person to prevail. I want to be lifted out of my discouragement and to live in the nation that I learned about in the fifth grade. I want the United States, established on the foundation of democracy, to be a nation that ensures the right to vote, free expression, just laws, and a setting in which all of us can pursue our dreams. Even with all of its limitations, I want our democracy to live up to the challenge of making a government of the people, by the people, and for the people. It will not be easy, and the challenges of COVID-19, climate change, and finding some unity in our profoundly diverse nation will test us in ways that will demand extraordinary wisdom and good judgment. At my age, in the time of a second naivety, I want a return to the government that I understood as I stood and recited the Gettysburg Address in the fifth grade. We govern best by honoring our foundational values rather than being driven by self-centered ambition. It is not an overstatement to say that our future as a nation depends upon it. DF

Sub-question 9h: What sort of changes would you make in the way our government is structured and the way it is run?

You speak of our activity in Birmingham as extreme. At first I was rather disappointed that fellow clergymen would see my nonviolent efforts as those of an extremist . . . Was not Amos an extremist of

justice? "Let justice roll down like waters and righteousness like a mighty stream." Was Abraham Lincoln an extremist? "This nation cannot survive half slave and half free." Was Thomas Jefferson an extremist? "We hold these truths to be self-evident, that all men are created equal."[17]

MARTIN LUTHER KING, JR.

In many ways, we are a broken nation as I write these words in the midst of COVID-19 and toward the end of the first term of President Donald Trump.[18] In a kind of tragic way, the coronavirus pandemic and the leadership style of Donald Trump have flowed together into raging, flooding river that threatens to drown many of our citizens. Our question about possible changes in the way our government is structured and run could not be more relevant. It is a question that has stimulated many books, endless pages in newspapers, and consistently it is the lead story in nearly every newscast. There is room for only a few paragraphs here, although I have a full-length book in my heart and mind. Therefore, I want to divide this brief essay into two simple categories of answers, structure and practice, leaving the expanded development of these categories for another time.

As I speak about structures, I want to say that I believe our current government structures, described in the Constitution, are generally adequate to guide a democratic government, or they would be if they were followed. For instance, the structural design of the check and balance system of three equal centers of governance, each with a different domain of responsibility, is wise and serves us well. But at the current time, there is a clear effort to increase the power of the presidency rather than preserve the balance of the three collaborative domains of government: Executive, Legislative, and Judicial. Currently the Executive Branch is demanding personal loyalty from the Justice Department and is in constant conflict with the House of Representatives, given that there is Democratic majority in the House. There is another structural issue that needs attention as we anticipate the election of 2020. There is almost universal agreement that our system of using the Electoral College to finalize presidential elections needs to be changed. This practice, although present in the

17. King, "Letter from a Birmingham Jail," April 1963. See https://www.africa. upenn.edu/Articles_Gen/Letter_Birmingham.html, esp. paras. 22 and 24.

18. It is also the time of protest about racism and profound concern about the way George Floyd was killed.

Constitution, either needs to be abolished or at least dramatically altered if we are to insure that our votes are actually going to determine the outcome. It is time to elect the President by a popular vote if we are to have a true democracy. I'll mention just one final structural issue, namely how it is that we divide up the electoral districts to give one party a clear advantage, called gerrymandering. A way must be found to determine electoral districts in a fair way.

In addition to possible structural changes, I want to say a brief word as well about what values should prevail in governmental practice. As we review governmental practices, we need to acknowledge the obvious, that human beings run all governments. Many of those in office may be gifted and committed to fairness. But the best of us have limitations of ability and do not always make good judgments. As far as possible, we should seek to find and elect those who govern with the following values:

1. The first, of course, is *justice*, the fundamental value of governance. The government must treat all of its citizens, and indeed all people who are present in the country, with fairness.

2. The second value is that the government must insure that all of its citizens have an *equal opportunity* for a good life, access to high quality education, adequate income and housing, good medical care, and safety.

3. And third, the government, in partnership with a vast array of private agencies, should have a good measure of *compassion and empathy.* These values will ensure that we are safe from foreign intervention and attack. Further, those who are marginalized and live "on the edge" because of limited education, minority or immigrant status, learning challenges, and illness will be cared for in wise and caring ways.

This list could be extended well beyond these three categories, but perhaps these will be suggestive. DF

Sub-question 9i: What sort of principles and policies should be central tour government?

A nation should not be judged by how it treats its highest citizens, but it lowest ones.[19]

NELSON MANDELA

True peace is not merely the absence of tension; it is the presence of justice.

MARTIN LUTHER KING, JR.[20]

If you want to go fast, go alone. If you want to go far, go together.

AFRICAN PROVERB

We are at an historic juncture; the year is 2020 and the entire planet is engulfed in a deadly pandemic along with social and political unrest. The invisible virus has exposed the United States health system to be inadequate and inequitable. A disproportionate number of minorities have died. Clearly, we need a health system that serves everyone regardless of income and race. The virus has taught us that we are unimaginably interconnected. If we neglect the health of one person, we will all suffer.

At the same time, many US cities are reeling from ongoing protests against police brutality and systematic discrimination against black- and brown-skin Americans. The shock sight of heavily armed and militarized police confronting unarmed citizens and depriving them of their right to protest gives rise to questions and concerns about the mindset of the government. Does it regard protesters as "the enemy" and their places of assembly as a war zone? Should an entire movement be maligned if a few actors get out of hand? Do city police need military equipment? Is it not time that we examine our bloated expenditure on defense forces deemed essential to protect us from vicious enemies at home and abroad? A classic story of the Mulla is in order: While giving the Mulla a tour of his impressive army, a just and pious king explained that the deterrent of armed forces had protected the kingdom from domestic and foreign

---

19. "Nelson Mandela Rules," 1.
20. King, "Realistic Look," para. 11.

enemies "No, your Majesty," replied the Mulla, "What is keeping you and your citizens safe is not your army but the justness of your decisions."

How do we deal with the injustice of racism and dangers of polarization? Legislation and education are critical, but what is desperately needed is human connection between the divided groups: police and minorities, black and white, rich and poor, Republican and Democrat. We need grassroots community programs that bring together polarized groups for dialogue and cooperation. Ongoing efforts to build intercultural trusts are the best antidote to fear and anger, and many ordinary citizens have astonishing ideas and goodwill to make this happen. The government can play an essential role in this endeavor by seeking their help.

On the international level our government must align its foreign policy with moral principles and stop supporting tyrants and despots for short-term advantage. These unethical alliances create enemies and ill will and will be the undoing of our liberal democracy. The Sufis say: "Whoever might perfume a scorpion will not thereby escape its sting."[21] Lastly, it is urgently critical that our government pay attention to environmental issues and work to reverse the damage caused by the current administration. This is a matter of survival not only just for us, but also for the entire world. JR

CHAPTER 9: HOW DO I HELP CREATE A MORE JUST, PEACEFUL, AND JUST SOCIETY AND WORLD?

Resources and Practices

Further Reading

1. Nena Bryans, *Full Circle: A Proposal to the Church for an Arts Ministry*

2. Thomas Byrom, *Dhammapada: The Sayings of Buddha*

3. Ibram X. Kendi, *How to Be Antiracist*

4. Martin Luther King Jr., "Letter from a Birmingham Jail"

5. Madelaine L'Engle, *Walking on Water: Reflections on Faith and Art*

6. Abraham Lincoln, "The Gettysburg Address"

21. Shah, *A Perfumed Scorpion*, 3.

7. Plato, *The Republic*

8. Alfred North Whitehead, *The Aims of Education*

Suggested Practices

Write a brief response to each of the following questions, describing social problems and what you might do to improve the setting in which you live.

1. How would you assess the quality of your education in informing you about issues of justice and peace? Do you think that public education should have the goal to inform students about injustice and other social problems such as global warming and world hunger?

2. How have you been influenced and motivated by the arts, and how have they helped you to better understand yourself, others, and the social environment in which you live?

3. In what ways do you wish that you might have been better informed about the causes of justice and peace, both where you live and in other regions of the world?

4. Does the setting in which you live have an educational and governmental structure that furthers the cause of justice and peace? What are the limitations of the current structure and programs?

5. Are there dimensions in your life that have lingering traces of prejudice against people who are different from you? People of color? People who came from different parts of the world and have a different culture and language? People of a different religion? People of a different political party? Are you making a conscious effort to make friendships with people of color? If not, why not?

6. What organizations and programs should be available in your community both to inform people about the quest for a more just and humane society and to offer programs and strategies to work for justice and peace?

7. What will be your next step to lend a hand in creating a more just and humane world?

Foundational Question 10

Is There Life for Me after Death or Is Death the End of Our Existence?

When this perishable body puts on imperishability,
and this mortal body puts on immortality, then the saying
that is written will be fulfilled:

"Death has been swallowed up in victory.
Where, O death, is your victory?
Where, O death, is your sting?"[1]

THE APOSTLE PAUL

ONE MIGHT WISH THAT the apostle Paul's strong belief in life after death could be easily matched and always provide the peace and comfort we need as death approaches. It was a more commonly held belief in his time, to some extent because it was part of his and his contemporaries' heritage and in part because he lived prior to the intellectual revolutions that have occurred since his time. We live on this side of the questioning mind and the perspective of science. The lens of our worldview is different. My own view, even though I have lived the vast majority of my life within the context of Christian faith, is that I don't know the answer to our question. Or at least I don't know in the sense of knowing by mathematical formulas, logical reasoning, or scientific certainty, in spite of the array of literature that has tried to *prove* eternal life.[2]

---

1. 1 Corinthians 15:54–55.

2. Often, the objective of proving eternal life is pursued by quoting what is considered authoritative scripture or pointing to the resurrection of Jesus. On a more

My approach to the question revolves less around the word *know* and more around the word *hope*.[3] Hope does have an emotional component, and it therefore tends to fluctuate in our consciousness. The presence of hope can be very vivid and gratifying when the future looks promising, or it can be diminished with the presence of fear. For most of us, there is some fear in our lives and hope gets nudged to the periphery. For example, we may fear pain or punishment, the breakdown of life-giving relationships, not having adequate income and good housing, or the loss of our job and a tangible purpose in life. Perhaps our greatest fear is related to our mortality.

As we get these fears under control, we tend to move toward a more hopeful outlook. As we sense that we can manage the range of challenges we all face in life, modest hope returns. As we regain a measure of peace about profound concerns such as our life calling, fulfilling relationships, and a sustaining spiritual orientation and practice, our hope becomes a life-giving reality. It is this hopeful spirit that we bring to the issues of mortality and eternal life.

I come to the issue of death with a hopeful spirit. I have lived my adult life with the belief in a God who is personal, loving, caring, and forgiving who welcomes me into eternity. I still approach this question with great humility. I am careful about not creating God in an image that just meets my needs, and I understand that God is beyond my full comprehension. Yet this view of a personal and loving God gives me the hope that as I pass away, I will enter fully into the mystery of God's presence and be filled with eternal bliss. With this view of God I can say with John Donne, "Death be not proud . . . and death shall be no more."[4]

I also have a measure of peace when I think about the possibility that there is no life after death. In these moments, in my heart of hearts, I tell death to stand down, that life has been rich and meaningful, and that

---

secular level, there have been a number of people reporting on the near-death experiences in which people have sensed that they had crossed over into a new realm.

3. See the book by Anthony Scioli and Henry B. Biller, *Hope in the Age of Anxiety* for a thoughtful development of how to sustain hope in troubled times. In the Christian context, I recommend John Macquarrie's book, *Christian Hope*.

4. See John Gunther's account of the illness and approaching death of his son in *Death Be Not Proud: A Memoir*. He opens by quoting John Donne's poem, "Death Be Not Proud," vi.

I will face it with the dignity of a well-lived life, one filled with a richness for which I am profoundly grateful.[5] DF

FOUNDATIONAL QUESTION 10: IS THERE LIFE FOR ME AFTER DEATH OR IS DEATH THE END OF OUR EXISTENCE?

The world is not conclusion;
A sequel stands beyond,
Invisible, as music,
But positive, as song.[6]

EMILY DICKINSON

I do believe that there is life for me after death, but I have little idea of what it might be like. Death is the introduction into the great mystery. What I know is that while I live, I trust God whose nature is love. God, who cares for me in this life, will care for me in whatever lies beyond this one. And that is enough for me to live and die in peace.

I love to celebrate All Saints' Day. As a Protestant believer, I combine All Souls' Day, which celebrates the faithful departed, with All Saints' Day that remembers the saints of the church both known and unknown. I see little difference between faithful departed and unknown saints. Paul's letters often address the saints living in various communities, and he refers to saints as the faithful followers of Jesus. On All Saints' Day I feel a deep connection to all those whose lives have carried out Jesus' teachings and who have preserved the church as the gathered community of the faithful. It is not just a rational thought for me; I sense a deep mystical union, as if the faithful hover near us, loving and supporting us.

We live our lives in trust that God's love continues beyond this lifetime. I spend little time thinking about life beyond death. My focus is on living this life with integrity and purpose and seeking to follow God's will and listening for God's call for my life. I know that I will die and, until then, I will pray and study, work and learn, trying to draw closer to

5. Katy Butler's book, *The Art of Dying Well*, is a helpful book on the practical issues of facing death.

6. See Emily Dickinson, "The World Is Not Conclusion" in Sloyan, *Sourcebook About Christian Death*, 108.

God so that I might serve the world in loving ways that create peace and justice for all. MB

FOUNDATIONAL QUESTION 10: IS THERE LIFE FOR ME AFTER DEATH OR IS DEATH THE END OF OUR EXISTENCE?

With God are keys to the Unseen, the treasures that none know but Him.

QUR'AN 6:59

Sell your cleverness and buy bewilderment![7]

RUMI

As the years mount up and I draw inexorably to the end of life, I am increasingly curious about what comes next so that I may use my remaining years to prepare for it. Alas, there are no definite guidebooks for that ultimate journey; our knowledge about the afterlife is wrapped in mystery and bewilderment. We may draw on insights and inklings from our holy books, but these are speculative and inconclusive.

We read in the Qur'an that the soul returns to God after death and is placed in a state of quietude called *barzakh*, where it awaits the Day of Judgment at the end of time. On that day, our bodies and souls will be reunited and we will be called to account for our earthly deeds and misdeeds, an accounting which will determine whether we will be assigned to heaven or hell. But are these verses to be taken literally or metaphorically? And what happens subsequently?

There are no clear answers, but there are some tantalizing clues that our journey continues in those invisible realms. The Prophet Muhammad said: "The grave is the first stage of our journey into Eternity."[8] The Qur'an teaches that God, who is the "Creator, Evolver, the Bestower of Forms" (59:24) and the "Lord of the Ways of Ascent," will "change your forms and create you again in forms that you know not" (56:61). Thus we will be incarnated again and again in our journey to union with God.

---

7. Chittick, *Sufi Path of Love*, 224.
8. Suhrawardy, *Sayings of Muhammad*, 18.

These incarnations will occur not on earth but in those heavenly realms. These revelations inspired Rumi to exclaim:

> When was I less by dying?
> I shall die as Man to soar
> With angels blest; but even from angelhood,
> I must pass on; all except God doth perish.
> When I have sacrificed my angel-soul,
> I shall become what no mind ever conceived.[9]

Sufi sages, who often instruct through teaching stories, can simply suggest that "It's not what you think" when asked about the afterlife. Two stories come to mind. In the first, a tomb for the fictional Mulla has a forbidding door with imposing padlocks and chains, but no walls. But that's not what we expect the tomb to look like! Precisely. Whatever we may expect about death and the afterlife, that's not how it will be. In a second story, a pious king visits a holy man who is on his deathbed and begs, "When the Light has completely graced you and you come into the nearness of Divinity, please remember me to God." The holy man replies: "When I step into that Presence and the Light of Splendor shines over me, I will no more remember myself. How do you expect me to remember you?" JR

Sub-question 10a: Knowing that we will die, how shall I live?

Help us to live as those who are prepared to die.
And when our days here are accomplished,
Enable us to die as those who go forth to live,

So that living or dying, our life may be in you.[10]

Our lives are finite. This time on earth is all that we get and it is the only chance we have to make a difference. It is the only opportunity we have to create relationships, and our only chance to experience this world in all of its wonder and pain. Somehow this awareness deepens my caring and concern. There isn't going to be another time to start over and do things differently. This is the moment to live, working as God's agents to create a world of peace and harmony where all creatures thrive.

9. Houston, *Search for the Beloved*, 210.

10. "A Service of Death and Resurrection," in the *United Methodist Hymnal*, 871.

As I read scripture, I see a concern for how people live now and how people can be faithful to God's will for creation. Humans are called to live the life we have been given as full and responsible participants in the ongoing process of creation. We partner with God in creating a world of love and justice. God's vision for the world is for shalom, where all of creation lives in peace and where there is justice for everyone. We are created in the image of God, and as such, we reflect God's deepest nature, which is love. As God's children we recognize that creation itself is God's gift, and we are invited to express appreciation and love for this gift and to care for it.

When we realize that "living or dying, our life is in you" we step away from fear knowing that no matter what happens, our life in God's love will continue. We don't do foolish things, of course. Rather we dare to stand up for the oppressed and speak out the truth that there must be respect for all people.

Our culture often ignores the reality of death, the fact that every life ends in death. There is much in our culture that disguises the reality of death. But if we acknowledge death, we then understand how precious is each moment and how important this day is. We become wise enough to prepare for our own deaths, writing wills and attending to the details that will surround the end of our lives. The conviction that we abide in God's unconditional love empowers us to go forth to live with integrity and courage, building relationships of love and support, and working for a more just society. MB

Sub-question 10b: In reference to life after death, does it really matter how I live?

As he was setting out on a journey, a man ran up and knelt before him, and asked him, "Good Teacher, what must I do to inherit eternal life?" Jesus said to him, "Why do you call me good? No one is good [perfect] but God alone. You know the commandments: You shall not murder; You shall not commit adultery; You shall not steal; You shall not bear false witness, You shall not defraud; Honor your father and mother." He said to him, "Teacher, I have kept all these since my youth." Jesus, looking at him, loved him, and said, "You lack one thing; go, sell what you own, and give the money to the poor, and

you will have treasure in heaven; then come, follow me." When he
heard this, he was shocked for he had many possessions.

MARK 10:17–22

As Jesus is asked a comparable question to 10b, he answered profoundly, "yes and no." Behind the answer of Jesus is his deep belief that *eternal life is unity and oneness with God*, and that it begins not necessarily when we die, but in the present as we open our hearts to God. Unfortunately, one part of the Christian understanding of this concern has been too preoccupied with whether God will allow us to "go to heaven" when we die. In order to "go to heaven" we must believe that our sins are atoned for by the crucifixion of Jesus. This argument, based in part on the Hebrew Bible's teachings about Torah (the Law) and the need for righteousness in the presence of God, does speak about religious practices such as the need for make sacrifices in order to be accepted by a righteous God. The apostle Paul, a well-educated and devout Jew (a Pharisee), picks up on this theme, and one part of his teaching speaks about the death of Jesus as a vicarious sacrifice that makes possible God's acceptance and our welcome to eternal life.[11]

I admire the measure of truth in this point of view that emphasizes the call of God to a righteous and spiritual life. But I think of this emphasis in a slightly different way, less as a need for an atoning sacrifice and more as a redeeming action and way of life. I summarize this concern in the Christian context as: "Jesus died *because* of our sins rather than *for* our sins." I cannot accept the view that God's angry judgment must be appeased by the death of Jesus. I hear Jesus saying to the rich young ruler to whom he was speaking something very central to his teaching. Underlying what he says is a view of God that emphasizes grace and loving presence. He is saying that eternal life begins now and that the essence of eternal life is living in harmony with the will and way of God.

Jesus, Paul, and for the most part the Christian church, have taught that God forgives us and graciously offers unconditional acceptance and love. It is this emphasis that is universal and timeless, not bound to the practices of a particular culture. I do not believe that God just sent Jesus to die for our sins as a vicarious atonement. Rather we hear God saying, in the teaching of Jesus, that God will forgive us, and that our eternal life,

11. See, for example, Rom 3:21–26. Anselm of Canterbury (c. 1033–1109 CE), in his book *Cur Deus Homo*, articulated the doctrine of vicarious atonement.

a life of abundance, purpose, and peace, begins now as we accept God's presence and love and begin to live a life that is God-centered rather than ego-centered. We enter and fully accept the reign or commonwealth of God, a way of life that draws upon the presence of God in order to live in harmony with the two great commandments, to love God with our whole being and to love our neighbor in the same way that we want to be loved. We become empowered to live in harmony with the teaching of God, and as we "cross the Jordon" we go to be eternally in presence of God.

In our passage from Mark's Gospel, we read that the so-called "rich young ruler" went away "grieving for he had great possessions." He had bought the lie that peace and happiness come with the abundance of possessions. Does that mean that he was eternally condemned? No, he still had the forgiving and unconditional love of God, but didn't make his life God-centered and therefore missed out on the present experience of eternal life, the joy and peace of God's healing and guiding presence, while he "played with his toys." But I trust he now experiences the bliss of being with God for eternity. Does this outlook make me a heretic? Perhaps, but I am a happy one, full of the peace and joy of accepting the most basic teaching of Jesus. In some ways, most of the teachings of nearly all of the world religions speak about living in harmony with Transcendence, however it is described in the language and culture in which it was generated. God understands and speaks all the languages of the human family and honors those who struggle to get it right. DF

Sub-question 10c: Do your beliefs or religious practices make a difference?

Dying, Christ destroyed our death.
Rising, Christ restored our life.
Christ will come again in glory.
As in baptism we put on Christ
So in Christ we may be clothed in glory.
Here and now dear friends, we are God's children.
What we shall be has not yet been revealed;
But we know when he appears, we shall be like him,
For we see him he is.[12]

12. "A Service of Death and Resurrection," in the *United Methodist Hymnal*, 870.

The truth of the Easter story is that we need not fear death. Christ's resurrection is the triumph over death. What appeared to be the end was in reality a new beginning. Rather than focusing on death, we turn toward life with hope. We are free to act with courage and take risks for the sake of the gospel. Our eyes are open to see the ordinary resurrections in our lives, where situations of death and destruction are transformed into places of hope and joy. When someone breaks free from addiction, when true forgiveness heals deep wounds, when a refugee family leaves a situation of danger and oppression and finds a new life of freedom: all of these are ordinary resurrections.

At the Annual Conference of the Pacific Northwest Conference of the United Methodist Church we sing "The Bishop's Song" which includes the lyrics: "Beloved! Beloved! We are the children of God and it does not yet appear what we shall be! But we know that when God appears, we shall be like God, we shall be like God. We shall see God face to face." There is this lovely tension between what we know: we are the children of God, and what we do not know: what we shall be. We live in this space, knowing that we are God's beloved and understanding that our human comprehension can never grasp the full divine reality. Because we trust so deeply in God's love and care, which is utterly reliable, we can face what we don't know without fear. MB

Sub-question 10d: Do you expect that there might be some kind of judgment at the end of your life about how you have lived and what you believe?

So whoever does an atom's weight of good will see it,
And whoever does an atom's weight of evil will see it.

QUR'AN 99:7–8

Out beyond ideas of right doing and wrongdoing there is a field. I'll meet your there.[13]

RUMI

---

13. Barks and Moyne, *Essential Rumi*, 36.

I believe that the Judgment Day mentioned vividly in the Qur'an is not about going to heaven and hell but about gaining clarity and self-awareness about our life on earth. It calls our attention to when we followed the right path and where we went astray so that we may be more mindful of the work we need to do to evolve into perfection in the celestial realms. On that phenomenal day, says the Qur'an, "piercing is your sight" (50:22), and it will be a time of "laying bare of truth" (69:1). Our bodies will rise from the grave and in the presence of angels and Divinity all of our good and evil deeds will stare us in our face. Startlingly, our bodies will testify against us about any wrongs we have done. Rumi surmises that our hands might say, "I stole money"; our lips, "I said meanness"; our feet, "I went where I shouldn't"; and our genitals, "Me too!" We shall become fully aware of our right doings and wrong doings.

Based on our level of attainment we will be placed in one of the levels of Heaven, from which we shall continue to progress into perfection and spiral into higher and higher states of unity with Divinity. The wise assure us that we shall move beyond paradoxes and contradictions as we grow in higher consciousness.

Sufi teachers are aware of the extraordinary paradox of being questioned and judged by the All-Compassionate and All-Aware God who created us. God already knows every intention, thought, belief, and deed of ours. These enlightened sages suggest that on Judgment Day we playfully make two requests of Divinity: "Please plead and advocate on my behalf with Yourself," and please do what is worthy of You, and not of me!"

No one knows why God sent us to earth as imperfect beings and placed in our souls a longing to evolve into the fullness of our being as we journey back to our Creator. Sages and prophets have urged us to purify ourselves and do righteous deeds on earth to the best of our ability. As we live this way, our ongoing journey on the Day of Reckoning, when we become aware of how we have fulfilled our responsibilities, will be less burdensome.

The fifteenth-century sage Kabir wrote: "If you do not break your ropes while you are alive, do you think ghosts will do it after?"[14] And the Prophet Muhammad advised shortly before his death: "It is better to blush in this world than in the next."[15] JR

---

14. Bly, *Kabir Book*, 36.
15. Sayed Ameer, *Spirit of Islam*, 117.

Sub-question 10e: Do you believe in heaven? If so, how do you envision it?

Blessed are you when people revile you and persecute you and utter all kinds of evil against you falsely on my account. Rejoice and be glad, for your reward is great in heaven, for in the same way they persecuted the prophets that were before you.

MATTHEW 5:11–12

We know that all things work together for good for those who love God and are called according to his purpose . . . No, we are more than conquerors though him that loved us.
For I am convinced that neither death nor life . . . will be able to separate us from the love of God . . .

ROMANS 8:28, 37–39

Within the Christian frame of reference, the belief in heaven has been a central doctrine of the church.[16] Given the centrality of this belief, one might expect a bit more description of heaven in the New Testament.[17] References to it tend to be focused on comforting those who struggle, suffer, and may have lost hope. The flow of these discussions often say that if you are faithful and suffer for the sake of your belief, remember that God will honor you in heaven and with eternal life. In the Sermon on the Mount (Matthew 5–7) one hears in the words of Jesus that it will be our reward for faithfulness, and as part of the Lord's prayer, we pray that God 's will be followed "on earth as it is in heaven." In the writings of Paul, the notion tends to be linked to the belief in the sovereignty of God, that because of God's great love, "all things" will come together and nothing, not even death, will separate us from God.

Once again, we find that the emphasis in the New Testament literature is that eternal life is a present experience. We may experience the fullness of God's presence by opening our hearts to the reign of God (the Gospels) and

16. There are many thoughtful and helpful books that address this question. I have found the one by Küng, *Eternal Life*, extremely helpful, although a bit dated.

17. It has been a central theme of much of the theology of the church, expressed in sermons and in the literature of Christian cultures, as for example, John Milton's *Paradise Lost*. The Gospel of John also guides our thinking about eternal life.

to the fullness of God's presence as we open our hearts to the Holy Spirit (the Pauline Epistles and the Gospel of John). I find this orientation both liberating and comforting. It is liberating in the sense that it frees me from the popular and somewhat distorted view that God dwells somewhere else (up there) and that when I die, I will travel where God (a very nice grandfather) lives, perhaps on a cloud with a small harp. I will not go to the fiery hot hell to suffer. It is comforting in the sense that I am reassured that I will continue to have a consciousness and identity. I will be able to continue in a new way, not described, that keeps me in harmony and relationship with the personal God of love.[18] It is spoken about by these first-century teachers, (e.g., Paul), through a premodern worldview, and once again, we must use wise hermeneutical practices that enable us to understand the message in our time and culture. We need to translate and bring forward this ancient literature in a way that is true to the ancient text, makes sense to us, and provides guidance and comfort. The work of integrating our scientific (evolutionary) understanding of reality with the Gospel narrative is always the task of the present generation.

Our question is, "Do you believe in heaven? If so, how do you envision it?" My answer is that I hope there may be some continuing consciousness, but it is more hope than firm belief. As I think about it, I find myself turning to the new understanding of time and eternity and hope that there will be life-giving understanding as we read with a different perspective about these vital subjects.[19] DF

Sub-question 10f: Do you think you will meet in heaven those who were close to you?

When the terminally ill patient can no longer deny his [or her] illness, when [s/]he is forced to undergo more surgery or hospitalization, when [s/]he begins to have more symptoms or becomes weaker

18. In another setting, I would like to integrate this understanding with the contemporary worldview of cosmology, time and eternity, evolution, and quantum physics. I have found the writing of Pierre Teilhard de Chardin to be helpful by providing new categories of understanding the future. Contemporary theologian, David Bentley Hart, addresses the subject in his recent book, *That All Shall Be Saved*. American philosopher, Ken Wilber, provides great wisdom about human consciousness in *The Spectrum of Consciousness*.

19. See, for example, the new book by the noted physicist, Brian Greene, *Until the End of Time: Mind, Matter, and our Search for Meaning in an Evolving Universe*.

*and thinner, [s/]he cannot smile anymore. His [her] numbness or
stoicism, his [her] anger and rage will be replaced with a sense of
great loss.*[20]

Elizabeth Kübler-Ross

In Elizabeth Kübler-Ross's classic work, *On Death and Dying*, she speaks
about the stages we go through as we anticipate dying. Acknowledging
each person's unique experience, she nevertheless points to common
stages. They are: 1. Denial and Isolation, 2. Anger, 3. Bargaining, 4. Depression, and 5. Acceptance. In her book, she provides a range of conversations of those at the dying stage of life to illustrate how common
this pattern occurs. As she writes, she does not pretend to be detached
as a scientific observer, but has engaged with great compassion those
who are at the end of life and how it is possible to have hope in these
circumstances. There are varieties of hope, and a central one is the belief in eternal life. One dimension of this belief that often occurs in my
conversations and in my own reflection is whether one may be able to
encounter those whom we have loved and have preceded us in death.[21] It
does *seem like only yesterday* that my older brother and I spent summers
on an Oregon farm with our grandparents. I have wonderful memories
of those months, the closeness to my brother, and the kindness and care
that my grandparents, coming from a profoundly different generation
and culture, gave us. Looking back, I feel like I had one foot dragging in
the old west, and horses (as well as cars) were an important part of transportation. Stories were told about the incompetence of the sheriff and
how justice sometimes had to be addressed by reaching for the rifle in
the gun rack. And the lakes, mountains, and forests were so beautiful and
peaceful, and we slept well in our bunk beds. My grandparents of course
are gone, and so is my brother who left a wife and two small children at
age twenty-eight. Across the years, as I am now in my ninth decade, I find
myself hoping that I'll be able to share stories with Bob when I die. We
were so close and had so much fun together.

20. Kübler-Ross, *On Death and Dying*, 85. I have made the slight changes in the
text regarding gender.

21. As an ordained minister, though serving more within the context of higher
education than the church, I have still been asked to care for the dying and lead funeral
services.

Another part of me, the mature and well-educated adult, knows that these hopeful reflections may not be even close to reality. I know I have constructed a child's fantasy about what heaven might be like. I am unsure there will even be consciousness beyond death, let alone an opportunity to chat with Bob in front of the fire on cold evening in the mountains of eastern Oregon. At my age, I have almost worked through most of the stages of dying. I find myself longing for more years, to be with my wife, our son, and our grandchildren, and to travel a bit more beyond the approximately seventy countries I have visited. And I also would like to do a bit more writing and provide pastoral care that is full of empathy and compassion. As I anticipate dying, I do not know whether I will meet my parents and brother; it is not likely that any form of continuing consciousness (eternal life) will be a reproduction of my life on earth. But perhaps there will be some form of consciousness filled with eternal bliss, perhaps a naïve and innocent hope. DF

Sub-question 10g: How do you deal with the fear/threat of death? How can we live in such a way that helps us accept our own dying? How does the knowledge that death is inevitable shape our living?

To God we belong and to God is our return.

QUR'AN 2:156

Childhood, youth and maturity, and now old age. Every guest agrees to stay three days, no more. Master, you asked me to remind you. Time to go.[22]

RUMI

Over the years three specific practices have softened my fear of death and deepened my understanding of life. First, I follow the example of the Prophet Muhammad who made it a spiritual practice to pray in grave-yards and attend the sick. I visit gravesites, attend funerals, participate in memorials, and spend time with those who are gravely ill. Little by little my fear of death has softened. I have begun to understand the insight that

22. Ladinsky, *Love Poems from God*, 11.

my fear is not about my death but about my not living fully. I realize the need not to enmesh myself in trivialities and to be humble, compassionate, and authentic. Time is precious and life is impermanent. To benefit fully from this practice, Sufi sages remind us to be completely present in the sacred moments of being with the dead and dying.

Second, every Friday I do an act of service and dedicate it to my beloved late parents. This weekly practice makes me aware that "every soul shall have a taste of death" (Qur'an 3:85). I discover that there is a gentleness and sweetness about this inevitable experience.

Third, I embrace difficult feelings that arise from the "little deaths" we all experience, such as a loss of a job, loss of a friendship or relationship, or shock of a sudden downturn in life circumstances. By acknowledging, honoring, and integrating these feelings, I have diminished my fear of death and seem to have more space for love and joy in my life.

Especially helpful are the conversations our community has after a member has passed away. No only do we honor our departed friend, but we also share thoughts and feelings about our own demise. Someone will lead a meditation on the meaning of death, and we become acutely aware of what we need to say and do right now in our own lives. Following this reflection, someone will invariably bring up the insight that when we die and look back on our earthly life, our dramas and melodramas, we shall laugh and laugh. Why not laugh right now while we are alive?

In the midst of vulnerability, laughter, and tears, we also tend to share a witty wisdom about our various physical frailties. For example, if my eyes are failing, Sufi wisdom teaches that it is because my soul has wept so copiously with longing for God that my sight has become cloudy and dim. If my spine is bent and sore, it is because it has borne the burden of my soul's grief at being parted from God.

These sessions usually end with poetry, and I particularly love a poem that says we have no idea of the joy the soul feels in returning home.

> A love-sick nightingale among owls
> You caught the scent of roses
> And flew to the Rose garden.[23]

---

23. Barks, *Rumi Bird Song*, 48.

Sub-question 10h: How do you "manage" the death of those who are very dear to you? How do you live with grief? What resources might bring you strength?

As far as I can see, grief will never truly end. It may become softer over time, more gentle, but some days will feel sharp, and grief will last as long as love does—forever. It's simply the way the absence of your loved one manifests in you heart. A deep longing, accompanied by the deepest love. Some days, the heavy fog may return, and the next day, it may recede once again. It's all an ebb and flow, a constant dance of sorrow and joy, pain and sweet love.[24]

LEXI BEHRNDT

There are so many kinds and shades of grief. Some deaths come at the end of a long and rich life. While we grieve, we are grateful for their presence in our lives and for the rich trove of memories they leave. If we survive a long relationship, we grieve their presence in our everyday lives. Each word, each action, each birthday or anniversary reminds us of our loss.

Other losses are more shattering: a sudden death, the loss of a child, or death by violence. Grief is intense, bringing its train of emotions: anger, blame, guilt, and more. Grief's journey is long and hard. In a sense we may never really accept that loss. We simply learn to live with grief, knowing that the pain ebbs and flows throughout our lives. People in our society tend to avoid the realities of intense grief, often in a trite and insensitive way urging someone to "get over it" and return to a "normal" life. But there is work to do as grief takes us on its own pilgrimage. Life will never be the same.

There are resources on this hard journey. The practice of gratitude helps us to find some tiny thing each day that brings a touch of joy. Friends and family who understand can walk beside us, sharing memories of the beloved or simply sitting in silence. They don't try to "fix" us but quietly accept us as we grieve.

Cultivating our own spiritual center provides comfort. We understand that God is present in our grief, understanding our sorrow, and comforts us as we grieve. We are assured that our beloved exists within God's presence.

---

24. Behrndt, "How To be Grateful When Life Is Hard," para. 19.

Sub-question 10i: Do you believe there is something we call "heaven and hell" or are these concepts a means of control by a religious establishment?

O Allah, if I worship You for fear of Hell,
burn me in Hell.
And if I worship You in hope of Paradise,
Exclude me from Paradise.
But if I worship You for Your own sake
Withhold not Your Everlasting Beauty.[25]

RABIA

It is said that the beloved eighth-century saint, Rabia, ran through the streets of Basra with a torch of fire in one hand to set fire to heaven and a pail of water in the other to quench the fires of hell. To those who listened, she declared that it is unworthy to worship God and live a life based on greed for the pleasures of heaven or fear of the punishing fires of hell. Either attitude can cause deformities in one's thinking and behavior.

To deepen this wisdom, consider a story by the eleventh-century Sufi master Al-Ghazali. Jesus comes across two groups of people whose faces are wrinkled with worry and bodies that are bent under the weight of anxieties. One group explains that their deformity is a result of intense fear of the blazing fires of hell, while the other group explains that their condition derives from an urgent desire for the sensual indulgences of heaven. Then he comes upon a third group, which has endured much but radiates love and joy. Asked the reason for their happy faces, they respond, "We love the Spirit of Truth. We have glimpsed Reality, and this has made us oblivious of lesser goals."[26] May we be like the people in that contented group!

Spiritual teachers point out that no matter how alluring heaven may be, measured by our earthly knowledge, our souls yearn for the singular fulfillment that comes from proximity to God. "That," says the Qur'an, "is the supreme felicity" (9:72). Hell is less a place of punishment and more a place of purification. Those who have not done their inner work will get

---

25. Vaughan-Lee, *Traveling the Path of Love*, 77.
26. Shah, *Way of the Sufi*, 58.

a second chance to cleanse and purify themselves before continuing their journey into mysterious realms.

This insight about hell is validated in a Hadith in which the Prophet and his companions were discussing the fires of hell when they saw a woman desperately searching for her child. When she found the child, the mother cradled and suckled the child with such love and care that the companions wept. Said the Prophet, "Do you imagine that this woman would ever throw her child into the fire?" "Impossible," replied the companions. Whereupon the Prophet declared, "Even more than this woman loves her child, does God love His servants."[27]

The Mulla also weighs in on the subject of hell. He once had a dream in which his wife sent him to hell to bring back fire for her cooking. "There is no literal fire here," said the angel in charge. "People who arrive in hell have an inner fire of rage and hate; the blaze burns from within."

CHAPTER 10: IS THERE LIFE FOR ME AFTER DEATH OR IS DEATH THE END OF OUR EXISTENCE?

Resources and Practices

Further Reading

1. Syed Ameer Ali, *The Spirit of Islam: A History of the Evolution and Ideals of Islam*

2. A. J. Arberry, *The Mystical Poems of Rumi*

3. Katy Butler, *The Art of Dying Well: A Practical Guide to a Good End of Life*

4. Elisabeth Kübler-Ross, *On Death and Dying*

5. John Macquarrie, *Christian Hope*

6. Anthony Scioli and Henry B. Billar, *Hope in the Age of Anxiety: A Guide to Understanding Our Most Important Virtue*

---

27. Suhrawardy, *Sayings of Muhammad*, 94.

Suggested Practices

1. Ponder those aspects of you life that give you hope. Write them down and share them with a trusted friend or counselor.

2. Explore ways that you might cultivate these dimensions and activities that bring you a more hopeful life.

3. Ponder those aspects of your life that cause you to feel despair, grief, and discouragement. Write these down as well and share them with a trusted friend or counselor.

4. Ask yourself whether faith and belief are factors in encouraging a hopeful spirit. Explore how they help and seek to cultivate them.

5. Reflect on the experience in your life in which you lost a person that was very important to you, a friend or relative. How would you describe the grief you felt and perhaps still feel? Find a close friend or counselor with whom you can share these feelings of grief.

6. What are the deepest and most important values in your life, such as love or joy, and ponder how these values help you deal with your mortality and that of those whom you love.

Postscript

IT HAS NOT BEEN possible for us to provide full and definitive answers to all ten foundational questions and each set of the nine sub-questions. Every question would be a good subject for a full-length book. Our goal was to suggest what might be a wise approach as we begin to answer these perplexing questions. We aimed for balance, perspective, and for life-giving insight that leads to a flourishing life. As we approached these questions, each of us discovered a range of other questions that might have been discussed and a great deal of writing filled with wisdom that we were unable to use. We agreed that we should stay focused, even though each of the questions suggested more important subjects to discuss. We kept our eyes on our goal and did not want be drawn away from making spiritual wisdom the heart of our writing. Even with this focus, we had to make difficult choices.

Our last foundational question with the nine sub-questions, relating to how we manage our mortality, was appropriately placed at the end. Yet it left all three of us as authors wanting to remind our readers not to forget that we need wisdom across our lifespan. To underline this point, we now provide a few more quotations on the value of wisdom, ones that we were unable to fit into the focus of answering the ten foundational questions and the additional sub-questions. They speak to a range of concerns and challenges we face in life and are drawn primarily from the Hebrew Bible, a primary source of wisdom for humankind, regardless of one's religious heritage. These quotations seek to define the place of wisdom in our lives.[1]

---

1. These selections are taken from a list I found in my files, and I am unable to give credit to the one who prepared it initially. I imagine it came from one of our teachers, and we express gratitude, wishing we could make our gratitude more personal.

1. Wisdom is "practical knowledge of the laws of life and the world based on experience."[2]

2. "Wisdom does not represent the actions of God in Israel's history; it deals with daily human experience in the good world God created."[3]

3. Wisdom is "a spirituality for the market place." "Wisdom spirituality accepts, indeed, blesses, life in the market place. It takes everyday life with the utmost seriousness. It asserts that ordinary human life."[4]

4. "Wisdom, as conceived in Proverbs as a whole, is not just a set of prepackaged traditional truths or wise sayings. It is the power of the human mind, both in its intellectual faculties and in the knowledge it can gain, hold, and transmit. God possesses it and, we are taught, it is ours as well."[5]

5. "Wisdom in ancient Israel . . . includes at least six important elements: knowledge, imagination, discipline, piety, and moral instruction."[6]

6. "The Hebrew concept of wisdom . . . refers to what is skillful, well made or well judged . . . In the wisdom literature it is most frequently used in the moral sense of skill in living within the moral order of Yahweh's world . . . Wisdom transcends human intelligence and cleverness, for it is rooted in trust in Yahweh."[7]

7. "The wisdom writings . . . work toward a personal liberation, a liberation that frees the individual from the psychic sources of personal or societal bondage—greed, lust, or inordinate pride or aggressiveness, for example. Wisdom, rather, sets out to motivate and educate the individual in the virtues that lead to life—the full joy-filled life of one who is humble, diligent, prudent, in control of emotions, faithful in relationships, compassionate, and God-fearing—in contemporary language, a mature, whole human being, able to love and be loved."[8]

Alas, there is so much more! Read with us. Most sincerely, Duncan, Mary, and Jamal.

---

2. Rad, *Old Testament Theology*, 418.

3. Murphy, *Tree of Life*, 1.

4. O'Connor, *Wisdom Literature*, 16.

5. Fox, *Proverbs 1–9*, 3.

6. Purdue, *Proverbs: Interpretation Bible Commentary*, 4.

7. Estes, *Hear, My Son*, 43.

8. Ceresko, *Introduction to Old Testament Wisdom*, 5.

The Questions

The Teachers of Spiritual Wisdom

Gaining Perspective on Life's Perplexing Questions

1. Who am I?
    a. Are we just a product of evolution (a very smart product) with the exclusive goals of survival and reproduction, or do we have an additional and more substantial identity?
    b. Are we fundamentally different from animals or is it simply that we have become more advanced in the evolutionary process?
    c. In that we are similar in many ways with animals and share nature with them, should we treat them much as we should treat human beings?
    d. Do animals suffer? Do we care if they feel pain? Do we have the right to eliminate them?
    e. What qualities in human beings make them distinctive?
    f. Do you think we were created "in the image of God"? Is there a self-aware and subtle, even a divine dimension to our identity?
    g. If we have the divine image, what does that mean? How might it shape the values that guide our lives?
    h. How do we awaken and become more aware of our divine identity? Why is it that we are not aware of divine image?
    i. Are there ways that we might transform our ego and self-centeredness and increase our capacity to live a God-centered life?

2. Why am I here?

   a.   Is there any deep and fundamental meaning in life? Is there
        a Transcendent Reality that gives order to the universe and a
        pattern for human life?
   b.   Does it really matter whether I have a clear meaning in life as
        long as I manage the challenges of life? If it does matter, how
        do I discover my special purpose in life?
   c.   Do we have some basic responsibilities and, if so, how do we
        integrate them into our lives?
   d.   How does our career and role in life fit into our understanding
        of our meaning in life?
   e.   Do you think there is a moment or period of time when
        we experience an awakening or enlightenment, perhaps a
        conversion to a new spirit and outlook? Does this happen a
        single time or is it a process?
   f.   Are there stages we go through or patterns of development
        that increase the understanding of our meaning and purpose
        in life? What is the journey that leads to an increased
        understanding of our meaning and purpose in life?
   g.   How do our meaning and purpose in life take shape in
        responsibilities? How can I prioritize my daily and often
        overwhelming tasks and duties?
   h.   Do you occasionally feel conflict between your immediate
        needs and desires and your sense of having a purpose in life?
   i.   How important to you is making money, having a good job,
        and "getting ahead"? Is life about gaining prestige, seeking
        pleasure, and having power over others? Or are there other
        ways of living that are more fulfilling?

3. What are my deepest values?

   a.   Do we choose our values or do they gradually emerge in our
        life experience?
   b.   Are there stages or patterns of growth in our moral
        development? If so, how would you describe them? Are they
        the same for all people?
   c.   What motivates us to engage in moral development? What
        motivates me to pursue a more mature ethical position?
        How much is our motivation conscious and how much is
        unconscious?

d. What guides our behavior? What are the sources we draw upon?

e. What does it mean to live an ethical life? Are you a moral person? How does one know that one is a moral person?

f. Is it important to honor and care for myself while caring for others?

g. If you believe in God, do you think we are invited to a God- or value-centered life rather than a self-centered life? Does belief in God make a difference?

h. Where do the universal values of love, integrity (honesty), and justice fit into your behavior? Is it possible for you to truly love another person (or persons) without self-interest playing a part?

i. Is there a model of an ideal person, such as Buddha, Moses, Jesus, Mohammad, Gandhi, Mary, the mother of Jesus, Fatima, Clare of Assisi, Mother Teresa, Dorothy Day, or someone you know well, that guides and motivates you?

4. Do you believe in God?

a. Do you think there is another layer of reality or an integral layer of reality often thought of as divine? Do you believe in a transcendent Other or Principle, the Ground of being, or a personal God?

b. Is there a spiritual dimension to our lives? If so, how do you understand it?

c. Do you believe in prayer as a way of connecting with God, and are your prayers primarily relational or more sincere requests to find God's will for your life and aid those for whom you care?

d. What is the difference between spirituality and religion, and do you use that difference consciously in the way you seek to find your way?

e. Where do you experience the holy? What leads you out of yourself into an encounter with the sacred? Does this dimension genuinely shape and influence your life?

f. Should we engage with others in interfaith understanding and collaboration?

g. Are you reluctant to cooperate with those who have different beliefs?

h. How do we know what is true? As Pilate asked Jesus, "What is truth?"

    i.   What part do faith and practice have in cultivating a relationship with God?

5. How do you and should you relate to other people?

    a.   How important is it to have close relationships and friendships?

    b.   What qualities or values must be present for you to have close relationships and friendships?

    c.   How much do you value having a loving family? Or miss having a family? What does a family look like? How can we choose our family? How do we deal with unhealthy relationships within families?

    d.   Is love and sharing life at a deep and true level with others important to you?

    e.   Are love, compassion, empathy, and caring the "heart" of living wisely and well? If not, what is?

    f.   What kinds of people do you enjoy the most? How do you stretch yourself to encounter and understand others whose life situations are different from yours?

    g.   What kinds of people are hardest for you to love and care about? How do you open yourself to understand their perspective? Is there any prejudice in you against others who are different from you?

    h.   How should we deal with relationships that are unhealthy and possibly harmful to us?

    i.   How do we find and build communities of meaning and purpose?

6. How should I take care of myself?

    a.   How do we develop and mature? How important is our environment in either nurturing or limiting our growth toward maturity?

    b.   How do we find a measure of peace, joy, and happiness?

    c.   How do we manage fear, insecurity, anxiety, anger, and sadness?

    d.   Are there stages of levels in our journey toward wholeness? What might they be? Is the journey linear or meandering?

    e.   Do you have a strong sense of self-worth and a good self-image? Or do you wish you had other qualities than those you have? How do you deal with self-doubt? Are you able to see yourself clearly?

f. Am I making good progress in my journey toward health and wholeness? For example, do I take good care of myself with diet, sleep patterns, and exercise?

g. What means or methods are helping me continue to grow and deepen?

h. On occasion, we need to "take care" of the deeper patterns or feelings in our sub- or unconscious life. How much do you feel influenced by them and how do we access those patterns that may harm us and heal them?

i. How do you relax? Do you have hobbies or like to play games? What brings you joy? Do the arts help you express your deepest self?

7. How important is it for me to belong to groups and organizations and have a supportive community?

a. Do the groups and associations you have sustain you, guide you, and motivate you?

b. Are there any risks and disadvantages in joining groups and associations? Are there ways to help organizations overcome their limitations and be more consistent with their stated goals?

c. What is our part in belonging to a supportive community? Is it easy for you to take the initiative and join a group or association of people?

d. How do we balance being alone and being with others?

e. Do you think of yourself as an introvert or an extrovert? How do you discern the difference?

f. Do you feel like you belong when you are in groups or do you often feel left out? Do you feel energized by being in groups or do you feel tired when the time with others is over?

g. Do you like yourself the way you are or would you like to develop better social skills? What ways are available to you to improve your interpersonal and social skills?

h. What is the difference between a healthy group or association and an unhealthy group or association?

i. What difference do groups or associations make in individual lives, in the community, and in the world?

8. Why do I suffer and why is there so much evil and suffering in the world?

    a. How do I cope when I feel discouraged and depressed?

    b. How do you find the strength and energy to engage with serious issues facing the world? What difference can you make? How can you deal with your own limited efforts?

    c. Is it possible to change these conditions? What conditions can be changed and what conditions are nearly impossible to change?

    d. On a grand scale, will humankind survive given the threats to our earth home? Or, as Einstein asked, "Is the earth friendly?" How do we find the strength to cope and help people deal with global warming?

    e. How should we address the challenges of climate change and global warming? How do we help create a more equitable economy? How should we deal with violence, both international and personal?

    f. What are the other threats or challenges we face, and how do we find the strength and energy to engage with these challenges? What difference can you make?

    g. What harsh truths do you prefer to ignore? How do you deal with or appease your conscience about these truths?

    h. Do you ever wonder why God allows evil and suffering to exist?

    i. Do you have answers or ways of explaining why evil and suffering exist?

9. How do I help to create a more just, peaceful, and humane society and world?

    a. What responsibility do we have to make a better world, and in particular, what role do the arts have in creating a better world?

    b. Do you occasionally feel helpless and unable to help in situations that cause suffering and damage to our earth home and those who live in it? For example, what might I do to help erase the lingering and very present prejudice against minorities in our country?

    c. Do you really care or just think we are here to satisfy our own needs and desires?

d. Are there threats to our liberal democracy and, if so, what are they?

e. What is the role of education and political leadership in government to guiding us to a more just, peaceful, and secure future?

f. What approach to education should we take? How would you rate your education? What role do the arts have in creating a better world?

g. Are you satisfied with our type of government?

h. What sort of changes would you make in the way our government is structured and the way it is run?

i. What sort of principles and policies should be central to our government?

10. Is there life for me after death or is death the end of our existence?

a. Knowing that we will die, how shall I live?

b. In reference to eternal life, does it really matter how I live?

c. Do your beliefs or religious practices make a difference?

d. Do you expect that there may be some kind of judgment at the end of your life about how you have lived and what you have believed?

e. Do you believe in heaven? If so, how do you envision it?

f. Do you think you will meet in "heaven" those who were close to you?

g. How do you deal with the fear/threat of death? How can we live in such a way that helps us accept our own dying? How does the knowledge that death is inevitable shape our living?

h. How do you "manage" the death of those who are very dear to you? How do you live with grief? What resources might bring you strength?

i. Do you believe there is something we call "heaven and hell" or are these concepts a means of control by a religious establishment?

Glossary

1. *Agape*: Greek word for unconditional and unlimited love.

2. Allah: the one and only God in Islam and the standard Arabic word for God.

3. Barzakh: An Islamic belief in a realm, not unlike purgatory, in which the soul awaits the Day of Judgment.

4. Basmala: The Islamic invocation, "In the name of God, Boundlessly Compassionate and Infinitely Merciful."

5. Compassion: Caring and active love that seeks to reduce suffering.

6. Community: a group of people with purpose and values in which one belongs, feels comfortable, and has goals that you affirm.

7. Consciousness: the quality of being aware of one's surroundings and how one thinks and feels about oneself and one's environment.

8. Ego: A general reference to one's inner life, the self, but often the term is used to describe self-centered behavior.

9. Empathy: The capacity to understand and care for the feelings and journey of another person or persons.

10. Faith development: An understanding of spiritual formation that maintains that we move through certain stages as we seek a deep spiritual dimension in life.

11. Gerrymandering: Arranging election districts to give an advantage to one political party.

12. Ground of Being: A term used by theologian, Paul Tillich, as a way of speaking about Transcendence or Ultimate Reality. It is often used as a term to refer to God in a non-anthropomorphic way.

13. Hadith: the accumulated sayings of the Prophet Muhammad.

14. Hafiz: Persian poet, 1315–90 CE.

15. *Hesed*: A Hebrew word that means love, and it is often translated from Hebrew into "steadfast love" or "loving-kindness."

16. *Hikmah*: Arabic name for God's presence, feminine in character.

17. Holy: the sense of the sacred in the environment, special objects (books, buildings, etc.), people with a religious vocation, settings with religious meaning, certain practices that put one in touch with the divine.

18. *Hokma*: Hebrew word meaning "wisdom."

19. Human development: a reference to a branch of psychology that focuses on the pattern of becoming a mature person. Often, stages of growth are identified as one moves through life.

20. *Ilm*: Arabic word, used often in the Qur'an, meaning "knowledge."

21. Image of God: The belief that we are born with characteristics that we often associate with God such as the capacity to love, show compassion (God is love), and to understand reality and to do what is right (God is light).

22. Islamophobia: The fear of Islam, often including Muslim people, and which results in prejudice against the religion of Islam.

23. Kabir: Fifteenth-century Muslim sage and poet, following the Sufi way.

24. Love: Word with many meanings, often defined by three Greek words: *eros*: attraction to that which is beautiful and profound; *philia*: the joys and commitments of friendship; *agape*: unconditional love.

25. Meditation: A time of mindfulness, quiet reflection, generally focusing on the present allowing relief from day-to-day worries and concerns and openness to the reality of the moment.

26. Mindfulness: Giving attention to reality and life goals, living in the present moment, setting aside insecurities, anxiety, and worry, a time to say, "Be still my soul."

27. Mulla: A Muslim title generally denoting "lord," and more generally refers to a noted scholar or religious leader.

28. Muhammad: The messenger and prophet, founder of Islam, born ca. 570, died 632 CE.

29. Naturalism: The view that the universe requires not supernatural cause and control, but is self-existent, self-explanatory, self-operating, and self-directed.

30. Panenthism: The theological view that God is both transcendent and yet immanent, fully engaged in the natural order.

31. Qur'an: The holy book of Islam, understood by Muslims to be the Word of God.

32. Religion: A set of beliefs and practices within a community that are generally related to the divine. These beliefs and practices include ethical systems, a form of worship, and a sustaining community.

33. Roma: the appropriate name for the group of people more commonly known as gypsies.

34. Rumi: Thirteenth-century Persian poet, scholar, and theologian.

35. Sacred naming: Making room in your heart and mind to be kind and caring about one's self. It is a process of saying supportive encouragement to one's self.

36. Sacred holding: Making room in your heart and mind to allow some feelings and thoughts about life and other people to mature so that you may become a "person for others."

37. Sangha: The intentional and spiritual community within Buddhism.

38. Salat: The daily ritual body prayer practiced by all Muslim as one of the Five Pillars of Islam.

39. *Shalom*: A Hebrew word meaning peace, one that is more than just the absence of war, but also one speaks about peace between others, and a deep sense of contentment in one's own life.

40. Slinking Whisperer: A name given to Satan in Islam.

41. Spirit: A word with many meanings, often pointing to the religious center in one's life; in reference to God, it often points to the presence of God, and is viewed in Christianity as part of the Trinity in Father, Son, and Holy Spirit.

42. Spirituality: The effort to incorporate the elements of our religious tradition into our lives in a way that provides guidance in life

leading to our development as persons growing toward wholeness (holiness), insight, and responsible living.

43. Sufism (Sufi): Mystic Islamic belief and practice that seeks to find divine love and knowledge through direct personal experience of God.

44. Torah: A reference to the Law in the Hebrew Bible, often used as a description of the first five books of the Hebrew Bible.

45. Tribal: Assuming that the beliefs and practices of one's religious community are correct and true and that other approaches are wrong; exclusive religious views and practices.

46. Unconscious: Not knowing or perceiving what is going on inside of you, and yet influencing your feelings and behavior.

47. Vocation: A sense of being called, in some cases to a particular career such as the ministry, or in other cases being called to a God-centered way of life.

48. Wisdom: The ability to understand reality and make good judgments and decisions in reference to your beliefs, values, and actions. Wisdom is often associated with feminine qualities such as intuition, insight, sensitivity, and compassion.

49. Wisdom traditions: A term generally associated with the teaching of the several religions of the human family.

Bibliography

Achbar, Mark, and Peter Wintonick. *Manufacturing Consent: Noam Chomsky and the Media*. American University, Washington DC: Necessary Illusions Productions, Inc., 1992.

An-Nawawi, Imaam. *An-Nawawi's Forty Hadith*. Cambridge, UK: Islamic Texts Society, 1997.

Armstrong, Karen. *The Lost Art of Scripture: Rescuing the Sacred Texts*. New York: Knopf, 2019.

Aslan, Reza. *God: A Human History*. New York: Random House, 2017.

Attar, Farid al-Din. *Muslim Saints and Mystics: Episodes from the Tadhikirat al-Auliya*. Abingdon, UK: Routledge, 2013.

Barks, Coleman. *Rumi's Little Book of Love and Laughter: Teaching Stories and Fables*. Newburyport, MA: Red Wheel/Weiser, 2016.

Barks, Coleman, and John Moyne. *The Essential Rumi*. New Jersey: Castle Books, 1995.

Barzun, Jacques. *Of Human Freedom*. Boston: Little, Brown, 1939.

Basho. "Spring." https://www.hakubai.org/spring.

Bass, Diana Butler. *Grounded: Finding God in the World*. New York: HarperOne, 1991.

Behrndt, Lexi. "How To Be Grateful When Life Is Hard." *Scribbles and Crumbs* (blog), November 19, 2015. http://www.scribblesandcrumbs.com/2015/11/19/how-to-be-grateful-when-life-is-hard/.

Berry, Thomas. *The Dream of the Earth*. San Francisco: Sierra Club, 1988.

———. *The Great Work: Our Way into the Future*. New York: Three Rivers, 1999.

———. *The Sacred Universe: Earth, Spirituality, and Religion in the Twenty- first Century*. New York: Columbia University Press, 2009.

Berry, Wendell. *The Unsettling of American Culture and Agriculture*. New York: Avon/Sierra Club, 1978.

Block, Peter. *Community: The Structure of Belonging*. 2nd ed. Oakland, CA: Berrett-Koehler, 2018.

Bloom, Howard. *The God Problem: How a Godless Cosmos Creates*. Amherst, NY: Prometheus, 2012.

Bly, Robert, ed. *The Kabir Book: Forty-four of the Ecstatic Poems of Kabir*. Boston: Beacon, 1977.

Bonhoeffer, Dietrich. *The Cost of Discipleship*. New York: Simon & Schuster, 1995.

The Book of Discipline of the United Methodist Church. Nashville: United Methodist, 2016.

Bourgeault, Cynthia. *Wisdom Jesus*. Boston: Shambhala, 2008.

Braden, Nathaniel. *Honor the Self: Self-Esteem and Personal Transformation.* New York: Bantam, 1983.

Breton, Denise, and Christopher Largent. *Love, Soul and Freedom: Dancing with Rumi on the Mystic Path.* Hazelden, City Center, Minnesota, 1998.

Brown, Lester B. *World on Edge: How to Prevent Environmental and Economic Collapse.* New York: Norton, 2011.

Brown, William P. *Seeing the Psalms: A Theology of Metaphor.* Louisville, KY: Presbyterian Publishing House, 2002.

Brueggemann, Walter. *Reverberations of Faith: A Theological Handbook of Old Testament Themes.* Louisville, KY: Westminster John Knox, 2002.

Bryans, Nena. *Full Circle: A Proposal to the Church for an Arts Ministry.* San Carlos, CA: Schuyler Institute for Worship and the Arts, 1988.

Buber, Martin. *I and Thou.* New York: Scribner's, 1958.

Bultmann, Rudolf with Five Critics. *Kerygma and Myth.* Translated by Hans Werner Bartsch. New York: Harper & Row, 1953.

Butler, Katy. *The Art of Dying Well: A Practical Gide to the Good End of Life.* New York: Scribner's, 2019.

Byrom, Thomas. *The Dhammapada: The Sayings of the Buddha.* Boston: Shambhala, 1993.

Cacioppo, John T., and William Patrick. *Loneliness: Human Nature and the Needs for Social Connection.* New York: Norton, 2008.

Campbell, Joseph. *Oriental Mythology: The Masks of God.* New York: Arkana, 1991.

Campbell, Joseph, with Brian Moyer. *The Power of Myth.* New York: Anchor, 1991.

Carroll, Sean. *The Big Picture: On the Origins of Life, Meaning, and the Universe Itself.* New York: Dutton, 2017.

———. *Something Deeply Hidden: Quantum Words and the Emergence of Spacetime.* New York: Dutton, 2019.

Ceresko, Anthony R. *Introduction to Old Testament Wisdom.* Maryknoll, NY: Orbis, 1999.

Chester, Michael P., and Marie C. Norrisey. *Prayer and Temperament: Different Prayer Forms for Different Personality Types.* Charlottesville, Virginia: The Open Door, 1991.

Chittister, Joan. *Following the Path: The Search for a Life of Passion.* New York: Crossword, 2012.

———. *Rule of St. Benedict: A Spirituality for the 21st Century.* Rev. ed. Lawrenceville, GA: Crossroads, 2010.

Chittick, William C. *The Sufi Path of Love: The Spiritual Teachings of Rumi.* Albany, NY: State University of New York Press, 1983.

Chopra, Deepak. *How to Know God.* Easton, PA: Harmony, 2001.

Christofferson, Travis. *Curable: How an Unlikely Group of Radicals is Trying to Transform our Health Care System.* White River Junction, VT: Chelsea Green, 2016.

Colledge, Edmund, and James Walsh, eds. and trans. *Julian of Norwich: Showings.* The Classics of Western Spirituality: A Library of the Great Spiritual Masters. New York: Paulist, 1978.

Cranmer-Byng, L., et al., eds. *The Wisdom of the East.* London: Dutton, 1920.

Curwood, Steve. "'We Scientists Don't Know How To Do That'... What a Commentary!" https://winewaterwatch.org/2016/05/we-scientists-dont-know-how-to-do-that-what-a-commentary/.

Dalai Lama. *The Compassionate Life*. Boston: Wisdom Publications, 2003.

———. *How To Expand Love*. Edited and translated by Jeffrey Hopkins. New York: Atria, 2005.

Davies, Kate. *Intrinsic Hope: Living Courageously in Trouble Times*. Gabriola Island, BC: New Society, 2018.

Davis, Ellen F. "Knowing Our Place on Earth: Environmental Responsibility from the Old Testament." In *The Green Bible*, I-59–64. San Francisco: Harper Collins, 2008.

Dawkins, Richard. *The Greatest Show on Earth: The Evidence for Evolution*. New York: Free Press, 2009.

———. *The Selfish Gene*. The New Edition. Oxford: Oxford University Press, 1989.

Delio, Ilia. *The Unbearable Wholeness of Being: God, Evolution, and the Power of Love*. Maryknoll, NY: Orbis, 2013.

del Rosario, D. J. "What If Online Worship Lasts for 6 Months?" *Bokeh Faith* (blog), March 23, 2020. https://www.revdj.com/new-blog/https/6moremonths.

De Witte, Melissa. "Instead of Social Distancing, Practice 'Distant Socializing' Instead, Urges Stanford Psychologist." *Stanford News*, March 19, 2020. news.stanford. edu/2020/03/19/try-distant-socializing-instead/.

Diamond, Jared. *Collapse: How Societies Choose to Fail or Succeed*. New York: Viking Penguin, 2005.

Dowd, Michael. *Thank God for Evolution: How the Marriage of Science and Religion Will Transform Your Life and Our World*. New York: Plume, 2007.

Eagleton, Terry. *Reason, Faith, and Revolution: Reflections on the God Debate*. New Haven: Yale University Press, 2009.

Eliade, Mircea. *From Primitives to Zen: A Thematic Sourcebook of the History of Religions*. New York: Harper & Row, 1977.

———. *A History of Religious Ideas*. Translated by Willard R. Task. 3 vols. Chicago: The University of Chicago Press, 1978, 1982, 1985.

Erikson, Erik H. *Identity: Youth and Crisis*. New York: Norton, 1968.

Ernst, Carl W., ed. *Teachings of Sufism*. Boston: Shambhala, 1999.

Esposito, John L. *Islam: The Straight Path*. 3rd ed. New York: Oxford University Press, 1998.

Estes, Donald J. *Hear, My Son*. Grand Rapids, MI: Eerdmans, 1997.

Fadiman, James, and Robert Frager. *Essential Sufism*. New York: HarperCollins, 1997.

Ferguson, Duncan S. *Exploring the Spirituality of the World Religions*. New York: Continuum, 2010.

———. *Lovescapes: Mapping the Geography of Love*. Eugene, OR: Cascade, 2012.

———. *The Radical Invitation of Jesus: How Accepting the Invitation of Jesus Can Lead to Living Faith and Fulfilling Life for Today*. Eugene, OR: Wipf & Stock, 2019.

———. *The Radical Teaching of Jesus: A Teacher Full of Grace and Truth*. Eugene, OR: Wipf & Stock, 2016.

Ferris, Timothy. *Coming of Age in the Milky Way*. New York: Morrow, 1988.

———. *The Whole Shebang: A State-of-the-Universe(s) Report*. New York: Simon & Schuster, 1997.

Finley, James. *Christian Meditation: Experiencing the Presence of God*. New York: HarperOne, 2004.

Forni, P. M. *Choosing Civility: The Twenty-five Rules of Considerate Conduct*. New York: St. Martin's Griffin, 2002.

Foster, Richard J. *Streams of Living Water: Experiencing the Presence of God*. New York: 1998.

Fowler, James W. *The Stages of Faith: The Psychology of Human Development*. New York: Harper & Row, 1981.

Fox, Matthew. *The Coming of the Cosmic Christ*. San Francisco: Harper & Row, 1980.

Fox, Michael V., ed. *Proverbs 1–9: A New Translation with Introduction and Commentary*. Anchor Bible 18A. New York: Doubleday, 2003.

Frank, Anne. *Diary of a Young Girl: The Definitive Edition*. New York: Knopf Doubleday, 2010. Kindle ed.

Frazer, James G. *The Golden Bough: The Roots of Religion and Folklore*. New York: Avenel, 1981.

Freud, Sigmund. *A General Introduction to Psychoanalysis*. Translated by Joan Rivers. New York: Doubleday, 1954.

Frevert, Patricia. *Welcome: A Unitarian Universalism Primer*. Boston: Skinner, 2008.

Friedman, Thomas. *Thank You for Being Late: An Optimist's Guide to Thriving in the Age of Accelerations*. New York: Macmillan, 2016.

Frost, Robert. *Collected Poems of Robert Frost*. New York: Halcyon, 1939.

Gibran, Kahlil. *The Prophet*. New York: Knopf, 2003.

Gilligan, Carol. *In A Different Voice: Psychological Theory and Women's Development*. Cambridge, MA: Harvard University Press, 1982.

"'Glass Walls' with Paul McCartney." https://www.peta.org/videos/glass-walls-2/.

Goleman, Daniel. *Emotional Intelligence: Why It Can Matter More Than IQ*. New York: Bantam, 1995.

Goldstein, Joseph. *Mindfulness: A Practical Guide to Awakening*. Boulder, CO: Sounds True, 2015.

Gore, Al. *An Inconvenient Truth: The Planetary Emergency of Global Warming and What We Can Do About It*. New York: Rodale, 2006.

Greene, Brian. *The Elegant Universe*. New York: Norton, 1999.

———. *Until the End of Time*. New York: Knopf, 2020.

Gunther, John. *Death Be Not Proud: A Memoir*. New York: Harper & Row, 1949.

Hanh, Thich Nhat. *How to Love*. Berkeley, CA: Parallax, 2015.

———. *Teachings on Love*. Berkeley, CA: Parallax, 1998.

Harari, Yuval Noah. *Homo Deus: A Brief History of Time*. New York: HarperPerennial, 2017.

———. *Sapiens: A Brief History of Humankind*. New York: Harper Perennial, 2015.

Hari, Johann. *Lost Connections: Uncovering the Real Causes of Depression—and the Unexpected Solutions*. New York: Bloomsbury, 2018.

Hart, David Bentley. *The Experience of God: Being, Consciousness, Bliss*. New Haven: Yale University Press, 2013.

———. *That All Shall Be Saved: Heaven, Hell, & Universal Salvation*. New Haven: Yale University Press, 2019.

Harvey, Andrew, and Eryk Hanut. *Light Upon Light: Inspirations from Rumi*. Berkeley, CA: Atlantic, 1996.

Heidegger, Martin. *Being and Time*. Translated by John Macquarrie and Edward Robinson. New York: Harper & Row, 1962.

Hick, John. *Evil and the God of Love*. London: Collins, 1968.

Hodgson, Peter. *God's Wisdom: Toward a Theology of Education*. Louisville, KY: Westminster John Knox, 1999.

Houston, Jean. *The Search for the Beloved: Journeys in Mythology and Sacred Psychology*. Los Angeles: Jeremy P. Teacher, 1987.

Jaynes, Julian. *The Origin of Consciousness in the Break Down of the Bicameral Mind.* 1976. Reprint, Boston: Houghton Mifflin, 1990.

Johnston, William J., ed. *The Cloud of Unknowing and the Book of Privy Counseling.* New York: Image, 1973.

Jung, Carl G. *The Collected Works of C. G. Jung.* Vol. 14, *Mysterium Coniunctionis.* Translated by G. Adler and R. F. C. Hall. Princeton, NJ: Princeton University Press, 1977.

———. *Modern Man in Search of a Soul.* New York: Harcourt, Brace & World, 1933.

Kaufman, Janet, and Ann Herzog. *The Collected Poems of Muriel Rukeyser.* Pittsburgh, PA: University of Pittsburgh Press, 2006.

Kazantzakis, Nikos. *Report to Greco.* New York: Touchstone: Simon & Schuster, 1975.

Keirsey, David, and Marilyn Bates. *Please Understand Me: Character and Temperament Types.* Del Mar, CA: Prometheus, 1984.

King, Martin Luther, Jr. "'A Realistic Look at the Question of Progress in the Area of Race Relations,' Address Delivered at St. Louis Freedom Rally." April 10, 1957. https://kinginstitute.stanford.edu/king-papers/documents/realistic-look-question-progress-area-race-relations-address-delivered-st.

Kohlberg, Lawrence. *The Philosophy of Moral Development.* New York: Harper & Row, 1981.

Kornfield, Jack. *A Path with Heart: A Guide Through the Perils and Promises of Spiritual Life.* New York: Bantam, 1993.

———. *The Wise Heart: A Guide to the Universal Teachings of Buddhist Psychology.* New York: Bantam, 2008.

Kübler-Ross, Elizabeth. *On Death and Dying: What the Dying Have to Teach Doctors Nurses, Clergy and Their Own Families.* New York: Macmillan, 1969.

Küng, Hans. *Does God Exist? An Answer for Today.* Translated by Edward Quinn. Garden City, NY: Doubleday, 1978.

———. *Eternal Life? Life After Death as a Medical, Philosophical, and Theological Problem.* Translated by Edward Quinn. Garden City, NY: Doubleday, 1984.

Ladinsky, Daniel. *Love Poems from God: Twelve Sacred Voices from the East and West.* New York: Penguin Group, 2002.

———. *The Subject Tonight Is Love: 60 Wild and Sweet Poems of Hafiz.* London: Penguin Compass, 2003.

Ladinsky, Daniel, trans. *Poems of Hafiz.* New York: Penguin, 1999.

Lash, Joseph P. *Helen and Teacher: The Story of Helen Keller and Anne Sullivan Macy.* Lebanon, IN: Hachette, 1997.

Lerner, Michael. *Revolutionary Love: A Political Manifesto to Heal and Transform the World.* Oakland, CA: University of California Press, 2019.

L'Engle, Madeleine. *Walking on Water: Reflections on Faith & Art.* Wheaton, IL: Shaw, 1980.

Levinson, Daniel J. *The Seasons of a Man's Life.* New York: Knopf, 1978.

Loizzo, Joseph, et al., eds. *Advances in Contemporary Psychotherapy: Accelerating Healing and Transformation.* New York: Routledge, 2017.

Lutkehaus, Nancy C. *Margaret Mead: The Making of an American Icon.* Princeton, NJ: Princeton University Press, 1999.

Macquarrie, John. *Christian Hope.* New York: Seabury, 1978.

Mafi, Maryam, trans. *Rumi Day by Day.* Charlottesville, VA: Hampton Rhodes, 2014.

Mahan, Brian J. *Forgetting Ourselves on Purpose: Vocation and the Ethics of Ambition.* San Francisco: Jossey-Bass, 2002.

Merton, Thomas. *No Man Is an Island.* Boston: Shambhala, 2005.

Metaxas, Eric. *Bonhoeffer: Pastor, Martyr, Prophet, Spy.* Nashville: Nelson, 2010.

Miles, Jack. *God: A Biography.* New York: Vintage, 1996.

———. *God in the Qur'an.* New York: Knopf, 2018.

Mills, C. Wright. *The Power Elite.* Oxford: Oxford University Press, 1956.

Mineo, Liz. "Good Genes Are Nice, but Joy Is Better." *The Harvard Gazette*, April 11, 2017. https://news.harvard.edu/gazette/story/2017/04/over-nearly-80-years-harvard-study-has-been-showing-how-to-live-a-healthy-and-happy-life/.

Mitchell, Stephen, trans. *Tao Te Ching.* New York: Harper Collins, 1988.

Murphy, Roland. *The Tree of Life.* New York: Doubleday, 1990.

Nasr, Seeied Hussien. *The Heart of Islam.* San Francisco: Harper Collins, 2002.

"The Nelson Mandela Rules." https://www.unodc.org/documents/justice-and-prison-reform/16-05081_E_rollup_Ebook.pdf.

Niebuhr, Reinhold. *The Nature and Destiny of Man: A Christian Interpretation.* New York: Scribner's, 1949.

Nurbaksh, Javad. *Traditions of the Prophet.* New York: Khaniqahi Nimatullahi, 1981.

O'Connor, Kathleen. *The Wisdom Literature.* Collegeville, MN: Liturgical, 1968.

O'Donohue, John. *Anam Cara: A Book of Celtic Wisdom.* New York: Harper Perennial, 1997.

Oliver, Mary. *Thirst.* Boston: Beacon, 2006.

Oswald, Roy M., and Otto Kroeger. *Personality and Religious Leadership.* New York: The Alban Institute, 1988.

Palmer, Parker J. *A Hidden Wholeness: The Journey Toward An Undivided Life.* San Francisco: Jossey-Bass, 2004.

Pearson, Anne M. "Gandhi and the Imperative of Interfaith Dialogue." *Young India*, September 2, 1927.

Pesso, Tana, with Penor Rinposche. *First Invite Love In: 40 Time-Tested Tools for Creating a More Compassionate Life.* Somerville, MA: Wisdom, 2010.

Plato. *The Dialogues of Plato.* Translated by B. Jowett. Vol. 1. New York: Random House, 1937.

Post, Stephen G. *Unlimited Love: Altruism, Compassion, and Service.* Philadelphia: Templeton Foundation, 2003.

Purdue, Leo G. *Proverbs: Interpretation Bible Commentary.* Louisville, KY: Westminster John Knox, 2000.

Putnam, Robert D., and David E. Campbell. *American Grace: How Religion Divides and Unites Us.* New York: Simon & Schuster, 2012.

Rad, Gerhard von. *Old Testament Theology.* Vol. 1, *The Theology of Israel's Historical Traditions.* New York: Harper & Row, 1962.

Rahman, Jamal. *Sacred Laughter of the Sufis.* Woodstock, VT: Skylight Paths, 2014.

———. *The Spiritual Gems of Islam.* Woodstock, VT: Skylight Paths, 2013.

Rifkin, Jeremy. *The Empathic Civilization: The Race to Global Consciousness in a World in Crisis.* New York: Penguin Group, 2009.

Roberts, Elizabeth, and Elias Amidon, eds. *Earth Prayers: 365 Prayers, Poems, and Invocations from Around the World.* San Francisco: HarperOne, 1991.

Rogers, Carl R. *On Becoming a Person.* Boston: Houghton Mifflin, 1961.

Rogers, Frank, Jr. *The Way of Jesus: Compassion in Practice*. Nashville, TN: Upper Room, 2016.

Rumi, Maulana Jalal Al-Din. *Jewels of Remembrance: A Daybook of Spiritual Guidance*. Translated by Camille and Kabir Helminski. Putney, VT: Threshold, 1996.

Runzo, Joseph, and Nancy M. Martin. *Ethics: In the World Religions*. Oxford: Oneworld, 2001.

Russell, Bertrand. *Why I Am Not A Christian*. New York: Simon & Schuster, 1957.

Sachs, Jeffrey D. *Common Wealth: Economics for a Crowded Planet*. New York: Penguin, 2008.

Sachs, Jonathan. *The Dignity of Difference: How to Avoid the Clash of Civilizations*. London: Continuum, 2002.

Sapolsky, Robert M. *Behave: The Biology of Humans at Our Best and Worst*. New York: Penguin, 2017.

Satir, Virginia. *Peoplemaking*. Palo Alto, CA: Science and Behavior, 1972.

Sayed Ameer, Ali. *The Spirit of Islam: A History of the Evolution and Ideals of Islam*. Cosimo Classics. New York: Cosimo, 2010.

Schell, Jonathan. *The Fate of the Earth*. New York: Knopf, 1982.

Schweitzer, Albert. *Out of My Life and Thought*. New York: A Mentor Book, 1953.

Scioli, Anthony, and Henry B. Biller. *Hope in the Age of Anxiety: A Guide to Understanding Our Most Important Virtue*. Oxford: Oxford University Press, 2009.

Shah, Idries. *A Perfumed Scorpion: The Way to the Way*. San Francisco: Harper & Row, 1981.

———. *The Way of the Sufi*. New York: Penguin, 1991.

Singer, Irving. *The Nature of Love*. Vol. 1, *Plato to Luther*. 2nd ed. Chicago: University of Chicago Press, 1984.

Sloyan, Virginia, ed. *A Sourcebook about Christian Death*. Chicago: Liturgy Training, 1989.

Smith, Houston. *The Soul of Christianity: Restoring the Great Tradition*. San Francisco: HarperSanFrancisco, 2005.

———. *The World's Religions: Our Greatest Wisdom Traditions*. San Francisco: Harper Collins, 1991.

Sölle, Dorothee. *Thinking about God: An Introduction to Theology*. Translated by John Bowden. London: SCM, 1990.

Sopolsky, Robert M. *Behave: The Biology of Humans at Our Best and Worst*. New York: Penguin, 2017.

Soulen, R. Kendall. "A Christian Theodicy: The Problem of Evil—Part 2." *Soulen and Soulen* (podcast), December 21, 2019. https://soulenandsoulen.com/2019/12/21/a-christian-theodacy-the-problem-of-evil-part-2/.

Steindl-Rast, Brother David. *Gratefulness, the Heart of Prayer: An Approach to Life in Fullness*. New York: Paulist Prayer, 1984.

Sternberg, Robert J., and Judith Gluck, eds. *The Cambridge Handbook of Wisdom*. Cambridge: Cambridge University Press, 2019.

Suhrawardy, Al Mumun Al. *The Sayings of Muhammad*. London: Archibald Constable, 1905.

Swimme, Brian, and Mary Evelyn Tucker. *The Journey of the Universe*. New Haven: Yale University Press, 2011.

Swinburne, Richard. *The Coherence of Theism*. 2nd ed. Oxford: Oxford University Press, 1993.

————. *Faith and Reason.* 2nd ed. Oxford: Clarendon, 1955.

Tagore, Rabindranath. *Fireflies.* New York: Macmillan, 1955.

Teilhard de Chardin, Pierre. *The Phenomenon of Man.* London: Collins, 1959.

Templeton, John. *Agape Love: A Tradition Found in Eight World Religions.* Radnor, PA: Templeton Foundation, 1999.

Thurman, Howard. *Meditations of the Heart.* Boston: Beacon, 1999.

Tippett, Krista. *Becoming Wise: An Inquiry into the Mystery and Art of Living.* New York: Penguin, 2016.

Tyson, Neil DeGrasse, and Donald Goldsmith. *Origins: Fourteen Billion Years of Cosmic Evolution.* New York: Norton, 2004.

Tzu, Lao. *Tao Te Ching.* Translated by Charles Miller. New York: Barnes and Noble, 2005.

United Methodist Hymnal. Nashville: United Methodist, 1989.

Vaughan-Lee, Llewellyn, ed. *Traveling the Path of Love: Sayings of Sufi Masters.* Inverness, CA: The Golden Sufi Center, 1995.

Vince, Gaia. *Transcendence: How Humans Evolved Through Fire, Language, Beauty, and Time.* New York: Basic, 2020.

Waldinger, Robert. "What Makes a Good Life? Lessons from the Longest Study on Happiness." https://www.ted.com/talks/robert_waldinger_what_makes_a_good_life_lessons_from_the_longest_study_on_happiness?language=en.

Wallace-Wells, David. *The Uninhabitable Earth: Life After Warming.* New York: Dugan, 2019.

Wesley, John. *The General Rules of the Methodist Church: The Book of Discipline of the United Methodist Church.* Nashville, TN: United Methodist, 2016.

————. *Works of John Wesley.* Edited by Albert C. Outler. 32 vols. Nashville: Abingdon, 1984.

Whinfield, Edward Henry. *Masnavi i Ma'navi: The Spiritual Couplets of Maulána Jalálu-'d-Dín Muhammad Rúmi.* Trübner's Oriental Series. London: Paul, 1898.

Whitehead, Alfred North. *The Aims of Education.* New York: Macmillan, 1949.

Wilber, Ken. *The Religion of Tomorrow: A Vision for the Future of the Great Traditions.* Boulder, CO: Shambhala, 2017.

————. *The Spectrum of Consciousness.* Wheaton, IL: Quest, 1993.

Williamson, Marianne. *A Return to Love: Reflections on the Principles of a Course in Miracles.* New York: HarperCollins, 1996.

Wilson, Edward O. *The Future of Life.* New York: Vintage, 2002.

————. *The Meaning of Human Existence.* New York: Liveright, 2014.

————. *On Human Nature.* Cambridge, MA: Harvard University Press, 1978.

————. *The Social Conquest of Earth.* New York: Norton, 2012.

Wright, Robert. "Islamophobia and Homophobia." *Opinionator* (blog), October 26, 2010.